# The Fateful Hoaxing of Margaret Mead

*Derek Freeman in Upolu, Samoa, 1946, with the
Samoan talking chief Magele (photo by Robert Gibbings)*

# THE FATEFUL
# HOAXING OF
# MARGARET MEAD

## A Historical Analysis of
## Her Samoan Research

## DEREK FREEMAN

**Westview Press**
A Member of the Perseus Group

*For Monica, but for whom . . .*

Copyright © 1999 by Westview Press, A Member of the Perseus Books Group

Published in 1999 in the United States of America by Westview Press, 5500 Central Avenue, Boulder, Colorado 80301-2877, and in the United Kingdom by Westview Press, 12 Hid's Copse Road, Cumnor Hill, Oxford OX2 9JJ

Library of Congress Cataloging-in-Publication Data
Freeman, Derek.
    The fateful hoaxing of Margaret Mead : a historical analysis of her Samoan research / Derek Freeman.
        p.  cm.
    Includes bibliographical references and index.
    ISBN 0-8133-3560-4 (hardcover)
    1. Mead, Margaret, 1901–1978.   2. Ethnology—Samoa.
3. Adolescence.   4. Ethnology—Fieldwork.   I. Title.
GN671.S2F727   1999
305.8'009961'3—dc21                                               98-26771
                                                                      CIP

The paper used in this publication meets the requirements of the American National Standard for Permanence of Paper for Printed Library Materials Z39.48-1984.

10   9   8   7   6   5   4   3   2   1

# Contents

# Illustrations

## Photos

*Second Photograph Section* following page 148

## Maps

# Acknowledgments

THE RESEARCH ON WHICH THIS BOOK is based began in 1987 in Fitiuta, Manu'a, when Galea'i Poumele, then secretary for Samoan affairs of the government of American Samoa, introduced me to Fa'apua'a Fa'amū. I am particularly grateful to Frank Heimans of Sydney for having recorded on video on November 13, 1987, the late Galea'i Poumele's conversation with Fa'apua'a Fa'amū concerning her relationship of 1926 with Margaret Mead.

In May 1988 and again in May 1993, the Samoan chief Unasa, Dr. L. F. Va'a of the National University of Samoa, traveled to Fitiuta to record, in Samoan, Fa'apua'a Fa'amū's answers to a series of detailed questions about her relationship with Margaret Mead and about Manu'a in the mid-1920s. The information he recorded during these visits to Manu'a is of exceptional historical significance. Unasa's contribution to the collection of the evidence contained in this book is thus, as I gratefully acknowledge, of quite fundamental importance. I am also grateful to Unasa for having interviewed Fa'apua'a's daughter Lemafai in Fitiuta in September 1995.

In 1990, Ralph Maud was instrumental in my becoming a Woodsworth visiting scholar of the Institute for the Humanities at Simon Fraser University in British Columbia. He also arranged for my wife, Monica, and me to visit Vancouver Island, where we were shown some of the places Boas had lived. Then, like a guiding spirit, he introduced me to Douglas Cole, who, as professor of history at Simon Fraser University, was working on a biography of Franz Boas. On March 16, 1990, after we had lunched together at the Faculty Club at Simon Fraser, Douglas Cole generously presented me with photocopies of the correspondence of 1925–1926 between Franz Boas and Margaret Mead, which he had obtained during the course of his own research from the archives of the American Philosophical Society.

On my return to Australia, I made a study of these letters and was immediately struck by their historical importance, and from that time until his unexpected death in September 1997, I was in active correspondence with Douglas Cole. Our common interest was in the life and ideas of Franz Boas. Early in 1995, Cole sent me the text of the first volume of his biography of Franz Boas, *"A Certain Work Lies Before Me": The Early Years of Franz Boas, 1858–1906.* It is based on historical research of the most meticulous kind, and I have drawn on this research in Chapter 1, "Franz Boas: The 'Incorrigible Idealist.'" I am, then, profoundly grateful to the late Douglas Cole for the assistance he gave to me from March 1990 right up to the month of his untimely death in 1997.

It was after reading the Boas-Mead letters of 1925–1926 that I decided late in 1990 to embark on a detailed historical study both of Margaret Mead's years as a student of Franz Boas and of the research she undertook in Samoa under his supervision. My first approach was to the archivist of the National Academy of Sciences, who sent me in July 1991 a copy of Mead's "roster file" for the years 1925–1930 from the archives of the National Research Council. I am grateful to Janice F. Goldblum for this invaluable assistance.

Early in 1992, I was given permission by the Manuscript Division of the Library of Congress to make "selected reproductions" from "Mead's field research materials on Samoa." I was able to do this in August 1992. For the assistance I received during my visit to that institution, I am most grateful to Mary M. Wolfskill, as well as to the interns Scott Wirz and Todd Essex.

I am also grateful for the assistance I have received from the Library of the American Philosophical Society, Philadelphia; the Library of the American Museum of Natural History, New York; the Nimitz Library of the U.S. Naval Academy, Annapolis; the Bancroft Library of the University of California, Berkeley; the Library of the Bishop Museum, Honolulu; the Hocken Library of the University of Otago, Dunedin; the Alexander Turnbull Library of Wellington, New Zealand; and the Library of the Australian National University, Canberra.

David Williamson's play *Heretic* is based, in part, on an early draft of *The Fateful Hoaxing of Margaret Mead.* Directed by Wayne Harrison, this play was first produced by the Sydney Theatre Company at the Drama Theatre of the Sydney Opera House on March 28, 1996. In Wellington, on February 28, 1998, my wife and I attended the first night of the quite outstanding production of *Heretic* by Ross Jolly and the Circa Theatre Company, which was part of the New Zealand International Festival of the Arts. For the rejuvenation that this provided, I am immensely grateful to Ross Jolly, as well as to David Williamson for his continuing interest in my work.

For their comments on the drafts of various sections of this book, I wish to thank Christopher Badcock, Laura Betzig, John Tyler Bonner, Thomas Bouchard, Don Brown, Joseph Carroll, Francis Crick, Helena Cronin, Richard Dawkins, Daniel Dennett, W. D. Hamilton, Peter Munz, Tim O'Meara, Vernon Reynolds, Matt Ridley, Marc Swartz, Dorothy Tennov, and George Williams.

For their interest in my research and much appreciated support over the years, I am also grateful to Aiono Fanaafi Le Tagaloa, George Appell, Irenäus Eibl-Eibesfeldt, Anthony Flew, James Fox, Martin Gardner, Larry Gartenstein, Phyllis Grosskurth, Gilbert Herdt, Stephen Hodgkin, Ian Jarvie, Alfred Katz, Mary Lefkowitz, Le Tagaloa Pita, Douglas Lewis, Loki Madan, Rodney Needham, Douglas Oliver, Lola Romanucci-Ross, Benson Saler, Melford Spiro, George Stocking, Donald Tuzin, and Gerard Ward.

The maps reproduced here are by Keith Mitchell of the Cartography Unit of the Research School of Pacific and Asian Studies of the Australian National University.

For advice and assistance in the preparation of this book for publication, I am deeply indebted to Phillipa Sandall Publishing Services, and in particular, I am grateful to Roger Sandall for his skilled editing of my drafts.

I am also most grateful to all those with whom I have had dealings at Westview Press and especially so to Michele Wynn for her expert editing of this book.

To my wife, Monica, to whom this book is dedicated, I am quite exceptionally grateful. For fifty years, she has accompanied me during fieldwork among the Iban of Sarawak and the Samoans of Western Polynesia as well as during my rethinking of the foundations of anthropology. Without her I would have been lost.

Finally, were this book of mine to be given an epigraph, I would, I think, choose these words of John Updike:

*Only the truth can be built upon. From a higher, inhuman point of view, only truth, however harsh, is holy.*

*Derek Freeman*

# Introduction

IN 1967, *Coming of Age in Samoa* was described by its author Margaret Mead as a "classic scientific study," and in 1988, *The Dictionary of Cultural Literacy*, a scholarly work of reference said to record "what every American needs to know," hailed it as a book that set "new standards for anthropological fieldwork" and "revolutionized the field of anthropology." The scientific status of *Coming of Age in Samoa* has already been discussed in my book of 1983, *Margaret Mead and Samoa: The Making and Unmaking of an Anthropological Myth*. Since around 1988, I have given my attention to the fieldwork on which Mead's conclusions rest, and my archival discoveries cast a highly revealing light on Margaret Mead's Samoan research of 1925–1926. From close examination of a wide range of evidence, it has emerged that her exciting revelations about sexual behavior were in some cases merely the extrapolations of whispered intimacies, whereas those of greatest consequence were the results of a prankish hoax.[1]

The historical analysis on which these conclusions are based arose from a series of dramatic and quite unforeseen events. In November 1987, I accompanied the documentary filmmaker Frank Heimans on a visit to American Samoa. Heimans was making a film about Mead's fieldwork there in 1925–1926 and hoped that while in Manu'a, he might be able to videotape someone who had known Mead. This seemed to me most unlikely. During our flight to Pago Pago, I told Heimans that from the intensive inquiries I had made in Manu'a in 1981, there was no possibility whatever of discovering surviving informants with whom Mead had worked in the mid-1920s. In this, however, I was mistaken.

Heimans's original letter seeking permission to enter American Samoa and to film there had been referred to Galea'i Poumele, secretary for Samoan affairs of the government of American Samoa. It so happened that Galea'i was indirectly connected with Mead's stay in Manu'a through his mother, Fofoa, who had died in 1936. Also, and more to the point, he knew something that neither Heimans nor I did: Mead's foremost Samoan friend of 1926, Fa'apua'a Fa'amū, who had been very close to Fofoa, was now living in Manu'a in one of the villages where Mead had worked some sixty years before. Aware of her potential importance as a witness since she was very much alive and well, Galea'i Poumele had asked Fa'apua'a Fa'amū whether she would be prepared to appear in a film being made about Mead—and she had agreed.[2]

Heimans and I were completely unaware of this when we reached Pago Pago in the second week of November 1987. Galea'i Poumele summoned us to our first meeting with him on Thursday, November 12, where he made a surprise announcement: On the following day, when we were scheduled to fly to the Manu'an island of Ta'ū, he would be flying with us. He said there was someone of importance he wanted us to meet.

When we reached Fitiuta on the morning of Friday, November 13, 1987, we were approached by a formally dressed, dignified Samoan lady who had obviously been expecting us. After greeting Galea'i Poumele, she announced that she had something to say and would like to have it recorded on video so that all might know of it.

She was, to my immense surprise, Fa'apua'a Fa'amū, at eighty-six years old still mentally alert and active. Although I had read about Fa'apua'a Fa'amū in Margaret Mead's *Letters from the Field*, published in 1977, I had never met her, nor had I been in any kind of communication with her. During my visits to Manu'a in 1967, 1981, and 1983, she had been in Hawaii, where she had gone to live in 1962 with her husband, Telemu Togia, and all but one of their seven children. It was only after the death of Telemu Togia in June 1986 that she had decided to return to her birthplace. In March 1987, she had taken up residence back in Fitiuta with her daughter Lemafai, the only one of her children who had stayed in Samoa.

All that I knew that Friday morning in 1987 was that although Fa'apua'a had not been one of the adolescents studied by Mead in 1925–1926 (at the time, Fa'apua'a was Mead's age—twenty-four years old), she had spent much time in Margaret Mead's company, as she was the *taupou*, or ceremonial virgin, of high chief Tufele Fa'atoia, district governor of Manu'a. And so, as she sat cross-legged on the *malae*,

or meeting ground, of Fitiuta, waiting to be questioned by the secretary for Samoan affairs of American Samoa, I was intensely curious
about what it was that Fa'apua'a wanted to have permanently
recorded. As Fa'apua'a was an elderly and high-ranking member of his
mother's generation, Galea'i Poumele treated her with the greatest respect.

The key excerpt from Galea'i Poumele's conversation with Fa'a-
pua'a Fa'amū, as videotaped in Fitiuta on that morning, was published
in 1989 in the *American Anthropologist*, both in Samoan and English.
The translation into English runs as follows:

> *Galea'i Poumele:* Fa'amū, was there a day, a night, or an evening,
>    when the woman [i.e., Margaret Mead] questioned you about
>    what you did at nights, and did you ever joke about this?
> *Fa'apua'a Fa'amū:* Yes, we did; we said that we were out at
>    nights with boys; she failed to realize that we were just joking
>    and must have been taken in by our pretences. Yes, she asked:
>    "Where do you go?" And we replied, "We go out at nights!"
>    "With whom?" she asked. Then your mother, Fofoa, and I
>    would pinch one another and say: "We spend the nights with
>    boys, yes, with boys!" She must have taken it seriously but I
>    was only joking. As you know, Samoan girls are terrific liars
>    when it comes to joking. But Margaret accepted our trumped
>    up stories as though they were true.
> *Galea'i Poumele:* And the numerous times that she questioned
>    you, were those the times the two of you continued to tell
>    these untruths to Margaret Mead?
> *Fa'apua'a Fa'amū:* Yes, we just fibbed and fibbed to her.[3]

Fa'apua'a had made this confession, she later explained, because
when she had been told by Galea'i Poumele and others about what
Margaret Mead had written about premarital promiscuity in Samoa,
she suddenly realized that Mead's faulty account must have originated
in the prank that she and her friend Fofoa had played on her when they
were with her on the island of Ofu in 1926. Innocuous though it
seemed at the time, that prank, she had come to realize, had had the
unintended consequence of totally misleading a great many people
about Samoa. And so she had decided, she said, to set the record
straight. During our half-hour conversation, which was in Samoan,

she mentioned how close her friendship with Margaret Mead had been. And she emphasized again and again that in telling Mead their far-fetched stories, she and Fofoa had only been joking *(taufa'alili)* and had never thought that she would take them seriously.

For anyone engaged in studying Margaret Mead's Samoan research, there could be no ignoring Fa'apua'a's testimony, which had entered the public domain through her own actions. From the excerpts from Mead's bulletin (Mead sent regular communications from Samoa, which she called "bulletins") of March 24, 1926, which had been published in 1977, it was known in 1987 that Fa'apua'a and "another Fitiuta girl" had indeed accompanied Mead to Ofu and Olosega in March 1926. Further, in her acknowledgments of March 1928 in the first edition of *Coming of Age in Samoa*, Mead had especially thanked both Fa'apua'a and Fofoa. There were thus substantive grounds for investigating Fa'apua'a's association with Margaret Mead in much greater detail than had been possible on November 13, 1987. Accordingly, a series of questions based on all of the available information on Mead's Samoan research was drawn up and arrangements were made for the Samoan chief Unasa, Dr. Leulu Felise Va'a, who was studying for a doctorate in anthropology from Australian National University and in 1988 was a lecturer in Samoan language and culture at the National University of Samoa, to travel to Fitiuta to question Fa'apua'a in more detail.[4]

When Margaret Mead arrived on the island of Ta'ū in November 1925, Fa'apua'a Fa'amū was Tufele Fa'atoia's *taupou*. Fa'apua'a's parents both belonged to the ancient polity, or *nu'u*, of Fitiuta, situated at the easternmost end of the island of Ta'ū. It was there, in the most remote settlement in Eastern Samoa, that Fa'apua'a Fa'amū was born on April 30, 1901. She was thus some seven and one-half months older than Margaret Mead, who was born in Philadelphia on December 16, 1901.

Since the mid-nineteenth century, Fa'apua'a Fa'amū's family had belonged to the Congregational Church of the London Missionary Society, in which her father was a lay preacher. As was customary, at about the age of twelve, she had gone to live in the household of the Samoan pastor of Fitiuta. At sixteen, she became, and has since constantly remained, a member of the Ekalesia, or communicant body, of her church. When she was in her early twenties, Fa'apua'a spent a year at the London Missionary Society's Atauloma Boarding School for Girls on the island of Tutuila, where she became fully literate in

Samoan and acquired some knowledge of English. She had been sent
to Atauloma by her father in the hope that she would become the wife
of a Samoan pastor. But instead, early in 1925, her life took another direction when she was twenty-three. As is required by Samoan custom,
only a *teine muli*, or virgin, can become a *taupou*. Thus, the title of
Laulauga was conferred upon the virgin Fa'apua'a Fa'amū, and she became the *taupou* of the high chief Tufele Fa'atoia. Although Fa'a-
pua'a's home remained in Fitiuta, from this time onward a good deal
of her time was spent fulfilling her role as *taupou* in Tufele's house at
Si'ufaga, only a few minutes' walk from the U.S. Naval Dispensary at
Lumā, where Margaret Mead took up residence on November 9, 1925.

Soon after her arrival in Si'ufaga, Margaret Mead met Fa'apua'a
Fa'amū. Both young women were twenty-four years old, and both occupied positions of great social prominence. During the first three
months of 1926, they developed a unique friendship, first in Fitiuta
and then on the islands of Ofu and Olosega. As they spent more and
more time in one another's company, their friendship became so fond
that after Mead had decided to cut short her stay in Samoa and had unexpectedly returned to the island of Tutuila to await the arrival of the
ship she was to board for Australia, Fa'apua'a made the long journey to
the port of Pago Pago so that she could say good-bye in person to
"Makerita," as she called her, before her American friend sailed away,
never to be seen again.

During the three weeks or so immediately following the days they
had spent together on the islands of Ofu and Olosega, Fa'apua'a wrote
to Mead from Fitiuta no fewer than nine times. And they continued to
correspond in Samoan after Mead had returned to New York. In these
letters, the originals of which are in the collections of the Manuscript
Division of the Library of Congress, Fa'apua'a wrote to Mead in the
most affectionate terms. For example, in a letter written in Samoan on
April 17, 1926, after having thanked Mead for the beautiful dress and
the soap she had sent to her in Fitiuta, Fa'apua'a went on to say: "You
are not forgotten to me. In my mind I constantly remember your kind-
ness to me. I constantly remember your love during the many days we
went about together. So, do not forget our good companionship that I,
for my part, will always remember." This letter from Fa'apua'a is clear
evidence that her friendship with Margaret Mead was by far the most
momentous relationship of her young womanhood. Mead, with the
knowledge of the Samoan language she had acquired in Tutuila during
September and October 1925, was the first female member of the rul-

ing American elite to associate with the young women of Manu'a. For Fa'apua'a, it was especially significant that she became the closest of all Margaret Mead's Samoan friends, and even after sixty-two years, as Unasa L. F. Va'a discovered in May 1988, her memories of the time that she and Mead spent together in 1926 were still coherent and vivid. When shown a photo of Mead taken in Samoa late in 1925, Fa'a-pua'a at once exclaimed: *"Talofa e!"*—an expression of affection and sympathy—and commented that this was just as Mead had looked when they became such close friends.[5]

Another account of Fa'apua'a in the 1920s has been given by the English writer and painter Aletta Lewis. Early in 1929, three years af-ter Margaret Mead had been there, Lewis spent several weeks in Manu'a as the guest of District Governor Tufele Fa'atoia. Soon after her arrival on the island of Ta'ū, Tufele introduced her to his *taupou*, Fa'apua'a, who, at twenty-eight years old, was still a virgin, as was re-quired by the *fa'aSamoa* (Samoan culture). Aletta Lewis, who called the Samoan *taupou* "a tremendously important person," described Fa'apua'a as having a "particularly aloof" manner with men and as be-ing "swathed in the cloak of her dignity." At the suggestion of Tufele, Fa'apua'a accompanied Lewis on a visit to the islands of Ofu and Olosega. It was a visit that Fa'apua'a still remembered in 1988, re-marking to Unasa L. F. Va'a that it was on this occasion that she first met her future husband, Telemu Togia. They were married at Fitiuta, in a Christian ceremony, in 1930.[6]

When Unasa first interviewed Fa'apua'a Fa'amū in Fitiuta, she had just turned eighty-seven years old. In his report on this interview, Unasa remarked that he had been "surprised to find an old lady who was so mentally alert and had such a remarkable memory." This had also been my impression in November 1987; during my discussion with Fa'apua'a, she was, without question, fully in command of her mental faculties. According to Unasa, Fa'apua'a "also had a good sense of humor and often laughed when she remembered some funny inci-dent from the past." On May 2, 1988, Unasa interviewed Fa'apua'a Fa'amū for a total of six hours and put to her over 250 questions deal-ing with her life history and with numerous aspects of her relation-ship with Margaret Mead during the first three months of 1926. Most of these questions had been prepared in advance, on the basis of what was already known from published accounts. Fa'apua'a's statements were recorded verbatim in Samoan. They provide a mass of detailed information of direct relevance to Mead's activities in Manu'a during 1926.[7]

When her answers to these questions had been written down and she had been told of the significance for anthropology of the avowals she had made, Fa'apua'a was asked if she would be prepared to swear *(tautō)* on the Bible that her testimony both on November 13, 1987, and on May 2, 1988, was true and correct. Fa'apua'a was very familiar with the procedure of swearing an oath on the Holy Bible (Tusi Paia) as to the truth of evidence. The swearing of such oaths is a common practice in Samoa. Furthermore, for Samoans like Fa'apua'a, who are devout Christians, the swearing of an oath on the Bible is the most serious of actions. As Tim O'Meara has noted, Samoans believe that swearing falsely on the Bible will result in sickness or death in the short term, with the final punishment for swearing falsely being eternal damnation at the hands of God (*'o le Atua*). As Robert Bolt has remarked of devout Christians like Thomas More, individuals "take an oath" only when they want to commit themselves "quite exceptionally" to a "statement" and, God having been called to act as witness and judge, when they do so, they fully believe that the inevitable consequence of perjury is outright damnation. It was within this same rubric of Christian belief that Fa'apua'a Fa'amū, a lifelong communicant, swore an oath on the Bible, on May 2, 1988, that all of the testimony she had given was true and correct; at the same time, she signed a formally witnessed deposition to the same effect. A copy of this deposition has been lodged with the executive director of the American Anthropological Association in Washington, D.C. Fa'apua'a Fa'amū's sworn testimony is of the sort that could be presented in a court of law. Having studied it in light of all that was known about Mead's Samoan research, I set about giving a brief preliminary account of Fa'apua'a's relationship with Margaret Mead. This account, entitled "Fa'apua'a Fa'amū and Margaret Mead," was published in the *American Anthropologist* in December 1989.[8]

With the publication of this detailed account in the *American Anthropologist*, the study of Margaret Mead's Samoan research entered an entirely new phase. Given the existence of Fa'apua'a Fa'amū's sworn testimony about the prank she and Fofoa had mischievously played on Margaret Mead when she questioned them about the sexual mores of the Samoans, there was, from 1988 onward, a conspicuous need to test this sworn evidence against the circumstances of Mead's

Samoan fieldwork. A meticulous examination of all of the available primary sources was required. For the conscientious historian, the point had been reached where there could be no avoiding this question: *What, in fact, actually happened during Margaret Mead's brief sojourn in the remote islands of Manu'a in the mid-1920s?*

For me, this question demanded systematic investigation. Issues of great anthropological significance were manifestly involved. As an emeritus professor of anthropology at the Research School of Pacific Studies of the Australian National University, I was fortunate to have the time and the resources for what, I fully realized, would be a major historical inquiry. And so, in 1990, I turned to the demanding but fascinating task of collecting for detailed study copies of all of the documents from the 1920s on Margaret Mead's Samoan research that I could possibly locate.[9]

In March 1990, when I was a Woodsworth visiting scholar of the Institute for the Humanities at Simon Fraser University in British Columbia, I had the good fortune to meet with Douglas Cole, a professor of history at Simon Fraser University who was working on a biography of Franz Boas. Boas, who was Margaret Mead's professor of anthropology from October 1922 onward, first at Barnard College and then in the Department of Anthropology at Columbia University, had "more influence" than anyone else "on the development of American anthropology," in the words of Robert Spier. Franz Boas became both the instigator and the official supervisor of Mead's "attempt" in Samoa "to determine how far the behaviour of an adolescent girl is determined by cultural environment."[10]

If it had not been for Franz Boas, Margaret Mead would never have gone to Samoa in 1925 and *Coming of Age in Samoa* would never have been written. Indeed, the history here presented is almost as much about the ideas and actions of Franz Boas as it is about those of Margaret Mead. I have, therefore, prefaced my account of Mead's entry into anthropology with a chapter on Franz Boas and the early development of Boasian culturalism.

The Professional Papers of Franz Boas are held in the library of the American Philosophical Society in Philadelphia. Professor Cole not only put me in touch with the manuscript librarian of the American Philosophical Society but also generously presented me with copies of the private correspondence of Franz Boas and Margaret Mead for the years 1925–1926, which he had obtained in the course of his own re-

search. These letters and the additional letters for 1927–1928, which I
obtained directly from the archives of the American Philosophical Society, contain much vitally significant information that made abun-
dantly clear the importance of making a thoroughgoing historical
study of Mead's Samoan fieldwork.

Margaret Mead conducted her Samoan fieldwork of 1925–1926, with
Franz Boas as her supervisor, as a National Research Fellow in the Bio-
logical Sciences of the National Research Council of the United
States. In 1991, I secured from the archives of the National Research
Council, which are now held by the U.S. National Academy of Sci-
ences, copies of all documents referring to Mead's tenure of this re-
search fellowship, as well as copies of her correspondence with the
National Research Council for the years 1925–1930.

Other important documents and photographs, dating from the
1920s, were obtained from the American Museum of Natural History,
New York; the Bancroft Library of the University of California, Berkeley; the Bishop Museum, Honolulu; the Hocken Library of the University of Otago; the Nimitz Library of the U.S. Naval Academy, Annapolis; and the Alexander Turnbull Library, New Zealand.

In 1992, I went to Washington, D.C., to research the relevant sections of the Papers of Margaret Mead and her South Pacific Ethnographic Archives, materials that occupy 580 linear feet of shelf space
in the Manuscript Division of the Library of Congress.

That Margaret Mead should have preserved with such thoroughness
the very extensive documentation of her Samoan research of 1925–
1926, thus making this documentation available for study in Washington, is the clearest possible evidence of her confident assessment of
the status of her research efforts. Furthermore, this action of hers con-
clusively confirms Margaret Mead's professional integrity, for, in lodg-
ing her papers in the Manuscript Division of the Library of Congress
she has, with a regard for the values of science and scholarship that is
permanently to her credit, made all of the field notes and other documents concerned with her Samoan fieldwork available for critical
evaluation.

The information about Margaret Mead's Samoan fieldwork in her
papers of 1925–1926 is exceedingly rich. Although she did not keep a
diary, she did record her actions and impressions (in some instances in
great detail) in a series of fourteen "news bulletins" that were written
for family and friends. The first of these bulletins is dated August 10,

1925, and was written aboard the S.S. *Matsonia*, en route to Hawaii; the last is dated March 24, 1926, and was written in the U.S. Naval Dispensary at Lumā, Taʻū, in Manuʻa. In all, these fourteen bulletins compose fifty-five pages, almost all business-size sheets, and all typed single-spaced. They total approximately 37,500 words. The bulletins, then, together with Mead's field notes, provide very detailed information not only about her five months of fieldwork in Manuʻa but also about the three months she spent on the island of Tutuila, during which she was either learning Samoan or awaiting the arrival from Honolulu of the S.S. *Sonoma*, on which she finally left Samoa on May 10, 1926, bound for France via Australia. Furthermore, the bulletins and field notes are supplemented by four particularly significant sets of correspondence.

The correspondence between Franz Boas and Margaret Mead (the original letters are preserved in the archives of the American Philosophical Society and in the collections of the Manuscript Division of the Library of Congress) extends from July 1925 (a fortnight or so before Mead set out for Samoa) to July 1926 (when she was in Paris on her way back to the United States). The correspondence began with Boas's farewell letter of July 14, 1925. Thereafter, from July 17, 1925, to July 13, 1926, Mead wrote a total of eighteen letters to Franz Boas about her Samoan research. Three of these letters were written during the weeks immediately before her departure from Holicong, Pennsylvania; one on board the S.S. *Sonoma* en route to Pago Pago from Honolulu; two from the island of Tutuila; ten from Manuʻa; one on board the S.S. *Chitral* en route to Perth from Adelaide; and one in Paris.[11]

During the eight months and ten days she spent in Samoa, Mead received six separate letters from her supervisor, Franz Boas, several of which had a profound effect on her fieldwork. In the first of these letters, dated November 7, 1925, Boas agreed, in principle, with Mead's decision to locate her research headquarters in the U.S. Naval Dispensary on the island of Taʻū. In his second letter of January 4, 1926, Boas fully accepted that Mead, following her appointment on December 23, 1925, as an assistant curator of ethnology at the American Museum of Natural History, would not want to seek reappointment as a research fellow of the National Research Council. This meant that her fieldwork in Manuʻa would last for only five months or so.

Most momentous of all, however, was Boas's response to Mead's letter of January 5, 1926, in which she asked her supervisor: "If I simply write conclusions and use my cases as illustrative material will it be acceptable?" Boas's reply, dated February 15, reached Mead on March 18, 1926, on the island of Ofu, where five days previously she had been the victim of a hoax about the sexual mores of the Samoans. The very next day, March 19, 1926, despite the fact that she had made no systematic investigation of the sexual behavior of her adolescent subjects, she wrote to Boas telling him she had decided to cut short her fieldwork in Manu'a and leave Samoa a month sooner than originally planned.[12]

Numerous other details about Mead's Samoan research are to be found in her extensive correspondence with the National Research Council, a correspondence that began with Mead's fellowship application of February 1925 and ended when the Board of National Research Fellowships in the Biological Sciences expressed "appreciation" of her "accomplishment" under her "fellowship" in a letter of February 1930.[13]

Another vitally important source of information is Mead's correspondence of 1925–1926 with members of the scientific staff of the Bernice P. Bishop Museum of Polynesian Ethnology and Natural History. In May and June 1925, there was an important exchange of letters between Mead and Professor Herbert Gregory, the director of the Bishop Museum, who suggested in January 1925 that Mead should locate her proposed fieldwork on heredity and environment in relation to adolescence somewhere in Samoa. Then in August 1925 in Honolulu, Gregory arranged for the Bishop Museum's senior ethnologist, Dr. Edward Craighill Handy, to give Mead instruction on the Samoans and the research she was proposing to do among them. The correspondence of Handy and Mead, especially after she had formally agreed to undertake ethnological research in Manu'a under Handy's guidance, is of crucial historical significance, for this involvement with the Bishop Museum had quite fateful consequences for the major investigation she was committed to carrying out, under Boas's supervision, for the National Research Council.[14]

Finally, there are Margaret Mead's letters to her paternal grandmother, Martha Adaline Mead. Born in 1845, Martha had lived with Margaret's family from the time of Margaret's birth in 1901 and became "the most decisive influence" in her life. It was to her paternal grandmother that Margaret Mead confided her innermost thoughts and feelings, particularly so after she had left home and taken up the study of anthropology. The fifteen letters that Margaret Mead wrote to her paternal grandmother from Samoa are thus a quite invaluable source of information.[15]

From these exceedingly rich sources—and especially from her bulletins and field notes—it was possible, after my return to the Australian National University from the Library of Congress, to construct a detailed chronology of Margaret Mead's activities from August 1, 1925, when she began her trip to Samoa at the Baltimore and Ohio Railway Station in Philadelphia, until October 11, 1926, when, after traveling in France, England, and Italy, she arrived back in the United States to take up her duties as an assistant curator of ethnology at the American Museum of Natural History in New York. Furthermore, it was also possible to construct a diary of Mead's day-to-day activities during her stay in Samoa, and so to follow the course of her fieldwork there in great detail. My historical analysis of Mead's fieldwork in Samoa is based on this record of her day-to-day activities there.

In 1989, after the testimony of Fa'apua'a Fa'amū had become known, the historian George Stocking expressed skepticism about "octogenarian recollections" of "events of sixty years before." To what extent is this attitude justified? In May 1988, it had been possible to seek from Fa'apua'a her recollections about various individuals with whom Mead had had dealings during her five-month sojourn in Manu'a. In her letter to Franz Boas of January 5, 1926, Mead gave detailed information about the family of Sotoa, the highest ranking *ali'i*, or titular chief, of Lumā, mentioning almost all of its members by name. When questioned in 1988, Fa'apua'a had clear recollections of both Sotoa and his wife To'aga (who was one of Mead's main informants). She also gave personal details about two adult male members of this family, Aviata and Numela, both of whom were well known to Mead, as the Sotoa household was immediately adjacent to the U.S. Naval Dispensary. Fa'apua'a correctly recollected the names of the Samoan pastors and schoolteachers who were stationed on the island of Ta'ū in 1926, people who are mentioned by name in the acknowledgments of March 1928 in the first edition of *Coming of Age in Samoa*. Indeed, in several instances, Fa'apua'a mentioned the names of the wives and the villages in other parts of the Samoan archipelago from which these pastors and teachers had come. Such detailed recollections (all of them validated by documents from the 1920s) fully confirm that in 1988, some sixty-two years later, Fa'apua'a, who turned twenty-four years old on April 30, 1925, did have precise memories of Manu'a as it was in 1926.[16]

Nonetheless, given Stocking's expression of skepticism, there was a need to check Fa'apua'a's recollections of the time she spent with Margaret Mead in further detail against independently established historical facts from the mid-1920s. By the end of 1992, a mass of reliable information about Manu'a in early 1926 and about Mead's activities there at that time had become available in the copies of Mead's Samoan papers that I had obtained from the Library of Congress. There was thus an opportunity to check Fa'apua'a's recollections of the events of 1926 in a more systematic way than had been possible in 1988. Accordingly, arrangements were made for Unasa L. F. Va'a (who was in Samoa conducting his own research for his dissertation in anthropology at the Australian National University) to revisit Fitiuta with a further series of questions based on Mead's Samoan papers of 1925–1926.

When Unasa interviewed Fa'apua'a in Fitiuta on May 3, 1993, she had just turned ninety-two years old. Although she was now five years older than when she had been interviewed on May 2, 1988, she was, according to Unasa, still "lucid" (as is evident in her words reported at the very end of this chapter) and "still able to remember well." In May 1993, then, it was possible to question Fa'apua'a in detail about the visit that she, Fofoa, and Mead had made to the islands of Ofu and Olosega on March 8–18, 1926. Fa'apua'a's replies fully confirmed the vividness of her memories of this historic visit. For example, she remembered, among other things, being seasick (*ma'i vasa*) during the crossing from Lumā to Ofu (on March 8), as she also was during the return crossing (on March 18); the presence of Dr. and Mrs. Charles Lane, whom she referred to as an *ulugali'i* (lit., a man and his wife) at the U.S. Naval Dispensary on Ofu; the *masi* (fermented breadfruit) served in Olosega; the roast pig presented in Sili; and how, the next day, she, Fofoa, and Mead were ferried across the narrow strait between the two islands, one at a time, in an outrigger canoe before walking back to Misa's guest house in the village of Ofu. All of these details are confirmed in Mead's own account, written on March 24, 1926, six days after she, Fofoa, and Fa'apua'a had returned to the island of Ta'ū.[17]

There is thus quite definite evidence that Fa'apua'a, in 1993, as in 1988, had substantially accurate memories of Manu'a in 1926, including the time that she and Fofoa had spent with Mead on the islands of Ofu and Olosega in March of that year. And this in turn argues for the historical reliability of Fa'apua'a's sworn testimony of November 13, 1987, and May 2, 1988. On May 3, 1993, for a second time, Fa'apua'a "swore on the Holy Bible" before witnesses that all of the testimony she had given to Unasa L. F. Va'a was to the best of her knowledge "true and correct in every way."

In the chapters that follow I present a historical analysis establishing that Fa'apua'a's testimony is fully consistent with all that is known from other primary sources about the course of Margaret Mead's fieldwork in Manu'a. Thus, the enigma of Margaret Mead's Samoan research, which has been at the center of the Samoa controversy since 1983, is effectively solved when the testimony of Fa'apua'a Fa'amū is systematically related to the evidence contained in Mead's papers. This is particularly borne out through a letter to Franz Boas that Mead wrote in Ofu village on March 14, 1926, immediately after her return there from the journey she had made to Olosega with Fofoa and Fa'apua'a, a journey that she describes in detail in her final bulletin from Manu'a.

The story I have to recount is intensely human, an extraordinary sequence of events of a kind that must have few parallels in the history of anthropological fieldwork. It is a story that needs to be told for the sake of Samoan studies, as well as for the sake of anthropology in general. I would emphasize, however, that I am quite uninterested in attributing blame in any way whatsoever in respect of events that occurred a full lifetime ago in unique historical circumstances.

What happened on the island of Ofu in March 1926, given all of the attendant circumstances, was virtually inevitable. This is indicated in the title: *The Fateful Hoaxing of Margaret Mead*. As I hope to make clear in the analysis that follows, Margaret Mead's hoaxing by Fa'apua'a and Fofoa was fated in at least five interrelated ways. First, she had brought with her to Samoa a fervent belief in the ideology, imparted to her by Boas, Ruth Benedict, and others, that human behavior is determined by cultural patterns. Second, her time-consuming involvement in "doing ethnology" for the Bishop Museum had created such a severe crisis for her official research on adolescent behavior that on Ofu, she was forced to turn to Fa'apua'a and Fofoa in the hope of finding a cultural pattern that would enable her to solve, once and for all, the problem Boas required her to investigate. Third, she had also brought with her to Manu'a the quite false preconception, derived from Edward Craighill Handy, that she would find that premarital promiscuity was the ruling cultural pattern in Samoa. Fourth, as one of Franz Boas's dedicated followers, she wanted, above all else, to reach a conclusion that would gratify him and that he would find acceptable. Fifth, it is commonplace for Samoans, like Fofoa and Fa'apua'a, to resort to joking behavior (*tausuaga*) when interrogated about sexual behavior, a customary response of which Mead had quite inadequate knowledge. Furthermore, in retrospect, the hoaxing of Margaret Mead on the island of Ofu in March 1926 was also a "fateful" happening because of the extraordinary influence that *Coming of Age in Samoa* (which is based on the untruths and hyperbole of Fofoa and Fa'apua'a) has had both on anthropology and the zeitgeist of the twentieth century.

My concern, I would emphasize, is purely with Margaret Mead's fieldwork in Samoa, undertaken at Boas's behest in 1925–1926, and with the writings she based on this fieldwork. The narrative I present needs to be followed in detail if this initial stage of Margaret Mead's anthropological career is to be adequately understood. I also discuss how Mead's conclusion of 1928 came to be quite generally accepted by other anthropologists. Finally, in the Afterword, I comment briefly on such things as my meeting with Margaret Mead at the Australian National University in 1964, the course of the Samoa controversy from 1983 onward, and the urgent need for a scientifically informed anthropological paradigm to replace Boasian culturalism.

When Fa'apua'a Fa'amū, Margaret Mead's close associate of 1926, who still spoke most lovingly in 1993 of her American friend, was asked at age ninety-two whether there was something she would like to say to those who had been taken in by the tall tales contained in *Coming of Age in Samoa*, she replied in Samoan, with memorable lucidity and wit:

> *Tatau i saenisi ona fa'aeteete i fa'amatalaga a tagata; tatau ona sa'ili muamua pe moni fa'amatalaga po'o ni tausuaga.*

This piquant admonition from a Samoan *tama'ita'i*, or lady of rank, who has come to occupy a unique position in the history of twentieth-century anthropology, reads in English:

> Scientists [i.e., anthropologists] should take care over the explanations people give to them; they should first check and make sure that what they are being told is true, and not just a joke.

It has been by patient and protracted historical research that the truth of what happened on the island of Ofu in March 1926 has finally become known. As my favorite Samoan proverb, which has a distinctly Popperian ring to it, avers: "It is in deep waters that the qualities of a canoe are tested."[18]

# 1

# Franz Boas:
# The "Incorrigible Idealist"

ALFRED KROEBER, WHO KNEW FRANZ BOAS WELL, wrote of him in 1943: "So decisive were his judgments, and so strong his feelings, that his character had in it much of the daemonic. His convictions sprang from so deep down, and manifested themselves so powerfully, that to the run of shallower men there was something ultra-human or unnatural about him. . . . In consequence, he was literally worshipped by some who came under his influence." "Dynamic and wiry," "well-proportioned in every limb in age as well as youth," Boas's "face and head" had in them, Kroeber said, "something aquiline, resolute, decisive and poised." For Kroeber, Franz Boas was "of the Titans—a self-disciplined Titan," with "a rugged, massive, powerful personality of great caliber, who drove his engine through to the accomplishment of whatever the task in hand seemed to him to be"; he was the *"facile princeps"* of his profession, who "saw through the fallacies of others" yet "refrained from committing his own."[1]

These are capacious claims, but they are matched by those of other American followers of Boas. In 1940, Robert Lowie ended a review in *Science* with the words: "In the anthropological science of his time Boas has been the great exemplar, fearless of authority, relentlessly self-critical, driven by a sacred thirst to ever new Pierian springs, gaining ever deeper insights into the nature of man." And, in 1941, Alexander Goldenweiser wrote of Boas as having come from nineteenth-century Germany, like some theomorphic culture-hero, to bestow clarification and scientific fiber upon American anthropology.[2]

Just who was this "great exemplar," this man George Stocking judged to have "shaped the character of American anthropology in the twentieth century . . . more than anyone else"? And what were the "underlying assumptions" of the Boasian culturalism that "from the late 1920s" became "fundamental to all of American social science," becoming by "the third quarter of the twentieth century . . . part of the intellectual baggage of a large proportion of educated Americans"?[3]

Franz Boas was born on July 7, 1858, into the Jewish community of Minden, a Westphalian garrison town, in a home in which (as he noted in 1938) "the ideals of the revolution of 1848 were a living force."[4] This was largely because of the friendship that Franz's mother, Sophie, had formed with Abraham Jacobi. In 1851, Jacobi had sent Sophie and her sister Fanny (whom he later married) a copy of the *Communist Manifesto*. Fleeing to England after having been imprisoned in Germany for his political activities, Jacobi visited Marx in London and stayed with Engels in Manchester before establishing himself as a physician in New York City. It was to his Uncle Jacobi that the twenty-three-year-old Franz Boas wrote in 1882 about a quite major intellectual transformation he had undergone.[5]

Although Boas claimed to have been "spared the struggle against religious dogma that besets the lives of so many young people," he did, for a time, receive religious instruction from a rabbi and was confirmed when he was thirteen years old. By sixteen, he was determined to "rise above others," and this would certainly have been his ambition when he left Minden on April 15, 1877, to begin his university studies. In his curriculum vitae, written upon completion of his college preparatory studies at the gymnasium, Boas had noted that his "favourite desire" was to study "natural science," especially mathematics and physics, and it was for courses in these subjects that Boas enrolled at the University of Heidelberg in April 1877.

Just five years later, in April 1882, he was writing to Abraham Jacobi about how he had become convinced that his "previous materialistic Weltanschauung" was "untenable." Remarkably, the twenty-three-year-old Boas had been converted to a form of neo-Kantian idealism that was to rule his thinking for the rest of his life. What, then, was the historical setting in which young Franz Boas, having taken a doctorate in physics at the University of Kiel, renounced scientific materialism to become a philosophical idealist? And what were the other historical influences that led to the emergence in the 1920s of Boasian culturalism?[6]

For some sixty years, from the time of the publication of Kant's *Critique of Pure Reason* in 1781 until a decade or so after the death of Hegel in 1831, German philosophy was dominated by varying forms of idealism, with the "transcendental" idealism of Kant being followed by the "subjective" idealism of Johann Fichte, the "objective" idealism of Friedrich Schelling, and the "absolute" idealism of Hegel. Then, in the middle years of the nineteenth century, the rise to prominence of Ludwig Feuerbach, "the father of German materialism," brought about a marked change. As Frederick Gregory has described in his *Scientific Materialism in Nineteenth-Century Germany*, Feuerbach's critique of idealism, together with "the proliferation and popularization of natural science," created a disenchantment with idealism, with Karl Vogt, Jacob Moleschott, and Ludwig Buchner being among the leading scientific materialists of the day.[7]

When Charles Darwin's *Origin of Species* was published in German in 1860, followed by T. H. Huxley's *Man's Place in Nature* in 1863, evolutionary theory soon became central to the scientific materialism that had emerged in Germany in the 1850s. Vogt's *Lectures on Man* of 1863 was followed in 1868 by Buchner's *Six Lectures* and Ernst Haeckel's *The Natural History of Creation*, and in 1868, the *Illustrierte Zeitung*, which paid close attention to science, reported that "all the educated" were familiar with Darwinism. By 1875, there was a German edition of Darwin's collected works, and in the judgment of Alfred Kelly, "Darwinism had carried the day at least in the scientific community"; furthermore, "materialism and Darwinism had become so intertwined that most Germans had come to assume that support for the one was tantamount to support for the other."[8]

As early as 1865, however, a countervailing movement began in German philosophy with the publication of Otto Liebmann's *Kant und die Epigonen*, each chapter of which ended with the words "back to Kant." This book, according to Lewis Beck, "came at the right time for it to be regarded as a clarion call to the formal establishment of neo-Kantianism as a distinct force in philosophy." But "the progenitor of a continuous school of neo-Kantians" was not Liebmann but Friedrich Albert Lange, whose *History of Materialism and Critique of Its Present Significance* was published first in 1866 and then again in 1873 in a revised edition. As Bertrand Russell noted in his introduction to the English translation of the 1873 edition of *History of Materialism*, Lange considered that materialism was refuted "by the psychology and physiology of sensation, which shows that the world studied by physics is a world dependent on our modes of perception, not a world existing independently on its own." Lange, then, was very much "an apostle of the Kantian view of the world," an idealist for whom the real was "of the nature of thought." Thus, for the neo-Kantians, reality was "a construct of the mind." They were convinced of the existence of "a world of values distinct from all that belongs to nature" and of "values, duties, norms and principles, separated by an unbridgeable chasm from the world of nature."[9]

This neo-Kantian philosophy took shape, as Klaus Kohnke has documented, during the late 1870s, years Franz Boas spent at university. They were particularly turbulent years. They had been preceded by the Kulturkampf, the conflict between the church and state in Prussia, in which Bismark and his supporters led an offensive against the Catholic Church. The name given to this conflict—the *Kulturkampf*—was coined by Rudolf Virchow, one of its leaders, who had first attained eminence in the field of cellular pathology and had then entered politics.[10]

With the waning of the Kulturkampf in the mid-1870s, the question emerged concerning whether evolutionary theory should be taught in schools. In September 1877, when Boas was still at Heidelberg, the fiftieth meeting of the German Association of Naturalists and Physicians was held in Munich. On September 18, Ernst Haeckel presented the association with his address, "The Evolution Theory of the Present Day in Its Relation to Science in General." He began by noting that no other theory had "so vividly claimed general attention for the last decade" and went on to claim that the theory of evolution enabled the solution of "the fundamental question of the position of man in nature"; it was vain, Haeckel said, "to try to keep a particular exceptional position for man, by constructing for him a special line of ancestors, separate from those of the vertebrata." Four days later, on September 22, in his address entitled "The Liberty of Science in the Modern State," Rudolf Virchow launched a caustic attack on Haeckel in particular and evolutionary theory in general. The crux of his attack was that "we cannot teach, we cannot designate it as a revelation of science, that man descends from the ape or from any other animal." As Haeckel subsequently noted, from this time on Virchow became the center of an "inveterate hostility" to Darwin's views as expressed in *The Descent of Man*.[11]

Virchow's denunciation of the theory of evolution also included a grave warning that if carried through to its extremely dangerous consequences by the Socialists, the theory might bring to Germany "all those horrors" that "similar theories" had brought to France—a reference to the murderous excesses of the Paris Commune of 1871. Virchow was widely extolled as a public-spirited hero. In the newspaper *Germania*, he was praised for his successful "club blows against the ape fanatics," and Adolf Bastian of the Royal Ethnological Museum in Berlin, who also had a "sovereign disdain" for Darwinism, jubilantly recorded in the *Zeitschrift für Ethnologie* that Virchow had freed science from a nightmare by banishing "the incubus called Descent." In 1878, when there were two attempted assassinations of the kaiser, the New Prussian *Kreus Zeitung* threw "all the blame" on "the theory of descent." In the words of Prince Von Bulow, "popular feeling was roused by these attempted assassinations" as it never had been since "the days of the Franco-German war." It was in this time of crisis, as Kohnke has shown, that neo-Kantian thinking came strongly to the fore.[12]

In October 1877, Boas moved to the university in Bonn, where he continued his studies in mathematics and physics and took a course in geography given by Theobald Fischer. Then, in October 1879, he transferred to the university in Kiel, where Fischer had become professor of geography. In Kiel, under the supervision of Gustav Karsten, director of the Physics Institute, Boas's research was on the optical properties of water, for which he received a doctorate in 1881. But he also attended Fischer's geography seminar, and this led him to decide that his future lay not in physics but in geography.

Another major influence during Boas's time at Kiel was Benno Erdmann, who had become a privatdocent in philosophy in 1877. Erdmann, in the words of Klaus Kohnke, "conceded to Kantian philosophy a surpassing significance" and was "one of the principal pillars of the 'Kant movement.'" In 1880, Erdmann was still a young man, and in May of that year, Franz Boas joined his seminar and came under the spell of his enthusiasm. One of the books that Erdmann enthused about to Boas was Lange's *History of Materialism*. Friedrich Paulson, a friend of Erdmann's, has left a vivid account of the impact of Lange's book on his own thinking. It came, according to Paulson, "like the answer to a cry of distress" and was read "with passionate interest." In its pages, "Kantian idealism appeared as the victorious challenger to dogmatic materialism." Lange and his book were given Paulson's "entire allegiance." During the early 1880s, Lange's *History of Materialism* had a comparable effect on the thinking of the young Franz Boas.[13]

Boas's passionate intellectual involvement with Lange began in May 1880 in Benno Erdmann's seminar at Kiel. Then, early in September 1881, after completing his examinations in geography, physics, and philosophy and receiving his degree, the twenty-three-year-old Boas went to Berlin to stay with the Lehmanns, who were family friends. Most of his time was spent with twenty-six-year-old Rudolf Lehmann, an ardent neo-Kantian, whose doctoral dissertation at the University of Berlin was on Kant's postulate of the existence of noumena, or "things-in-themselves," devoid of all phenomenal attributes. The two young men had a great deal in common and spent much of their time poring over Lange's *History of Materialism*. On September 29, 1881, Boas had to return to Minden to begin a year of compulsory military service.[14]

When Franz Boas wrote to Abraham Jacobi from Minden on April 10, 1882, recording how he had become convinced that his "previous materialistic Weltanschauung" was "untenable," he was still on military duty. It would seem likely that his conversion to neo-Kantian idealism had occurred either during or soon after his study with Rudolf Lehmann of Lange's *History of Materialism* in Berlin in September 1881. It was certainly a momentous conversion, for it led directly to the mentalistic assumptions on which Boasian culturalism, as it has come to be called, was based.

His military service over, Boas returned to Berlin early in October 1882, with his new Kantian weltanschauung. He was intent on undertaking geographical research in Baffin Land. Soon after his arrival, he was introduced to both Adolf Bastian and Rudolf Virchow. Bastian befriended Boas and early in 1883 arranged for Virchow to give him instruction. In a lecture that he gave five months after the death of Charles Darwin on April 19, 1882, Haeckel spoke of Virchow's "unqualified antagonism" to evolutionary theory. For Boas, however, Virchow had a "cold enthusiasm for truth," and it is evident that much of Virchow's "unqualified antagonism" to evolutionary thought was communicated to Boas. As his student Paul Radin has noted, Boas "always took a prevailingly antagonistic position" to the theory of evolution. And so much so, as J. J. Williams noted in 1936, that by the mid-1930s, Boas had succeeded in "suppressing the classical theory of evolution among practically the entire group of leading American ethnologists."[15]

After his year of geographical research in Baffin Land, Boas traveled to New York, where he became engaged to Marie Krackowiser in September 1884, whom he had met two years earlier in Germany. Unable to find suitable employment in the United States, he went back to Berlin. Bastian appointed him to a temporary assistantship at the Royal Ethnological Museum, where he worked briefly early in 1886 with the members of a touring group of nine Bella Coola Indians from British Columbia. Then, having qualified as a privatdocent in geography at Berlin University, he returned to New York City in July 1886, in the hope of finding a position that would enable him to marry Marie Krackowiser. When nothing could be found, he headed off to British Columbia on a fund-raising collecting trip for just over three months. In academic terms, he was still a geographer, and when he got back to New York, he submitted an article to *Science* that he had been working on for some time. It was entitled "The Study of Geography." This led in January 1887 to a two-year appointment at $150 a month as assistant editor of *Science* in New York, "with special responsibility for geography." This was enough to enable him to settle in America and marry Marie Krackowiser, which he duly did on March 10, 1887.[16]

Boas's "The Study of Geography," which appeared in *Science* on February 11, 1887, is informed throughout by the Kantian idealism to which he had become converted at the age of twenty-three. It also contains an echo of Virchow's opposition to Darwin in Boas's dismissive reference to those scientists "who try to construct the evolution of organisms in details which, at the present time, at least, can neither be proved or refuted." When he was in the Arctic, "at a time when the temperature outside his igloo was below -40 degrees C, and he was suffering acutely from hunger," Boas, as Stocking has described, "spent the 'long evenings' with 'a copy of Kant.'" In his review of John Watson's *The Philosophy of Kant*, which appeared in *Science* on August 17, 1888, Boas offered the opinion that "undoubtedly the study of Kant is the best introduction to modern philosophy, and a powerful means of guarding students from falling into a shallow materialism or positivism." Here, evolutionary theory is certainly implicated, and Boas's idealist stance is directly comparable to Virchow's rejection of the monism of Ernst Haeckel at Munich in 1877.[17]

In 1943, soon after Boas's death, Ruth Benedict, who knew him well, remarked that it had "never been sufficiently realized how consistently throughout his life Boas defined the task of ethnology as the study of 'man's mental life,' 'fundamental psychic attitudes of cultural groups,' man's 'subjective worlds.'" As early as 1888, Benedict pointed out, Boas had asserted that "the data of ethnology prove that not only our knowledge but also our emotions are the result of the form of our social life and the history of the people to whom we belong." Ruth Benedict was quoting from Boas's own translation into English of 1940 of a lecture entitled "The Aims of Ethnology" that he gave, in German, in New York on March 8, 1888. In March 1888, at twenty-nine years, Boas was a geographer, with no inkling of "the biology of behavior" and lacking the ethnographic experience to warrant his making these idealist assumptions about the human species. Nonetheless, his fervent neo-Kantian convictions and his marked aversion to evolutionary theory led him, even before he had become an anthropologist, to define anthropology in these categorical terms. Boas consistently adhered to this idealist and antievolutionary orientation, as Ruth Benedict noted in 1943, for the rest of his anthropological career.[18]

This career began in the fall of 1889, when he commenced teaching anthropology at Clark University in Worcester, Massachusetts. This appointment ended unhappily after only three years, but in 1894, Boas was afforded the opportunity of addressing the Anthropology Section of the American Association for the Advancement of Science. In this address, he once again adopted an idealist stance. In opposition to an "evolutionary standpoint," he advanced what he called "the true point of view" of Theodor Waitz. This was that "the faculty of man does not designate anything but how much and what he is able to achieve in the immediate future and depends upon the stages of culture through which he had passed and the one he has reached."[19]

Boas took this idealist "point of view" from the first volume of Waitz's *Anthropologie der Naturvolker.* Published in Germany in 1859 and in English translation in 1863, it has a preface dated Marburg, October 1858. Theodor Waitz, who was born in 1821 and who became a professor of philosophy at the University of Marburg in 1848, had been much influenced by the Kantian thinker J. F. Herbart, who was appointed to Kant's former chair at Konigsberg in 1809. Waitz's idealist stance was highly congenial to Franz Boas, and from 1894 onwards, it became the basis of his own approach to anthropology. Friedrich Lange, whose *History of Materialism* had such an effect on the young Franz Boas, also thought highly of Waitz's "excellent *Anthropologie der Naturvolker.*" Thus, Lange's *History of Materialism* was almost certainly the source of Boas's introduction to Waitz.[20]

Throughout his entire anthropological career, Boas continued to rely on what he called in 1894, with neo-Kantian zeal, "the true point of view" of Theodor Waitz. In 1909, for example, he identified Waitz as one of the "great minds" who had "laid the foundations of modern anthropology." In 1924, in a paper that led to his formulation of the problem that he required Margaret Mead to investigate in Samoa, he again cited the assertion by Waitz that he had used in 1894, describing it as the "view" that had come to be the basis of all anthropological research into the cultural history of mankind. And Boas again avowed this unqualified acceptance of Waitz and his idealist assumptions in 1934 (in the *Encyclopaedia of the Social Sciences*), at the end of his professional career.[21]

Franz Boas, therefore, following Theodore Waitz, was an ardent cultural determinist. In an address he gave soon after he became professor of anthropology at Columbia University in 1899, he depicted culture as "controlling all our actions since the time of our birth." Then in 1904, he gave it as his opinion that the time was "rapidly drawing near when the biological branch of anthropology" would be "finally separated" from the rest of anthropology. "Anthropology, pure and simple," he predicted, would "deal with the customs and beliefs of the less civilized peoples only." And so, from this time onward, as Stocking has noted, "the whole thrust" of Boas's thought was "to separate biological and cultural heredity." Further, it is in this "context," in Stocking's judgment, that Boas's work has "its full historical significance."[22]

It was a "thrust" that Boas successfully imparted to his students at Columbia. The first and most influential of them was Alfred Kroeber, who, if anything, came to evince an even greater zeal for cultural determinism than did Boas himself. Thus, in his "Eighteen Professions" of 1915, which Stocking has called "a kind of manifesto of Boasian anthropology," Kroeber totally excluded evolutionary theory by laying it down as axiomatic that "heredity cannot be allowed to have acted any part in history." This was followed in 1917 by another paper in the *American Anthropologist* in which Kroeber asserted that culture, or "the superorganic," as he called it, was "without antecedents in the beginnings of organic evolution," from which "the superorganic" was entirely separate and which it transcended "utterly." Then, on the basis of this unsubstantiated supposition, convinced he was standing "at the threshold of glimpsing vague, grand forces of predestination," Kroeber instigated a massive intellectual schism, proclaiming that there was an abyss between cultural anthropology and evolutionary biology, an "eternal chasm" that could not be bridged. It was Kroeber, then, as Clifford Geertz has acknowledged, who delivered what Boas had promised.[23]

Later in 1917, Robert Lowie, another of Boas's early students, gave unqualified support to Kroeber's separatist claims, declaring culture to be "a thing sui generis," and propounding, in oracular fashion, the maxim *"omnis cultura ex cultura."* This maxim was conspicuously an ideological formula, for in asserting that cultural phenomena can only be understood in terms of other cultural phenomena, Lowie was setting up a closed system, predicated on Kroeber's claim that there was an "eternal chasm" between evolutionary biology and cultural anthropology.[24]

In 1916, Boas had claimed that "in the great mass of a healthy population the social stimulus is infinitely more potent than biological mechanism." This claim was an exemplification of what Leslie Spier, who became Boas's student in 1916, has called "the compelling idea" of the "life's work" of Franz Boas: *"the complete molding of every human expression—inner thought and external behavior—by social conditioning."* It was this "compelling idea" that moved Kroeber and Lowie in their proclamations of 1917. Thus, by 1922, when Margaret Mead became a student of Franz Boas at Barnard College, the Boasians had established their independence from biology by ideological fiat. The breach with evolutionary theory was complete, and Boasian culturalism was poised to become one of the leading ideologies of the twentieth century.[25]

There remained, however, a quite crucial problem. The categorical claims of Kroeber and Lowie, and of Boas himself, had in no sense been empirically demonstrated, especially not to Boas's adversaries in the still very active nature-nurture controversy.

From the days of his youth, Franz Boas had been an inveterate fighter. In his first duel, or *Mensur*, at the University of Heidelberg, which he fought when he was nineteen after some of his fellow students had mocked the piano playing of an acquaintance, he received a large wound on the front of his head, "a piece of scalp four by half a centimetre" being cut away; but his adversary came off much the worse, with "three cuts from ear to nose that required eight stitches." Numerous other duels, in which Boas was the victor, followed.[26]

In 1924, what Boas wanted above all else was the vindication of his idealist weltanschauung by a clear-cut victory in the nature-nurture controversy, in which he had been a leading protagonist since its inception. To this end, he completed two separate articles bearing on this impassioned controversy, one for the *American Mercury* of October 1924, and the other for the *Nation* of January 28, 1925. In the

*American Mercury* article, having extolled the cultural determinist views of his mentor, Theodor Waitz, Boas went on to complain of being beset by the "fundamental difficulty" of "differentiating" between "heredity and environment." Then over the next few months, in an attempt to solve this problem, about which he had long made up his own mind, he devised "a study in heredity and environment based on the investigation of the phenomena of adolescence," with the requisite fieldwork to be done by one of his graduate students, the twenty-three-year-old Margaret Mead.[27]

This was not at all what Margaret Mead herself wanted to study; her heart was set on ethnological research in the Tuamotu Islands of the remote South Pacific. However, so deeply was Boas the "incorrigible idealist," embroiled in the nature-nurture controversy of the 1920s, that he imposed his "study of heredity and environment" upon her, while agreeing, at her insistence, that she could undertake the study that he was imposing on her in American Samoa.

The chapters that follow chronicle the momentous consequences of this imposition, while tracing in detail the history of Margaret Mead's Samoan research and of her relationship with Franz Boas from 1922 when she became his student at Barnard College until 1928, when *Coming of Age in Samoa*—every word of which had been given Boas's approval—was published in New York City. No sequence of events has had a greater effect on anthropology in the twentieth century.

# 2

# At Barnard:
# Studying with Franz Boas
# and Ruth Benedict

WHEN MARGARET MEAD WAS AT COLLEGE in New York City
in the early 1920s, it seemed, so she thought, that she could
"make one of three choices." She could become "a scientist" or
"an artist," or she could "go straight into politics and try to improve
the state of the world right away."[1]

At seventeen, when she went to De Pauw University in Greencas-
tle, Indiana, she intended to "become a writer" and took courses in
English composition and literature. But in Indiana, what she most
longed for was to be in New York City, "where Mencken and George
Jean Nathan were publishing *Smart Set*," where the *Freeman*, the
*New Republic*, and the *Nation* flourished, and where Luther Cressman, to whom she had become secretly engaged soon after her six-
teenth birthday, was a student at the General Theological Seminary.
In September 1920, having with some difficulty gained her father's approval, she entered Barnard College of Columbia University, where
she continued to major in English.[2]

With the protracted horrors of World War I finally over, the early
1920s in the United States were a time of great hope for the future.
Throughout her life, as she herself put it, Mead always "made it a
practice to try to alter the climate of opinion" so that "new ideas"
might "bud and flower." It was to this end that her literary talents
were put from the very outset of her academic career. At De Pauw

University, she had made "quite a name for herself by writing and presenting a college pageant." On September 3, 1921, in Holicong, Pennsylvania, where she had grown up, a pageant by Margaret Mead written at the conclusion of her first year of study as an English major at Barnard College was presented by the Buckingham Women's Club. Entitled "The Buckingham Child's Quest," it concluded with the child of Buckingham, her hand "clasped fast" in the hand of the "Spirit of Tomorrow," freeing the "Spirit of the People," while the "Spirit of Tomorrow" uttered these visionary words:

> The rosy hues of sunrise
> I have culled from the lightening sky,
> Oh, despise not the dream of Tomorrow,
> When a new made world bids the Past goodbye.[3]

While "still very young," she was moved deeply by the image in *The Ballad of Sir Patrick Spens* of the young moon holding the old moon in its arms. This, according to Jean Houston, became a "seed image" for the young Margaret Mead "that flowered as she grew up into thinking of the whole world as needing care." Although her mother "did not believe in a personal God," at the age of ten, young Margaret was baptized, at her own request, into the Episcopal Church.[4] She had come to believe in God. From childhood onward, and throughout her life, she strongly believed in human betterment. One of her earliest aspirations was "to be known for having made a difference in the world." In January 1913, when just eleven, she wrote in her school exercise book:

> To live and love and loved be,
> To work the blessed day,
> To do, to fare, to fight—be free,
> This is my prayer alway.[5]

When she was sixteen, as she relates in the prologue to her autobiography, she was enthralled by the text "All things work together for good to them that love God," set "like a flowered valentine on the office wall of an old country doctor"; and her studies of "faraway peoples," like the Samoans, were undertaken, she tells us, "so that Americans might better understand themselves." The 1920s, as C. P. Snow noted, were a "period of ideals." Like Snow's George Passant, Mar-

garet Mead was conspicuously "a child of the twenties." Like George
Passant, she "wanted to build a better world," to work, as she put it
some years later, "towards the welfare of all mankind in all places on
the face of the earth." And so, from the outset of her anthropological
career, Margaret Mead enjoyed "writing exhortatory articles." She described the imposing staff she took with her everywhere from 1960
onward as her "pastoral rod." Thus, in addition to being "a research
scientist," Margaret Mead was also, in the words of Rebecca West, "a
genius of the prophetic sort," as is evident in her pageant of 1921,
written when she was only nineteen, with its "dream of Tomorrow,
when a new made world bids the Past goodbye."[6]

It was this vision of a "new made world" culled from the dawn skies
of Pennsylvania that Mead carried with her when, in her senior year at
Barnard College, she was attracted to anthropology. Before the 1920s
were out, it had been given unfettered expression in another literary
production, culled this time from the fabled South Seas, that was to
make her world famous. It was very much a vision of utopia that
Mead provided in *Coming of Age in Samoa*, and this idealist vision
was one to which she had been deeply drawn as a teenager, long before
she had ever studied anthropology.

At the beginning of her second year at Barnard, realizing that "cre-
ative writing" would not "provide a central focus" for her life, Mead
decided to concentrate instead on the study of psychology, under Professor Harry L. Hollingworth. This she supplemented, during the first
semester of 1922, with a course in zoology given by Professor Henry E.
Crampton, an authority on the evolution of the land snails of the islands of the South Pacific. During this course, Henry Crampton mentioned his research in Tahiti, and as her class notes record, Miss Mead
was required to study the problem of heredity and environment. Then,
in the fall of 1922, a few months after completing her course in zoology with Professor Crampton and while still at Barnard College, she
became a student of Professor Franz Boas and of his teaching assistant
Dr. Ruth Benedict.[7]

As Mead has described, the Department of Anthropology at Columbia in the early 1920s was "a small embattled group." During World
War I, his "pacifism" and his German origin had made Franz Boas "a
target for the inflamed feelings of the period," and "his relations with
his colleagues were stormy." Even in 1922, "although much of the
rancor of the wartime period had cooled," Boas was still "virtually a
professor without a department, his work pared to the bone." Thus,

there were no undergraduate courses in anthropology at Columbia, but during the academic year of 1922–1923, Boas did teach, for the last time, the introductory course in general anthropology that for some years previously he had been presenting at Barnard College. It was this course that Mead elected to take, discovering in anthropology, "a fascinating field in which she could combine her interests in the arts, in writing and in speaking" as well as "in people, in science" and "in the fate of human beings."[8]

When Margaret Mead became his student in 1922, Boas was in his sixty-fifth year. For Mead, Boas was "the greatest mind she had ever encountered." She very quickly became his devoted follower, and in her research in Samoa on "heredity and environment" in relation to adolescence, of which Boas was both the instigator and the supervisor, she was, from beginning to end, acting as his agent.

In fall 1922, Ruth Benedict, who had completed her doctorate in anthropology at Columbia with Boas as her supervisor a few months earlier, became Boas's assistant at Barnard. Her main role was to extend Boas's teaching by taking groups of students on visits to the ethnological collections of the American Museum of Natural History. Occasionally, she would take his classes, as on January 5, 1923, when she lectured on diffusion, commenting afterward in her diary: "Stumbled into anti-evolution. n.b. never argue that point again, its dead." Ruth Benedict was very much a Boasian, and her influence on Margaret Mead, from the outset of Mead's anthropological career, was almost as marked as was that of Franz Boas himself.[9]

Ruth Fulton was born in New York City on June 5, 1887, the daughter of a medical doctor, Frederick Fulton, who died before she was two. Brought up in various parts of New York state in a "staunchly Baptist family," she created "her world" largely from the Bible, according to Stocking, peopling it with Blakean figures "of a strange dignity and grace, among whom her father was identified with Christ." Her graduation in 1909 from Vassar College, where she majored in English, was followed by travel in France, Italy, Germany, Switzerland and England with two Vassar friends. She then taught for three years in girls' schools in Los Angeles and Pasadena and, in 1914, married Stanley Benedict, a professor of biochemistry at Cornell Medical School, and settled in suburban Long Island.[10]

For several years, she sought fulfillment in various literary projects, including a "pet scheme" to "write a series of biographical papers" about "restless and highly enslaved women of past generations." Then in 1919, if only casually at first, she became intrigued with anthropology. The New School for Social Research had been founded in downtown Manhattan early in 1919. In the fall of that year, Ruth Benedict enrolled in a course called "Sex in Ethnology," given by Dr. Elsie Clews Parsons, who had received a doctorate in sociology from Columbia University in 1899, and then, in 1900, had married Herbert Parsons, a Republican politician with whom she traveled widely.[11]

In 1915, after having spent a vacation among the Pueblo Indians of the Rio Grande, Dr. Parsons decided to take up anthropology. To this end, she consulted Alfred Kroeber and Robert Lowie, as well as another of Boas' followers, Pliny Earle Goddard of the American Museum of Natural History. She also consulted Boas himself and became his close friend, from 1915 onward receiving from him, in Kroeber's words, "measured but massive sympathy." Indeed, by May 1919, Parsons and Boas were doing fieldwork together at Laguna Pueblo. Franz Boas was the anthropologist whose "methodology and theoretical perspective" had decisively influenced Elsie Clews Parsons when she taught her "Sex in Ethnology" course at the New School for Social Research, which she had helped to found. Thus, from the very beginning of her own contact with anthropology, Ruth Benedict was exposed, through the teaching of Elsie Clews Parsons, to the influence of Franz Boas.[12]

In 1920, Benedict continued her studies at the New School under Alexander Goldenweiser. Goldenweiser, after completing his doctorate under Boas in 1910, had become an instructor in anthropology at Columbia, only to be dismissed, to Boas's displeasure, in 1919. Boas had then found a position for his brilliant if wayward student at the New School, where he quickly established himself as an outstanding lecturer in anthropology. The "mercurial" Goldenweiser, as Mead called him, was very much a protégé of Boas, and in later years, he wrote of the "glowing enthusiasm and colossal knowledge" of Professor Franz Boas, which for many years had served as his "guidance and inspiration." He was also very much influenced by Kroeber and Lowie. Goldenweiser was thus a leading proponent of the extreme form of cultural determinism that entered American anthropology in the year 1917; and in 1920 and 1921, he effectively imparted this way of looking at things to his student Ruth Benedict.[13]

During these years, Ruth Benedict took four courses with Goldenweiser: "Groundwork of Civilization" and "Early Society and Politics" in 1920; "Early Economics and Knowledge" and "The Diffusion of Civilization" in 1921. And she also took a course with Lowie, who lectured on primitive law at Columbia before he left to become an associate professor at the University of California at Berkeley.[14]

Then, on the recommendations of Alexander Goldenweiser and Elsie Clews Parsons, Ruth Benedict was accepted by Franz Boas as a doctoral candidate at Columbia University. With his "customary disregard for administrative rules," Boas got Ruth Benedict credit for the courses she had taken at the New School for Social Research. She completed her doctorate under Boas's supervision in spring 1922, after only three semesters of study. In the summer of that year, she went to the Morongo Indian Reservation in southern California to study the culture of the Serrano Indians, under the "introductory tutelage" of Professor Kroeber. Thus, when Margaret Mead first encountered her in the fall of 1922, Ruth Benedict had been influenced not only by Franz Boas but also by three of his leading students, Alfred Kroeber, Robert Lowie, and Alexander Goldenweiser, and had become a strong advocate of their ideas.[15]

The introductory course given by Professor Boas and his teaching assistant Dr. Benedict, for which the twenty-year-old Margaret Mead enrolled in her final year at Barnard College, began in the fall of 1922. Within a few weeks, anthropology began "to come alive" for her. Professor Boas, "with his great head and slight frail body, his face scarred from an old duel, and one eye drooping from facial paralysis," spoke "with an authority and a distinction" greater than she had ever met in a teacher. By the end of the first semester, Mead had become so enthusiastic about anthropology and had talked so much with other students about Boas's course that the class registration doubled. This enthusiasm was also excited by Ruth Benedict's "vivid delight" in such things as "Northwest Coast art," which "gave life to the clarity and order of Professor Boas' presentation of man's development through the ages."[16]

In Mead's class notes, totaling some 215 pages, made during Boas's lectures between October 4, 1922, and May 16, 1923, the idealist assumptions of Boasian culturalism are quite explicit. On November 6, 1922, Franz Boas told his Barnard class, which included Mead, that "we act actually on the basis of what is handed down to us"; on November 24, that "the adjustment of emotion depends upon the culture in which we live and the whole set of controls is dependent on the culture"; and, on December 6, that "in primitive society the ideal is conformity, and any attempt to deviate is not tolerated."[17]

This emphasis on what Mead was to call a few years later "the phenomenon of social pressure and its absolute determination in shaping the individuals within its bounds" was, as Mead's class notes show, the anthropological leitmotiv of the course of lectures that Franz Boas gave during the academic year 1922–1923 at Barnard College. This was in accord with Boas's doctrine of "the complete molding of every human expression—inner thought and external behavior—by social conditioning." On April 27, 1923, at Barnard College, he summarized his position in these two highly significant sentences: "It is very important to realize that the pattern of thought which develops in a large area is an important characteristic of every aspect of cultural life. One of the more important conclusions we can draw from the study of anthropology is that we find this tendency to conform to a pattern."[18]

This is a succinct statement by Boas of the doctrine of the cultural patterning of human thought and action that Benedict and Mead were to make peculiarly their own and, with Boas's active support, to develop into a major anthropological movement. Furthermore, it was with this doctrine of the cultural patterning of human thought and behavior that Mead operated in Manu'a in American Samoa in 1926, where it decisively influenced both the inquiries she made and the conclusions to which she came.

From the very outset of Benedict's studies with Boas, the concept of pattern was central to her thinking, as is evident in her first anthropological paper, "The Vision in Plains Culture," written in 1921 when she was his student. Thus, in June, 1922, after having read a reprint of this paper, Edward Sapir, who in 1917 had radically questioned the extreme cultural determinism of Kroeber's "The Superorganic," wrote to Benedict from Ottawa, asking if she took the same "extreme view" that "no matter what patterns rise, no matter how unsuitable they seem *a priori* for the guidance of human behavior, human psychology can and does accommodate itself to them as it accommodates itself to practically any physical environment." To take this view, said Sapir, one would have to be "a kind of culture fatalist."[19]

This, however, was precisely the view that Benedict, inspired by the doctrines of Boas, and by those of Kroeber, Lowie, and Goldenweiser, did in fact take. In a review of F. C. Bartlett's *Psychology and Primitive Culture*, written at about this time, Benedict defined "man" as having "responses" that "have been conditioned from birth by the character of the culture into which he was born" and numbered herself among those who hoped "to achieve some understanding of human behavior" through the study of "cultural patterns." In her paper "The Science of Custom," which set the stage for the writing of her *Patterns of Culture*, judged by G. W. Stocking Jr. to be "the single most influential work by a twentieth-century American anthropologist," Benedict declared that "traditional patterns of behavior set the mold" into which "human nature" flows and, further, that the cultural pattern of a people "fashions as it will the instincts of the people who live within it, remaking them in conformity with its own requirements." As is evident in these assertions, Ruth Benedict was an uncompromising cultural determinist, and the anthropological ideology for which she became famous was directly derived from the teaching of Franz Boas and the writings of Alfred Kroeber and Robert Lowie.[20]

This ideology and this teaching were cogently communicated to Margaret Mead. As Mead herself describes, Ruth Benedict, by 1922, had "found Professor Boas" and "sense," and after they had become intimate friends in 1923, Benedict conveyed to Mead "a double feeling of urgency": the need to "learn everything" that Boas had to offer during the last course of lectures that he was giving at Barnard College, as well as the need to "rescue the beautiful, complex patterns that people had contrived for themselves to live in, that were being irrevocably lost all over the world."[21]

When Ruth Benedict entered anthropology, she was, as Mead described her, "a gentle wraithlike figure, her hair going prematurely grey and never staying in place, dressed with a kind of studied indifference, just deaf enough to miss a great deal of what was being said before others recognized it, and painfully shy—the beauty which had been hers as a young girl misted over by uncertainty and awkwardness." As Boas's teaching assistant at Barnard College, she "spoke so hesitatingly that many students were put off by her manner." But Margaret Mead and her fellow student Marie Bloomfield were "fascinated" by Dr. Benedict, whose "comments humanized Boas' formal lectures." On visits to the American Museum of Natural History, they would "ride down and back on the Broadway streetcar with her." This led to their being invited to a seminar at which Ruth Benedict discussed John Dewey's book of 1922, *Human Nature and Conduct*, and by the beginning of 1923, a friendship had begun to form between Boas's thirty-five-year-old teaching assistant and her twenty-one-year-old student Margaret Mead. They had lunch together on Monday, January 8, and Wednesday, January 17, and "tea until 5.30" on Thursday,

January 18. Then, in Mead's words, they were "precipitated" into "a much closer relationship" early in February 1923—by the shock of the suicide of Marie Bloomfield.[22]

When this tragic event was reported in the newspapers, Ruth Benedict wrote to Mead, saying, "I shall be thinking of you today and wishing people could be of more use to each other in difficult times" and suggesting that Mead should come to her apartment. This Mead did, on the evening of Thursday, February 8, to be consoled by Ruth Benedict's understanding, and from this meeting onward, their friendship became much more intimate. At this same time, Ruth Benedict's marriage to Stanley Benedict was in crisis. As she noted in her diary early in 1923, it was as if they had "no crumb in common" and "inhabited the opposing poles." And so, in her isolation and loneliness, Ruth Benedict turned eagerly to her relationship with Margaret Mead, whose "zest of youth" and "admiration," as she noted on March 7, 1923, rested her "like a padded chair and a fireplace."[23]

On that day, Ruth Benedict had discussed with Margaret Mead the notion that she might enter anthropology. A few days later, on March 11, 1923, in a long letter to her paternal grandmother, who was "the most decisive influence" in her life, Mead announced that anthropology had become her "chief enthusiasm." She continued:

> I would so like to be an anthropologist. For contact with modern civilization is killing off primitive cultures so fast; in a hundred years there will be no primitive people; the work is so urgent, and there are so few people who even understand the importance of the work, let alone being willing to do it. However, it is so non-lucrative that I fear I'll have to do other things first. Boas has let me come into his other graduate course too. So I am having seven hours of lectures a week in anthropology and I'm doing barrels of reading.[24]

In this same letter, Mead also noted that Dr. Benedict belonged to a committee that tried to "popularize anthropology and make at least a few of its ideas common coin." Two days later, over lunch, Ruth Benedict again did her utmost to persuade Margaret Mead to take up anthropology, writing afterward in her diary: "I hope she does it. I need a companion in harness." This tipped the balance. On March 20, 1923, Margaret Mead told Franz Boas of her desire to work for a doctorate in anthropology at Columbia. At first Boas "poured cold water" on the idea. He then advised her to go to Harvard. He had, however, been impressed by Mead's "helpful participation in class discussion" to the extent of excusing her from taking the required examination; and he also knew of the very high regard in which she was held by Dr. Benedict. Eventually, Boas agreed to accept Mead as a doctoral candidate in anthropology at Columbia beginning in the fall of 1923, despite her background of only two semesters of undergraduate study of the subject at the time of her acceptance.[25]

On June 6, 1923, Miss Margaret Mead of Barnard College received a Bachelor of Arts degree from Columbia University, "with honorable mention." In her final year, she had demonstrated her intellectual brilliance by achieving excellence not only in anthropology but also in economics, English, psychology, and sociology. On graduation at twenty-one, she was elected to the Barnard section of the New York chapter of Phi Beta Kappa. She had been editor of the *Barnard Bulletin* and a member of the Barnard College debating team and had shown herself to be an individual of quite exceptional intellectual abilities. In addition, she was engagingly vivacious, with a rare capacity to communicate with others in a way that enthused them. In a letter sent to her soon after her graduation from Barnard College, one of Mead's fellow students wrote to her, saying, "I love everything you write, poems, letters, editorials, and I get a thrill whenever I read them and realize that I know you."[26]

To her disappointment, given her resolve to work for a doctorate in anthropology at Columbia, Mead had narrowly failed to win the Caroline Duror Fellowship, Barnard's only graduate fellowship. But in its stead she received a "no-red-tape fellowship" of $300 from her mentor and well-wisher, Ruth Benedict. As Mead herself recorded, "by electing anthropology as a career," she was also "electing a closer relationship" with Ruth Benedict and, as Margaret Caffrey, Benedict's biographer, has described, the two women eventually entered into an intimate sapphic relationship. In this relationship, they "read and re-read each other's work, wrote poems in answer to poems," and shared their "hopes and worries," especially "about anthropology." Ruth Benedict's influence on Margaret Mead's thinking from 1923 onward, and especially during Mead's Samoan research and the writing of *Coming of Age in Samoa,* was thus most immediate and of profound significance. As a direct result of her encounters with Boas and Benedict during her senior year at Barnard College, the exceptionally talented young Margaret Mead had, at the age of only twenty-one, been recruited into the select company of those whose approach to the understanding of human behavior was through the study of "cultural patterns."[27]

# 3

# Funding the Samoan Research Project: A National Research Fellowship

O N SEPTEMBER 3, 1923, in the Episcopal church where she was a communicant, just outside the village of Buckingham in Pennsylvania, Margaret Mead was married to Luther Cressman, the newly ordained theologian to whom she had been engaged since December 31, 1917. They were, according to Cressman, both virgins. After a brief honeymoon at Cape Cod, they took up residence in New York City in an apartment at 419 West 119th Street, eager to resume their separate studies at Columbia University.[1]

New York City in the early 1920s was, in Luther Cressman's words, a "vortex of new ideas derived from discoveries in science, reaction to and reflection on the lessons of the war, and an awareness that a new phase of life for the Western world had come on stage with the Russian Revolution and the world's response in fear and hope." For Rebecca West, writing at about this time, New York's skyscrapers, "more angular than pagan temples, more solid than cathedrals," had, "unexpectedly enough, a religious quality." She described the scene in these words: "At the base of the mountains of masonry walk crowds of people who are exhilarated as if they breathed high mountain air; for the atmosphere of New York, which is so full of electricity that you may give yourself a shock if you draw your hand along the brass rail of your bed, runs like wine in its people's veins." This was the New York—"a swirl of excited nothingness," as Eugene O'Neill called it—where Mead, in the fall of 1923, embarked on her graduate studies in anthropology, living life to the full. On a weekend early in November 1923, she attended a concert by Cecilia Hansen, a new Russian violinist, went to an exhibition by Frances Cugat, a new Spanish artist, and read Willa Cather's latest novel, *A Lost Lady*.[2]

During her first year of graduate work, in addition to her anthropological studies, Mead had the major task of completing a thesis in psychology, which she had become committed to writing before Ruth Benedict persuaded her to take up anthropology. It was on a topic suggested to her by Franz Boas, involving the analysis of the intelligence testing of Italian and American children in Hammonton, New Jersey. Mead was able to show that the scores of Italian children were influenced by language, social status, and other extraneous factors and to reach the important conclusion that the "classification of foreign children, in schools where they have to compete with American children on the basis of group intelligence test findings alone, is not a just evaluation of the child's innate capacity and may be prejudicial to the child's welfare by placing him with children of less intelligence."[3]

For this thesis, which is another indication of Mead's concern with the betterment of social conditions, she received a Master of Arts degree from Columbia University on June 4, 1924. This research, as Mead noted, concluded her "relationship with psychology." It was, however, an experience that led her to give considerable time to psychological testing during the course of her fieldwork in Samoa.[4]

In the fall of 1923, Mead obtained part-time employment at $85 a month as an assistant to Professor William F. Ogburn, head of the Department of Sociology and Economics at Barnard College and the editor of the *Journal of the American Statistical Association*. This, for Mead, was a most important relationship, as Ogburn became a main supporter of her application in 1925 to the National Research Council for a National Research Fellowship in the Biological Sciences to work in Samoa. In her final year at Barnard College, Mead had taken a course by Ogburn based on his book of 1922, *Social Change with Respect to Culture and Original Nature*, in which he adopted the same ideological stance as had Kroeber and Lowie in 1917. The principal conclusion of Ogburn's teaching was, in Mead's words, that "the nature of man had to be derived from cultural materials," a view identical with that held by Boas and Benedict, as well as by Kroeber, Lowie, and Goldenweiser. Ogburn, by whose teaching she became "convinced," was thus a major influence in the formation of the anthropological assumptions with which Mead began her graduate studies at Columbia in 1923 and that two years later she took with her to Samoa.[5]

When Mead began her study of anthropology, the historical development of cultures was a topic of consuming interest, of which Boas, in his course of lectures at Barnard College in 1922–1923, made frequent mention. Thus, in fall 1923, when Mead suggested as the topic of her doctoral dissertation "the problem of the stability of cultural elements" in relation to attempts "to reconstruct the history of a primitive culture," Boas readily agreed. Boas told her she might work on Siberia, which would mean learning Chinese and Russian, or on the Low Countries, for which she would have to have a command of French, Dutch, German, and medieval Latin, or on Polynesia, where she "could do with only French and German."[6]

Mead had determined to complete her graduate course within two years, and despite her "extremely heavy schedule," was soon immersed in the study of Polynesia, concentrating on the "complexes of canoe-building, house-building and tattooing in Hawaii, Tahiti, the Marquesas, New Zealand and Samoa." On February 19, 1924, she wrote to her grandmother, saying: "I am spending my days in the midst of Polynesia. Very soon I shall speak it in my sleep." She then went on to recount that on the previous Saturday morning, when she was "half asleep," she had got "a very convenient hunch" that she thought was "going to prove valuable." It was "the idea that the keynote of the special development you find in Samoa is due to the particular emphasis placed on village communities rather than on rank or religious hierarchies." Although it might not lead to anything, this "hunch" was at least a "point of departure for discussion," as she had to "make a report on all Polynesia" in a month's time at Boas's seminar.[7]

In preparation for this seminar, held the last week of March 1924, Mead "worked like a Trojan," as she knew "how many aching voids" there were in her knowledge. It "went off pretty well," however. "It was delightful"—so said Dr. Boas to Dr. Gladys Reichard, his successor as full-time instructor in anthropology at Barnard College, who told Dr. Pliny Goddard of the American Museum of Natural History, who told Mead herself. With some assistance, she had made enlarge-ments of various Polynesian "tattooing designs," which she displayed along one side of the seminar room. The next day, at lunch, Boas turned to her and commented: "I didn't know you were such an artist." To which Mead replied: "They were only copies, Dr. Boas." "Well," he remarked, "I couldn't do it." This, Mead felt, was "unconscious and most complete praise." With this seminar on Polynesia, she had made her mark as one of the most gifted of Boas's graduate students.[8]

A few months later Mead's research was sufficiently advanced for her to consolidate her position as a stellar student by presenting a paper entitled "Rank in Polynesia" at the Ninety-Second Meeting of the British Association for the Advancement of Science, held in Toronto, August 6–13, 1924. The meetings of Section H (anthropology), held in the Anatomy Building of the University of Toronto, were "very well attended." Among those participating were A. C. Haddon and C. G. Seligman from England, D. Jenness and T. F. McIlwraith from Canada, as well as two of Boas's former students, one of them Alexander Goldenweiser and the other Edward Sapir, of whose book *Language,* published in 1920, Robert Lowie had declared: "I know of no general work put forth by American anthropological scholarship of which we have more reason to be proud." Mead, a twenty-two-year-old graduate student from Columbia, was thus addressing a distinguished anthropological audience in presenting, on the basis of her library studies, "an analysis of the idea of rank as found in Samoa, Hawaii and New Zealand." Once again, she had demonstrated her intellectual prowess.[9]

It was, as Sapir reported, a decidedly successful meeting, with "the exchanges, both scientific and personal" among the British, American, and Canadian anthropologists present being "cordial and stimulating." It was especially stimulating for the young Margaret Mead, for whom associating with Sapir, "the intellectual giant of Boasian anthropology" and his fellow anthropological illuminati was a major formative experience. In particular, while learning "the delight of intellectual arguments among peers," she discovered that each ethnologist had "a field of his own" and "a people to whom he referred in his discussions." Ruth Benedict had already convinced Mead of the urgent need for ethnographical research. She returned to New York wanting a "people" on whom she could base her "intellectual life." As the "idea flowered," finding her own "people" became "a driving force" in her life. One of Mead's fellow graduate students was Isabel Gordon, whose paper "Cultural Stability Among the Mountain Whites of Tennessee," had been read by title at the British Association for the Advancement of Science meeting in Toronto in August. Cultural stability was the very topic on which Mead was working. But the last thing she wanted was to do fieldwork in the United States among American Indians, "where everybody else seemed well established." Instead, although she well realized the difficulty of going there alone, her heart was set on certain of the untouched islands of Polynesia, about which she had been so eagerly reading. By early September 1924, she was bending all her energies on trying to persuade Isabel Gordon to "go to the South Seas" with her.[10]

At this time, Mead was hard at work on her doctoral dissertation in a room in a tower of the American Museum of Natural History. To get there she had to climb "a narrow iron stairway" and then "thread long corridors" lined with "shelves of pottery" and by "locked storerooms marked 'Africa' and 'Madagascar.'" The place had a "pungent, spicy, penetrating odor all its own, compounded of old baskets, pottery dust, chemical preservatives, dried hides and hair, and perhaps the sacred drugs of dead Indian medicine men." From the room where she worked, "six stories down and a block away" was "the hum of the city," and from the window, which the old Cockney keeper told her she must be sure to close, she could "look out for blocks over the city towards the East River." The American Museum of Natural History, with its zoologists, botanists, paleontologists, and anthropologists, was "a very world in itself"—and one that she liked immensely.[11]

In the fall of 1924 as she worked on her dissertation, Mead had ranged before her on a long table in her tower room such books as W. Ellis's *A Narrative of a Tour Through the Sandwich Islands*, J. B. Stair's *Old Samoa*, F. E. Maning's *Old New Zealand by a Pakeha Maori*, H. D. Skinner's *The Morioris of the Chatham Islands*, and W. W. Gill's *Songs and Myths from the Southern Pacific*, as well as bound volumes of the *Journal of the Polynesian Society*. In volume 28 of this journal, which is listed in the bibliography of her dissertation, Mead would have come upon the writings of Reverend Père Hervé Audran, a French missionary, on the Paumotu, or Tuamotu Islands, an archipelago of atolls to the east of Tahiti, and upon an intriguing cosmological drawing made in 1869 by a Tuamotuan named Paiore. In earlier volumes, there was a dictionary of the Paumotuan dialect compiled by Edward Tregear.[12]

As a result of her stirring experiences in Toronto, Mead had resolved to do fieldwork as soon as she could complete her doctorate.

With her husband's collaboration, she worked out a scheme that would make this possible. Her plan was to do field research on cultural change, an idea that had grown directly out of the dissertation on which she was working. What she had in mind was a specifically ethnological study having to do with the general theory of culture. By September 1924, Mead had devised just such an ethnological project, one she planned to undertake somewhere "in the South Seas," beginning—if she could get a fellowship—in about mid-1925. The Tuamotu Islands, as she noted at the time, were "still unexplored ground," and it was to these remote islands of central Polynesia that Mead, in the fall of 1924, adventurously determined she would go to carry out an ethnological project that would put her in the same class as the celebrated ethnologists she had encountered at the Toronto meeting. Her personal commitment to this ethnological project in the South Seas was intense.[13]

In marked contrast, while Mead was pursuing her research on Polynesia at the American Museum of Natural History, Boas remained deeply involved in the nature-nurture controversy of the early decades of the twentieth century. He had entered this great controversy on the side of the environmentalists, with an article in the *Scientific Monthly* of November 1916, in which he asserted that "in the great mass of a healthy population, the social stimulus is infinitely more potent than the biological mechanism." For Boas and his followers, this was an issue of quite crucial importance. When Ruth Benedict reviewed A. L. Kroeber's 1923 work, *Anthropology*, in the *Nation* in January 1924, she praised it as "the first book" to make available "the fundamental point of view of modern American anthropology." Her review was entitled "Nature and Nurture," and its third paragraph ran as follows:

> The fundamental question, as Mr. Kroeber conceives it, to which the labors of anthropology are directed, is in how far the forces at work in civilization are cultural, and in how far organic or due to heredity; what is due to nurture, in the rhyming phrase, and what to nature. It is first of all necessary to be able to recognize those elements that are received from tradition, those which are ours because we have been brought up in a particular group or country. Only then can we presume to discuss that residue which is due to heredity and to the psychology of the individual.[14]

This, as his article in the *American Mercury* of October 1924 made clear, was also the view of Franz Boas, and soon after it had appeared, he devised "a study in heredity and environment based on an investigation of the phenomena of adolescence among primitive and civilized peoples" that he hoped would provide an unambiguous answer to what, together with Kroeber and Benedict, he judged to be a quite "fundamental question." In this way, he might be able to win the vexing nature-nurture controversy in a satisfyingly decisive manner. His plan was for this study to be done among American Indians with funds from the National Research Council. The investigator he had in mind was his brilliant young doctoral student, Margaret Mead, who already had a master's degree in psychology.[15]

The U.S. National Research Council was set up in 1916, after consultations between the National Academy of Sciences and President Woodrow Wilson, when, as *Scientific American* noted, "science, education, industry and the federal government" joined hands for the first time "in a plan for the promotion of research, as such, without stipulations or preoccupations as to the immediate 'practical terms.'" In 1923 came the announcement that the National Research Council had been "entrusted by the Rockefeller Foundation with the expenditure of a sum of $325,000, available between July 1, 1923, and June 30, 1928, to promote research in the biological sciences, including Zoology, Botany, Anthropology and Psychology by post-doctorate research fellowships." The "special funds" that had been provided by the Rockefeller Foundation were administered by a Board of National Research Fellowships in the Biological Sciences, the members of which in 1924–1925 were: Frank R. Lillie, chairman, professor of embryology, University of Chicago; H. H. Bartlett, professor of botany, University of Michigan; C. E. McClung, professor of zoology, University of Pennsylvania; M. M. Metcalf, zoologist, Orchard Laboratory, Oberlin, Ohio; T. H. Morgan, professor of experimental zoology, Columbia University; W.J.V. Osterhout, professor of botany, Harvard University; C. E. Seashore, professor of psychology, University of Iowa; E. L. Thorndike, professor of educational psychology, Teachers College, Columbia University; Clark Wissler, curator of anthropology, American Museum of Natural History; and R. S. Woodworth, professor of psychology, Columbia University.[16]

In April 1923, after completing his doctorate at Columbia, Melville J. Herskovits had been awarded a National Research Fellowship in the Biological Sciences for a research project in physical anthropology that was both sponsored and supervised by Franz Boas. As Stocking has noted, the Herskovits project, like the "study in heredity and environment in relation to adolescence" that Boas devised in 1924 for Mead to undertake among American Indians with a National Research Fellowship in the Biological Sciences, was "related to the overall pattern" of Boas's long-term research program on "questions of race and culture." Appealing as this plan was to Boas, it created a major quandary for Mead, who at this time, according to her husband, was a "brilliant," "goal-oriented" young woman, at times "wilful" and "stubborn," with her heart set on ethnological research in the Tuamotu Islands of Polynesia. As Mead subsequently declared: "I didn't even want to study the adolescent girl. I wanted to study change. I wanted to find out in a society that was changing whether people felt more strongly about new things or old things. That was the problem I was interested in."[17]

When she was growing up in Pennsylvania, the young Margaret Mead had "resented furiously" her father's "entirely arbitrary intrusions" into the everyday lives of herself and her younger siblings. As early as 1923, she and Ruth Benedict had begun to refer to Professor Boas as "Papa." This was an expression of the affection they both felt for him. It was a feeling they very much shared. In one of her letters, Ruth Benedict refers to the things that she and Margaret Mead had been "brought up on" with their "mother's—or Papa Franz's!—milk." And now, in the final year of her doctoral course, on the ground that Polynesia was "too dangerous" a place, Papa Franz was directly intruding into Mead's affairs to deny her her precious ethnological project.[18]

The Social Science Research Council had declined to give her a grant because she was "too young," and so, with no other source of funding available, "going into the field at all" depended on reaching some kind of compromise with Professor Boas. In this predicament, Mead did what she had "learned to do" when she had "to work things out" with her father. She knew that there was one thing that mattered more to Boas than "the direction taken by anthropological research." This was that he should not behave "like a Prussian autocrat." And so, she repeated over and over that by insisting that she work with American Indians, he was preventing her from going where she really wanted to work. Unable to bear the "implied accusation" that he was "bullying" her, Boas finally agreed that she could go to somewhere in Polynesia to study heredity and environment in relation to adolescence, as long as it was not to the remote Tuamotus but to "an island to which a ship came regularly." This proposal Mead reluctantly accepted, even though the problem that Boas was requiring her to investigate, and if at all possible solve, was very different indeed from the ethnological research on which her heart had been set. She had now to locate a suitable Polynesian archipelago in which to work on Boas's problem.[19]

For many years, the main center for research in Polynesia had been the Bishop Museum in Honolulu. Its director in 1924 was Dr. Herbert E. Gregory, formerly the Silliman Professor of Geology at Yale University. Gregory was in the habit of making annual visits to the Eastern states in fulfillment of his continuing duties as a member of the staff of Yale University and as chairman of the Committee on Pacific Investigations of the National Research Council based in Washington, D.C., which he did from October 1924 to January 1925. During this visit, as was his custom, he called at the American Museum of Natural History to confer with the curator of anthropology, Clark Wissler, who was also a member of the Committee on Pacific Investigations and a consultant to the Bishop Museum.[20]

In a letter that Mead wrote to Gregory on May 5, 1925, she mentions having talked with him during the previous January, when she was working on her dissertation in the tower of the American Museum of Natural History. Gregory had pointed out to Mead that her prospects "of doing effective fieldwork" would be "very much enhanced" if she could "work in close affiliation and consultation with the staff of the Bishop Museum." Applicants for a National Research Fellowship in the Biological Sciences were required to nominate an institution at which their proposed research could be "prosecuted to the best advantage." Accordingly, Mead asked Gregory for a letter that she could attach to her application to the National Research Council. Although no record of their meeting has survived, Mead would have grasped the opportunity in January 1925 to discuss her proposed research in Polynesia with Gregory while he was visiting New York. However, it is known that on his return to Honolulu in January 1925, Herbert Gregory wrote a formal letter to Margaret Mead, a copy of which has survived in the archives of the National Research Council, and that she included it with her application of February 1925 for a National Research Fellowship in the Biological Sciences.[21]

Gregory dictated and signed this letter as soon as he got back to the Bishop Museum. The senior ethnologist at the Bishop Museum, Dr. Edward Craighill Handy, had visited both American and New Zealand Samoa in 1923. Gregory was thus in a position to provide Mead with

the reliable information she was seeking. So important is this letter of
Gregory's for understanding the extraordinary course that Mead's
Samoan research eventually took that it deserves to be cited in full. It
is headed Bernice P. Bishop Museum of Polynesian Ethnology and
Natural History, Honolulu, Hawaii, and dated January 23, 1925. It
reads:

My dear Miss Mead,
I am pleased to learn of your plan for psychological studies in con-
nection with anthropological work now being done in Polynesia.
The importance of that work is obvious and would be included in
the scientific program of the Bishop Museum if funds were available. Samoa is a promising field and one in which it is entirely
feasible for a woman to work. In American Samoa the United
States Navy has established several hospitals and schools in out-
lying districts; in New Zealand Samoa the Agricultural Department is coming into close touch with the natives. Because of its
relations with government officials, missionaries and native leaders, the Bishop Museum can assist you with introductions. If you
undertake this work, I suggest that you join the Museum staff as a
Volunteer Associate and spend perhaps a month in Honolulu on
your way to the field, studying Samoan material and consulting
with members of the staff who have worked in those islands.
Very truly yours,
Herbert E. Gregory, Director

In 1925, the ships of the Oceanic Steamship Company called at Pago
Pago in American Samoa about once every three weeks on their voy-
ages between Honolulu and Sydney. This met Boas's requirement that
Mead must work on a Polynesian island "to which a ship came regu-
larly." With an assurance from the director of the Bernice P. Bishop
Museum that Samoa was "a promising field" where it was "entirely
feasible" for her to work on the project she would be undertaking for
Boas, Mead, with Boas's approval, quickly decided on American
Samoa as the site for her proposed fieldwork.
During the following weeks, while continuing to act as an editorial
assistant to Professor Ogburn, attending Boas's lectures at Columbia,
and writing her doctoral dissertation, Mead also found time to prepare
her application to the National Research Council for a National Research Fellowship in the Biological Sciences. The completed application

was received in Washington, D.C., on February 27, 1925. On the main application form, she gave as the "subject" of her "proposed research": "A Study in Heredity and Environment based on an Investigation of the Phenomena of Adolescence among primitive and civilized peoples," with "Fieldwork to be done in Samoa." Attached to the main application form, as required, was a "plan of research," in which the purpose of Mead's proposed investigation, of which Boas had been the instigator, was made unambiguously clear. Its first paragraph read: "This investigation aims to provide data from a primitive culture which can be compared with observations made in our own civilization, in an attempt to throw light on the problem of which phenomena of adolescence are culturally and which physiologically determined." It was proposed, Mead stated, "to make an intensive study of the adolescent girl in one primitive culture, that of the Samoan islands." By confining the investigation to one culture, it was hoped to "avoid the errors due to interpretations based on insufficient knowledge of the whole cultural milieu." She proposed "to spend a year in actual fieldwork in Samoa," which had been chosen because she was "familiar with the literature relating to the Polynesian area" and could, therefore, begin her investigation "with a useful working knowledge of the culture." The "native culture in American Samoa" was, she believed, "still sufficiently primitive" to make the study she was proposing "practicable." She noted in her application that she would be supported in her proposed research in Samoa by the Bernice P. Bishop Museum of Honolulu, and she attached a copy of the letter she had received from its director, Dr. H. E. Gregory, in which he had suggested that she should join the staff of the Bishop Museum as an associate.[22]

During her tussle with Boas about where she would undertake the research on heredity and environment that he had imposed on her, Mead had told her father that her professor was trying to make her work with "Americans, already heavily contacted," instead of letting her go "where things were interesting." "Partly out of sheer counter-suggestibility to the proposal made by Boas, but also out of his genuine capacity to share in another person's ambitions," her father, in support of her desire to work in Polynesia, offered to pay her fare around the world. She was thus able to include in her application the information that she would be able to pay her own "transportation expenses" from the United States to Samoa and back. This meant, she noted, that the "full stipend" of any fellowship she might be awarded could be "utilized" during her "twelve months in the field."[23]

The referees nominated by Mead were Professor Franz Boas of Columbia University and, at Barnard College, Professor William F. Ogburn, Professor Harry L. Hollingworth, and Dean Virginia C. Gildersleeve. She requested that they send letters directly to the secretary of the Board of National Research Fellowships in the Biological Sciences "as to an applicant's attainment and promise in research" as indicated by "ideals, ability, originality, judgment, enthusiasm, industry and personality." In her letter of February 17, 1925, Dean Gildersleeve noted that Miss Mead, who had "an exceptionally good record as a student at Barnard College," was "a young woman of real scholarly promise." Hollingworth, noting that Mead, "specializing in psychology as an undergraduate," had been his student "for several years," was "glad to testify," on February 13, 1925, to her "thorough competence" to "study the phenomena of adolescence among primitive peoples (Samoa), with special reference to the analysis of physiological vs. cultural influences." She had, Hollingworth wrote, "a high level of intelligence, and an independence and initiative such as are quite uncommon."[24]

Even more enthusiastic, in his letter of February 27, 1925, was Professor William F. Ogburn, whom Mead had studied with at Barnard and whose personal assistant she had become in fall 1923. He thus knew Mead better than any of her other referees, including Boas himself, and had "learned to know her method of work and type of mind very well indeed." "I am," Ogburn wrote, "very enthusiastic about Miss Mead. She has a splendid mind and is wonderfully well trained along the lines of precision and accuracy. She is fertile in ideas and yet knows very well the meaning of facts and evidence. She is a person who carries through a project and finishes her work on time. She knows what the carrying out of a project means. She has much ambition and is a very hard worker and I predict for Miss Mead great success in any intellectual undertaking."[25]

Whereas Ogburn addressed this remarkably percipient appreciation of the young Margaret Mead to the Board of National Research Fellowships of the Biological Sciences, as had Hollingworth and Gildersleeve, Franz Boas wrote directly to Professor R. S. Woodworth, chairman of the Division of Anthropology and Psychology of the National Research Council. Woodworth had been Boas's colleague for many years and as professor of psychology at Columbia was familiar with the research on which Mead had based her master's thesis of 1924, "Intelligence Tests of Italian and American Children," an abstract of which she included with her application. Woodworth was thus well acquainted with her exceptional capabilities, and Boas, in each of his letters to Woodworth, the first written on February 24 and the second on April 23, 1925, just a week before the Board of National Research Fellowships in the Biological Sciences was due to meet in Washington, D.C., was rather more concerned with the research project he had devised for her to undertake than with Mead herself. In the second of his letters to Woodworth, Boas noted that Margaret Mead was "a very energetic person," who he felt "very confident" would "go on with her anthropological work." He then went on to delineate the problem that Mead would be attempting to solve on his behalf. "We are always confronted," Boas wrote, "with the difficulty of telling what part of our behavior is socially determined and what is generally human." Mead's object, he said, was "to study girls belonging to the entirely different culture of Samoa and to see in how far the phenomena which we find among ourselves may prevail there also, or in how far they may be replaced by a different kind of behavior." Woodworth, so Boas hoped, would be willing to support Mead's application for a fellowship of the National Research Council, "both on account of her own future work and on account of the problem she intends to investigate." For Boas, it is evident, the problem he had set Mead to solve—a problem about which he had very decided views of his own—was of consuming importance to him.[26]

With Boas as sponsor and with Mead being so talented and highly qualified, her application for a fellowship of the National Research Council was virtually certain to succeed. Boas himself had been a member of the Division of Anthropology and Psychology of the National Research Council in its early years, and when he resigned at the end of 1919 on an issue of principle, he was described in a unanimous resolution as "the most eminent anthropologist in America and a man of unimpeachable devotion to his ideals."[27]

Among those who venerated Franz Boas was Dr. Pliny Earle Goddard, curator of ethnology at the American Museum of Natural History. While he was a lecturer in anthropology at Columbia from 1915 to 1920, Goddard had edited the *American Anthropologist* and, from 1917 onward, had coedited the *International Journal of American Linguistics* with Boas. Early in 1925, Goddard was moved to write to the colleague he so admired:

Dear Professor Boas,
Congratulations on the work you have done, and that which you have caused to be done. Congratulations for the admiration and

love your many students have for you. May your school become established and made permanent, and that while you are its leader.

P. E. Goddard[28]

Pliny Goddard had gotten to know Mead when she was working at the American Museum of Natural History. He also knew of the high regard in which she was held by Boas. On March 3, 1925, Goddard took it upon himself to write to Dr. F. R. Lillie, chairman of the Board of National Research Fellowships in the Biological Sciences, about Miss Margaret Mead, who was hoping to "teach anthropology" and who, "to complete her training," needed to do fieldwork, which for anthropology is "as essential as a laboratory is for biology." Miss Mead's "intellectual equipment," wrote Goddard, was "very unusual"; she was "keen, critical, very industrious, and persistent in overcoming obstacles." He recommended her "most heartily" for the fellowship for which she had applied.[29]

When Lillie and the members of his board met in Room 209 in the National Research Council building in Washington, D.C., on the morning of Thursday, April 30, 1925, Miss Margaret Mead was duly "appointed to a National Research Fellowship in the Biological Sciences for the year 1925–1926."[30]

When news of the award reached Mead in New York that same day, she and various of her Barnard College friends, who together had formed a group called the Ash Can Cats, were in the midst of preparing "to hang a May basket woven of willow withes and filled with wild flowers" on the doorknob of Edna St. Vincent Millay's house in Greenwich Village. With the publication of her *A Few Figs from Thistles* in 1920—the year, according to F. Scott Fitzgerald, during which the veil finally fell and the Jazz Age began to flower—Edna St. Vincent Millay had become the darling of those in Mead's generation who were exuberantly defiant of convention. For young women in particular, her irreverent wit and satiric cynicism made her a "symbolic figure—the 'free woman' of her age." When she was at Barnard, Mead and the other Ash Can Cats had chosen "as a motto" the lines that most appealed to each of them from Edna St. Vincent Millay's *A Few Figs from Thistles*. Mead chose Millay's Second Fig:

> *Safe upon the solid rock the ugly houses stand:*
> *Come and see my shining palace built upon the sand!*

But she "liked equally well" the First Fig:

> My candle burns at both ends;
> It will not last the night;
> But ah, my foes, and oh, my friends—
> It gives a lovely light.

In retrospect, these "figs," taken together, are a poignant comment on Mead's Samoan research efforts—as, in the eye of history, they have turned out to be. But in 1925, when both Boas and her father had let her have her way, she was "simply gleeful," and in a poem of her own, she wrote elatedly of a young girl who, with her skipping rope, had torn "a star out of the studded sky."[31]

In a letter dated May 2, 1925, Professor Lillie, the chairman of the Board of National Research Fellowships in the Biological Sciences, formally notified Miss Mead that her appointment was "to a Fellowship for twelve months at a stipend of $150 a month, beginning any time in the year 1925, after June 30"; she was entitled to "six weeks' vacation within the period of a twelve months' appointment." Her appointment, she was told, was "subject to the following conditions": "(1) that you satisfy the requirements for the degree of doctor of philosophy in Columbia University before the Fellowship begins; and (2) that you carry out the research in substantial accordance with the plans presented in your application and under the advice of Professor Boas of Columbia University."[32]

The second of these conditions is of particular significance. All the members of the board that on April 30, 1925, decided to appoint her to a fellowship would have fully understood the fundamental importance for the behavioral and biological sciences of Mead's planned "attempt," by her research in Samoa, "to throw light on the problem of which phenomena of adolescence are culturally and which physiologically determined." Several of them had participated in the nature-nurture controversy of the immediately preceding years. Most of them, as biologists, would have accepted the conclusion of Professor E. G. Conklin in his book of 1915 (which by 1925 was in its fifth edition) that both heredity and environment are "necessary to development." In the *Yale Review* of 1924, T. H. Morgan had noted that "while much individual variability is due to minor genetic factors, and this is inherited, some individual variability is due to the environment and this is not inherited." And this, judging from his paper "The

Gene and the Ontogenetic Process," published in *Science*, would also have been the view in 1925 of Frank R. Lillie, the board's chairman. R. S. Woodworth, in his psychology textbook of 1921, recognized the importance in human behavior of both nature and nurture, or "native and acquired traits," as he called them. It is fully understandable then that Mead was formally required by the Board of National Research Fellowships in the Biological Sciences to concentrate in her research in Samoa on "the problem of which phenomena of adolescence are culturally and which physiologically determined." It was a research project markedly different from the ethnological fieldwork that Mead had hoped to be able to do on one of the untouched islands of Polynesia and on which her heart was still secretly set.[33]

Professor Boas was well known to a number of the members of the board, and especially to Dr. Clark Wissler and to Professors Morgan, Thorndike, and Woodworth, all of Columbia. The board, as its records show, viewed Boas as the "official sponsor" of Mead's proposed research on heredity and environment and, further, as Lillie's letter to Mead of May 2, 1925, shows, required that Boas become the official supervisor of Mead's research in Samoa. Mead duly discussed Lillie's letter with Boas. On May 12, Boas wrote to Lillie informing him that Margaret Mead, of whose ability he thought "very highly," had during the previous week "passed her examination for the Ph.D." He believed that the problem on which she was proposing to work was "of very great importance." "I shall, of course," Boas told Lillie, "be very glad to advise her so far as I am able." And so, with his acceptance of the position of official supervisor of Margaret Mead's Samoan research, Franz Boas became personally responsible for the way in which the research project he had devised was carried out and, in particular, for the scientific standing of any conclusions that Mead, with his concurrence, might base on this research.[34]

# 4

# Professional Researcher Status:
# A Bishop Museum
# Associate in Ethnology

WITH BOAS'S LETTER TO LILLIE of May 12, 1925, the conditions laid down by the Board of National Research Fellowships in the Biological Sciences had been met. On May 26, Mead's fellowship appointment was confirmed by Lillie's secretary, "to begin as of August 1, 1925." On June 24, Mead was notified of Professor Lillie's further advice that she should obtain "letters of introduction and identification" from the Bishop Museum. In fact, Mead had written to Dr. Herbert Gregory as early as May 5, 1925, informing him of the award of her fellowship by the National Research Council for the "investigation of the adolescent girl in a primitive culture as a study in heredity and environment" and seeking "close affiliation" with the staff of the Bishop Museum. Gregory's response was immediate. At a meeting of the trustees held on May 21, 1925, Miss Margaret Mead, on Gregory's recommendation, was appointed an associate in ethnology on the staff of the Bernice P. Bishop Museum for the period June 1, 1925, to December 31, 1926. In a letter dated June 2, 1925, Gregory wrote to Mead again, enclosing "a brief list of ethnological topics requiring study in Samoa" and inquiring whether any of these topics fitted into her own research program. It had occurred to him that Mead might "assume the task of collecting information" for a separate publication by the Bishop Museum "on some such topic as Samoan family life, birth, marriages, death, care of children, etc." Her assistance, Gregory told her, would be "welcome."[1]

Mead reported that after she had "agreed to study the adolescent girl" and Boas had "consented" to her working in Samoa, Boas gave her "a half hour's instruction" in preparation for the fieldwork that she would be carrying out on his behalf. Although she had to be "willing to waste time just sitting about and listening" in pursuing her study of adolescent girls, Boas instructed her, she must "not waste time doing ethnography, that is, studying the culture as a whole." Furthermore, her appointment to a fellowship had been confirmed on the condition, communicated to her by Professor Frank Lillie in his letter of May 2, 1925, that her research in Samoa be carried out "in substantial accordance" with the plans presented in her application, plans that were specifically concerned with an investigation that aimed to "provide data" from Samoa "in an attempt to throw light on the problem of which phenomena of adolescence are culturally and which physiologically determined."[2]

Yet in June 1925, within a few weeks of the confirmation of her fellowship, Mead had before her an open invitation from no less a person than the director of the Bishop Museum to undertake the very kind of ethnological inquiry interdicted by Professor Lillie and which Professor Boas, her official supervisor, had instructed her not to waste time doing. On the eve of her Samoan research, this was an immense temptation. Was she to heed the instructions she had been given by Lillie and Boas, or was she, confident in her own abilities, also to tackle ethnological research of the kind proposed by Gregory, in addition to the problem devised by Boas and approved by the National Research Council? It was on ethnological research that she had set her heart some time before Boas had imposed on her his study of heredity and environment in relation to adolescence. From her reply to Gregory of June 16, 1925, about which she consulted neither Boas nor Lillie, it is evident that Mead had an intense desire to complete the kind of ethnological research in which she was really interested while in Samoa. She thought it "very probable," she told Gregory, that she would be able to make a study of the kind he had proposed. She could not, however, enter into any definite undertaking until she had been "in the field for a couple of months" and had some idea of how much time would be "absolutely necessary" to complete the "particular problem" for which she had been awarded her fellowship by the National Research Council.[3]

Thus it was, while still in New York, that Mead foreshadowed the private agreement into which she eventually entered with the Bishop Museum to undertake wide-ranging ethnological research in Samoa of either nonexistent or quite marginal relevance to the problem for which her fellowship had been awarded. She made this commitment in defiance of the explicit instructions of both her supervisor, Franz Boas, and Frank Lillie, chairman of the Board of National Fellowships in the Biological Sciences of the National Research Council, that while in Samoa, she was to give all of her time to researching "the problem of which phenomena of adolescence are culturally and which physiologically determined," because of the complexity of the topic. Moreover, in Honolulu, in August 1925, during the course of extensive discussions with the Bishop Museum's Herbert Gregory and its senior ethnologist, Dr. Edward Craighill Handy, Mead was further encouraged with the promise that her findings on the ethnology of Samoa would be published by the Bishop Museum. This, for the twenty-three-year-old Margaret Mead, at the very outset of her anthropological career, was a most powerful inducement. On November 1, 1925, over a week before setting out for Manu'a, without having consulted or informed either her supervisor or the National Research Council, she entered into an agreement with the Bishop Museum to undertake wide-ranging ethnological research. Mead's desire to engage in ethnological research somewhere in the South Seas was proving irresistible. Although in her report to the National Research Council of January 6, 1926, she did note that "some of the aspects of Samoan culture" were "being studied in cooperation with the B. P. Bishop Museum in the light of general Polynesian problems," she failed to inform either Franz Boas or the National Research Council that in addition to her official "investigation of the adolescent girl" as "a study in heredity and environment," she was, in fact, also working on an "ethnology of Manu'a" for publication as a bulletin of the Bishop Museum.[4]

With her letter to Gregory of June 16, 1925, then, Mead clearly foreshadowed the course that her research in Manu'a was to take. Thus, after she had been there just over three months, she virtually abandoned her research on Boas's problem to devote her time for some four weeks to an ethnological project that she had devised in collaboration with the Bishop Museum. And this despite the fact that just a fortnight before she set out for Samoa, Boas had reiterated his earlier instruction to her. In his farewell letter to her of July 14, 1925 (see Appendix)—by which time Mead had already entered into her under-standing with the Bishop Museum, of which he knew nothing—Boas wrote that he presumed that her work in Samoa would be of such a character that "a great deal" of what she was "particularly interested in" could be "obtained only indirectly." This would leave a lot of time for other things. "Here," Boas cautioned, "there is a practical danger that when this happens some of the regular ethnological questions may become so attractive to you that you may be tempted to slight the principal object of your trip." These words, in Boas's letter of July 14, 1925, were percipient, for by devoting almost all of her time to the investigation of "ethnological questions" from the third week of February 1926 onward, Mead did indeed "slight the principal object" of her trip. It was the "practical danger" that this slighting created for the overambitious young Margaret Mead that led directly to her fateful hoaxing on the island of Ofu at the end of the second week of March 1926.[5]

In his letter to Mead of July 14, 1925, Boas had impressed on her not to forget her health in the tropics. "If you find that you cannot stand the climate," he wrote, "do not be ashamed to come back. There are plenty of other places where you could solve the same problem on which you propose to work." Two days later, he was writing urgently to Ruth Benedict about another aspect of Mead's health. Edward Sapir, who had just had "a long talk" with Boas, was concerned with what he claimed was a "latent neurotic situation." Furthermore, Sapir was intent, according to Boas, on trying to "compel" Mead, on the eve of her departure, to "give up" her trip to Samoa. Although Boas recognized that Mead was "high strung and emotional," he was quite unable to trust Sapir's judgment. Sapir, he thought, had "read too many books on psychiatry." "It has seemed to my mind ever since I prevented her going to Tuamotu," Boas confided to Benedict, "that it would be much worse to put obstacles in her way that prevented her from doing a piece of work on which she had set her heart, than to let her run a certain amount of risk." In Boas's opinion, to compel Mead at this late stage to give up her Samoan research, as Sapir had proposed, would be "disastrous." This was also the opinion of Benedict in her reply to Boas of July 18, 1925. She had known for a long time about all of the things that had "alarmed Sapir." In the spring of 1925, she had sent Mead to two doctors "of the highest standing, one a neurologist." They could find nothing organically wrong. In Benedict's opinion, Sapir was "unduly alarmed" about Mead's "mental condition."

He had written to Benedict of "his anxiety about Margaret's going," and she was "trying to reassure him."[6]

What neither Benedict nor Boas seems to have realized is that Sapir's anxiety was very largely prompted by self-interest. In April 1924, Sapir's wife, Florence, to whom he had been married since 1911 and by whom he had three children, died in Ottawa. In August of that year at the Toronto meeting of the British association, Sapir, then aged forty, was much taken by the vitality of the twenty-two-year-old Margaret Mead. On September 8, back in New York, Mead wrote to Benedict about a letter she had received from Sapir, describing him as "the most brilliant person" and "the most satisfying mind" she had "ever met." Her relationship with Sapir, she told Benedict, was "such a satisfactory friendship, defaced by no tiresome preliminaries . . . and founded on such sure ground of like-mindedness." These feelings were reciprocated by Sapir. On December 30, 1924, being now in love with her, he composed a sonnet to Margaret Mead, which he entitled "Ariel":

> Of the heedless sun are you an Ariel,
> Rising through cloud to a discovered blue
> The windy, rocking landmarks travel through
> And clamber up a crazy pinnacle.
> Be wild, oblivious, nor think how fell
> One mocking angel and a frightened crew
> Through all the sunny pools of air into
> The dark and wondrous ritual of Hell.
>
> For you have footing poised and in your breast
> The interchange of breath, both quick and slow.
> Reckless, be safe. The little wise feet know
> Sun-way and cloud's and sudden earthen aim,
> And steps of beauty quicken into flame
> Wherein you burn up wholly in arrest.[7]

To her husband, Luther Cressman, Mead was, at this same time, a "flaming torch . . . not a torch of 'smoky pine,' but of a pine knot that flamed brightly as the resin caught fire," at times throwing "shadows" that were "surprisingly grotesque" and at other times "images" that were "brilliantly clear." It was probably of Mead's preternaturally intense enthusiasms, when she would seem to "burn up wholly in ar-

rest," that Sapir spoke to Boas in mid-July 1925, in his attempt to put
an end to her Samoan research. His true desires became evident a
week later when Mead traveled to New York from Holicong, Pennsylvania, for an important meeting with Dr. Pliny Goddard, curator of
ethnology at the American Museum of Natural History. After having
received the immensely exciting news from Pliny Goddard that on her
return from Samoa, she could look forward to becoming an assistant
curator of ethnology at the museum, Mead had gone in a highly elated
state to dine with Sapir at a New York hotel. Soon she would be leaving, as a research fellow of the National Research Council and as an
associate in ethnology of the Bernice P. Bishop Museum, to do fieldwork in the South Seas, fieldwork that would establish her profession-
ally. And from Samoa, she would be voyaging on around the world to
travel in Europe before returning to a secure job at the great museum
in New York City that she so loved and where she had first dreamed of
visiting Polynesia. Sapir, however, who was about to take up a position at the University of Chicago, had other plans for her and did his
utmost over dinner to persuade her to divorce Luther Cressman and
become his wife and the stepmother of his three children, even though
this meant forgoing fieldwork in Samoa, as well as all of the other stirring prospects before her. She would, he told her, "do better to stay at
home and have children than go off to the South Seas to study adolescent girls." Although Mead had been enormously impressed by Sapir's
remarkable intellect after encountering him in Toronto, she now
found his narrow-minded and self-centered demands insufferable and
expressed her feelings in what she later called "a bitter little verse of
feminine protest":

> Measure your thread and cut it
> To suit your little seam,
> Stitch the garment, tightly, tightly,
> And leave no room to dream.

To which she added the even more caustic lines:

> Head down, be not caught looking
> Where the restless wild geese fly.[8]

When Kroeber, on a visit to New York, had heard that Mead was going to Samoa to undertake the investigation that Boas had devised for

her, he had exclaimed: "I'd have given anything in the world to have worked on a problem like that!" But when he had first heard of it, Sapir was far less sympathetic. "Good for Margaret!" he wrote on January 26, 1925, in a letter to Ruth Benedict. "She'll enjoy Samoa, but the thought of a grind of fieldwork out there somehow makes me yawn. How perverse can we be!" As they journeyed westward together by rail for their separate destinations in Samoa and Zuni at the beginning of August 1925, Mead and Benedict decided that Sapir had been unforgivably perverse, especially in his devious and high-handed approach to Boas. As they sat together, "overlooking the Grand Canyon," which they "both loved," they found that they very much "preferred each other" to Sapir. Mead, certainly, was finished with him. Once she was in Samoa, when Sapir wrote telling her he had "fallen in love with someone else," she "made a bonfire of all his letters" on a beach on the island of Ta'ū, standing over the dissolving ashes, with no regrets at all.[9]

Mead returned to Holicong from her emotional meeting with Sapir, more determined than ever about going to Samoa. She at once wrote to Boas telling him of her discussions with Pliny Goddard and sending to Boas the various addresses at which he could write to her after she had left the United States for the islands of Polynesia. There was no mention of the importunate Sapir. Deeply concerned as he was about Mead's welfare in Samoa, Boas had suggested to Goddard that she be offered a position at the American Museum of Natural History. As Boas explained to Mead, this was to ensure that while in Samoa, she would be free of anxiety about her future. Immediately after Boas and Sapir had their "long talk," Boas told Mead in his letter of July 17, 1925, that he wanted her "to be as much at ease as possible, and not to worry about anything." He also put to Mead the suggestion that she might, during the academic year of 1926–1927, become instructor in anthropology at Barnard College in place of Gladys Reichard, who would be going to Germany on study leave. This suggestion shows just how highly, as early as 1925, Boas rated Mead's capabilities. He even thought that she might be able to "combine" working at the American Museum of Natural History with teaching at Barnard College. Mead, "very much flattered" by Boas's notion of her "substituting in the Barnard job," was hesitant. When Gladys Reichard returned, it would leave her "more completely without prospects" than if she had her fellowship "for another year." This comment in Mead's letter to Boas of July 19, 1925, written just before she went to New York to meet with Pliny Goddard, is of particular interest. Before Goddard had assured her of a position at the American Museum of Natural History, one of the options that Mead had in mind, it is evident, was to extend her stay in Samoa beyond one year by applying for an "additional year" of her National Research Council fellowship. Had she done this, she could have done fieldwork in Manu'a for eighteen months or so instead of, as actually transpired, for only some five months.[10]

Dr. Pliny Goddard, besides enormously admiring Franz Boas, had come to have a high regard for the exceptional abilities of Margaret Mead. He was most enthusiastic at Boas's suggestion that Mead be considered for appointment as an assistant curator in ethnology. And although the Board of Trustees of the American Museum of Natural History did not formally approve her appointment until December 23, 1925, at their meeting in New York ten days before she left for Samoa, Goddard was able to assure her that her appointment was virtually certain. When she wrote to Boas on July 24, 1925, after returning to Holicong from her meeting with Goddard, Mead ruled out any possibility of a temporary lectureship at Barnard College, as "the Museum administration would not approve." She was committed instead, she told Boas, to her promised assistant curatorship in ethnology, which she would take up as soon as she returned from Samoa.[11]

This unexpected development, which had stemmed from Boas's concern for her welfare, was to significantly influence the course of Mead's Samoan research. In her application for a National Research Council fellowship of February 1925, Mead had given "university teaching and research" as her "future professional career." Then, late in July 1925, just before her departure for Samoa, she had enthusiastically come to accept that in all likelihood her future career would be at the American Museum of Natural History. This, joined with the insistent promptings she was to receive from Gregory and Handy of the Bishop Museum, led her during the course of her Samoan fieldwork to devote more and more time to ethnological research that had no bearing on the problem she had been sent to Samoa to investigate. Again, her promised position at the American Museum of Natural History beginning in mid-1926 also meant that she no longer needed to think in terms of renewing her fellowship for a second year. And so, when she parted from her husband, Luther, at the Baltimore and Ohio Railway station in Philadelphia at the beginning of August 1925 to travel by train to San Francisco en route to Samoa, it was agreed between them, Luther having been awarded "a fellowship to travel in Europe," that they would meet again in Marseilles in the spring of 1926, which was less than a year away.[12]

When Margaret Mead set out from Philadelphia in 1925 she was "most enthusiastic," as Ruth Benedict assured Franz Boas, both about her trip to Samoa and about returning to New York to take up her job as an assistant curator in ethnology. Since her childhood, she had always been told: "There's no one like Margaret," and as Luther Cressman has described, she "carried the lance high for anthropology." At twenty-three years and seven months of age, she had completed Boas's introductory course in anthropology at Barnard College, and for twenty months at Columbia University while working toward her doctorate, she had continued her study of anthropology with Professor Boas. In Mead's eyes, Franz Boas was "first of all a scientist," a man who had "built a science" and under whom she had been "enchanted" to study. She did not doubt that in Samoa she would be "doing scientific work" and would "have to live up to scientific standards." Wherever Boas "held control," according to Mead, "he was uncompromisingly strict and brooked no opposition." Further, he was "very definite about what he wanted done." His influence, she says, "spread through American anthropology like an animated veto, seldom exercised but haunting the imagination of those who had absorbed . . . his methodological standards of enough facts first." Yet as Mead also recorded, Boas "almost never" discussed "scientific method" with his students. "He never loaded us down," she recounted, "with talk about the paraphernalia of science; we heard nothing about hypotheses or paradigms and we did not discuss formal epistemology. In his teaching Boas presented material in such a way that his students simply absorbed the correct procedures." Further, although in 1925 Mead was setting out to do anthropological fieldwork on a most difficult problem that Boas himself had devised and that he considered to be of "very great importance," before she left for Samoa, he gave her only "a half-hour's instruction." Thus, despite her high academic attainments, when she set out for Samoa in 1925, Mead "really did not know much about fieldwork" and "realised only very vaguely what a commitment to fieldwork and writing about fieldwork meant," as she herself has acknowledged. In Samoa, where she was officially a research fellow of the National Research Council working under Boas's supervision on a problem of which he was the instigator, she continued to regard him as her "professor." Boas believed that her research would "indicate that culture is very important." Her great "hope" was that she would not "disappoint" him.[13]

The anthropological concept that was uppermost in Mead's mind when she set out for Samoa was that of "pattern," which in 1925, as Mead recorded, was "used to describe the way any part of cultural behavior was organized." "I remember," Mead recounted, "walking down Amsterdam Avenue with a fellow student in the spring of 1925, and seeing two people meet, each greeting the other in passing, 'Good evening. Isn't it a lovely evening?'" At which Mead and her companion turned to one another and said in one breath, "Pattern!" One of the main pieces in the personal anthology that Benedict compiled for Mead to take with her to Samoa was Amy Lowell's poem "Patterns." It describes a woman "held rigid" in her "stiff, brocaded gown," who had herself become a "pattern," endlessly walking "patterned garden-paths" as she grieves for her fiancé, killed "in a pattern called a war." For Benedict and Mead, in 1925, the concept of cultural pattern was of absorbing importance. As Mead herself put it, "individuals" were identified and studied "so that the pattern of the culture could be explicated." The "final summary statement" of the course she had taken with William Fielding Ogburn was, Mead reported: "Never look for a *psychological* explanation unless every effort to find a *cultural* one has been exhausted." In this formulation, according to Mead, "psychological" refers to "the innate, generic characteristics of the mind," whereas "cultural" refers to "the behavior learned as a member of a given society." This conclusion of Ogburn's was closely paralleled by Benedict's belief, derived directly from the teaching and writings of Boas, Kroeber, and Lowie, that it is "the traditional patterns of behavior" that "set the mold" into which "human nature" flows.[14]

For both Benedict and Mead, during the years immediately before Mead's departure for Samoa, "the nature of man had to be derived from cultural materials." As Benedict subsequently put it: "The life-history of the individual is first and foremost an accommodation to the patterns and standards traditionally handed down in his community; from the moment of his birth the customs into which he is born shape his experience and behavior." Thus, if a pattern in the culture she was studying could be "identified" by an anthropologist, the behavior of its members could, it was believed, be directly inferred from the content of this pattern. It was by this article of faith that Mead's research in Samoa was to be primarily informed, despite the wholly unresolved problem of what Benedict called the "exceptions," those who had not "easily taken the traditional forms of their culture." The existence of these "exceptions" or "deviants," as they were termed, could not be ascribed to any cultural pattern, and so posed, for Benedict, an intractable problem. Thus, Mead has written of Benedict's "searching" in the mid-1920s for "an explanation of deviance" and of how she took with her to Samoa "all the questions about deviance" that had been "raised" by Benedict. This, then, was the newly formulated and entirely untested cultural determinist ideology with which the twenty-three-year-old Margaret Mead set out for Samoa. It had been derived directly from Benedict and Boas, and she well knew what they expected of her.[15]

Mead was accompanied on her journey as far as the Grand Canyon by Ruth Benedict. From there, Mead traveled on by rail to San Francisco while Benedict turned back to "the red terraced hills of Zuni," discovering in herself "a great fondness" for the place. When the two were in Rome together, in September 1926, they had markedly differing appreciations of Michelangelo's frescoes on the ceiling of the Sistine Chapel. Their separate dispositions are also evident in their differing responses to the Grand Canyon. The shy and self-effacing Ruth Benedict was "most impressed by the effort of the river to hide, a torturing need for secrecy which had made it dig its way, century by century, deeper into the face of the earth." In contrast, what the ebullient and highly imaginative Margaret Mead "loved best" were "the endless possibilities of those miles of pinnacled clay, red and white, and fantastic, ever-changing their aspect under a new shadowing cloud." At one moment she would see "a castle with a great white horse of mythical stature standing tethered by the gate, and, further over, a great Roman wall." Then, when the light changed, "the Roman wall had become a friendly street in Thrums, and unexpected cattle were grazing in a forgotten gully." In numerous ways, Ruth Benedict and Margaret Mead complemented one another, and, as Benedict confided to her sister, one of the "deepest satisfactions" of her life was the privilege of "stirring up" Margaret Mead's interest in anthropology and then watching her "carry the torch into fields" where she herself could not go. This, Mead was about to do, while Benedict wrote to her like an elder sister, counting off the "three week gaps between letters" as "the Indians do with their prayerstick plantings." Indeed, during the first month after their parting, Benedict wrote to her talented protégé no fewer than seven times, enjoining her to love the venture on which she was embarked "because you are you and indomitable in the long run" and telling her, encouragingly, that she was "quite prepared" to have her speaking Samoan "in three months."[16]

After a brief stop in Los Angeles, which she thought "a self-conscious, prettifying place, run by real estate men for other real estate men" and which she "hated," Mead traveled on by night train to San Francisco. There was a full moon, and she awoke during the night, when the train was running right beside the sea, for her "first glimpse of the Pacific." In Berkeley, she talked once more with Kroeber, who in New York had been so enthused by the problem she was to research. Then, from San Francisco, she mailed a farewell note to her husband, Luther. So shocked was he when he opened it a fortnight later back in Pennsylvania that he had to sit down on the running board of the car against which he had been leaning. It ended: "I'll not leave you unless I find someone I love more." By that time, his wife was in Honolulu, "the Paradise of the Pacific," as she called it in her letter of August 11, 1925, written on the day of her arrival there from San Francisco in the luxury liner, S.S. *Matsonia*. Her foray into Polynesia had begun.[17]

# 5

# In Honolulu:
# At the Bishop Museum

HONOLULU IN THE 1920S was an American city, a place where, as Somerset Maugham described it, "shacks" were "cheek by jowl with stone mansions" and "dilapidated frame houses" next door to "smart stores with plate glass windows," where "electric cars" rumbled noisily along the streets; "Fords, Buicks and Packards" lined the pavements, and the shops were "filled with all the necessities of American civilization." In Honolulu, on the morning of Tuesday, August 11, 1925, Margaret Mead was met with "necklaces of flowers" by Mrs. May Dillingham Frear. May Dillingham, who came from one of Hawaii's old missionary families and who had been a friend of Mead's mother at Wellesley College, had returned to Honolulu to marry Walter F. Frear, the governor of the Hawaiian Islands from 1907 to 1913. She welcomed her friend's daughter with open arms. The Frears' main abode was a house "up in the mountains," twenty minutes' drive from Honolulu. Mead, who had come to work at the Bishop Museum, was given the run of their lavish town house, where for the next two weeks she lived "in charming surroundings" with all her needs "noiselessly supplied" by Japanese servants. It was, Mead felt, "like being invited quite casually into heaven." "Basking in the Frear and Dillingham prestige," she could not "have had a more felicitous beginning" to her field trip. After a breakfast of papaya and Chinese oranges, she was driven around Honolulu to be impressed by the exuberance of the subtropical vegetation and the way in which the flame trees grew "all over the Ford advertisements." Mrs. Frear was able "to command any resources she needed," and her influence, which extended even to Samoa, smoothed Mead's path "in a hundred ways."[1]

Mead was also greeted on disembarking from the *Matsonia* by Herbert Gregory, director of the Bishop Museum, and by his secretary, Stella Jones. In her letter of June 16, 1925, accepting appointment as associate in ethnology of the Bishop Museum, Mead had informed Dr. Gregory that en route to American Samoa, she would be visiting Honolulu from August 11 to 24. "I hope to spend my time in Honolulu," she told him, "in consultation with you and the members of your staff." This was an arrangement that Gregory greatly welcomed. After she had settled in at the Frears' town house, Mead had lunch with Dr. Gregory, and was then taken, with several others, on a forty-mile sightseeing drive across the island of Oahu. Arrangements were also made for her to be driven the five miles to the Bishop Museum each morning by its malacologist, Dr. C. Montague Cooke Jr., a specialist on the land snails of the Pacific, who discussed with her his own plan to make a field trip to American Samoa early in 1926.

In 1924 in the *American Anthropologist*, W. C. McKern drew attention to the "recent renaissance of scientific interest in Polynesia." This renaissance had begun with the first Pan-Pacific Scientific Congress, held in Honolulu from August 2 to 20, 1920, with Professor Gregory as its chairman. It had been organized on behalf of the National Research Council of the United States by Herbert Gregory and Clark Wissler. Its Anthropology Committee had formulated, in response to a request from the Bishop Museum, "a plan for the development and coordination of anthropological research in the islands of the Pacific, particularly in Polynesia." By 1920, the Bishop Museum, with Professor Gregory of Yale University as its new director and with a donation of $40,000 from Bayard Dominick, a Yale graduate and a member of the New York Stock Exchange, was already organizing a series of ethnological expeditions to various parts of Polynesia. It was the beginning of what Ernest Beaglehole called "a new chapter in Polynesian research."[2]

By June 1920, an expedition had already sailed for the Marquesas Islands. And that same year, ethnological and archeological research was launched in Tonga, the Austral Islands, and Hawaii. In all of these activities, Director Herbert Gregory of the Bishop Museum, who had shown such an interest in having Mead do ethnological research in Samoa, was prominently involved. Of all the Bayard Dominick

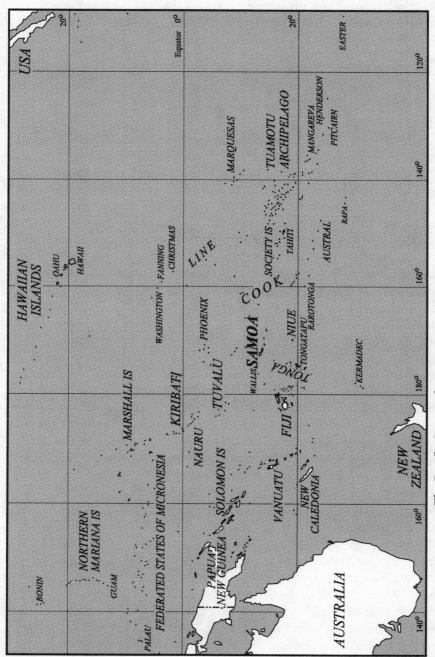

*The Pacific Ocean, showing Samoa, the Marquesas,
the Tuamotu Archipelago, and the Hawaiian Islands*

expeditions, by far the most significant for Mead's Samoan research was the one to the Marquesas Islands, a place that Herman Melville made known to the Western world in *Typee,* and in rhapsodic lines such as these:

> *Marquesas and glenned isles that be*
> *Authentic Edens in a pagan sea.*[3]

Edward Smith Craighill Handy, whose writings on Polynesia were so to influence Margaret Mead, was born in Roanoke, Virginia, in 1892. After graduating with a Master of Arts from Harvard in 1916, he served for a time in the U.S. Navy before returning to Harvard to take his doctorate in anthropology in 1920, with a dissertation on Polynesian religion. His chief interest while at Harvard was in Polynesian ethnology, and this led to his appointment on June 1, 1920, as research associate in ethnology at the Bishop Museum and as leader of "the Marquesas party of the Bayard Dominick Expedition." The other members of the party were his wife, Willowdean Chatterson Handy, and Ralph Linton (A.B., Swarthmore College; A.M., University of Pennsylvania), a research associate in archaeology of the Bishop Museum. Edward Craighill Handy was in the Marquesas Islands from September 21, 1920, to June 21, 1921, during which time he sought "a complete general picture of the ancient culture." When he returned to the Bishop Museum, where he had been appointed to the position of ethnologist on its scientific staff, he concluded in his report to Gregory that although there were "marked differences from what is usually considered the typical Polynesian complex," the "culture of the Marquesan islanders was basically and essentially Polynesian." He then settled down to write his monograph *The Native Culture in the Marquesas,* which was published in 1923 as Bulletin 9 of the Bishop Museum, just in time for it to be studied by Margaret Mead in New York in the course of writing her doctoral dissertation on "cultural stability in Polynesia." In the *Journal of the Polynesian Society* of 1924, H. D. Skinner ranked Handy's monograph as likely to "always remain the most important single contribution to Marquesan ethnology." In the published version of her dissertation, Mead cited Handy's *The Native Culture in the Marquesas* some fourteen times. She thus made extensive use of Handy's "admirable treatise," as E. W. Gifford called it in the *American Anthropologist* of 1924, and came to rely on it as the best account available to her of a Polynesian culture in her own approach to the ways of the Samoans and, in particular, to their sexual behavior.[4]

During 1923, Edward Craighill Handy, as ethnologist of the Bishop Museum, accompanied by his wife, Willowdean, as associate in Polynesian folklore, spent seven months on ethnological research in the Society Islands. In Handy's estimation, the Society Islands were "of prime importance as a center of cultural diffusion in Polynesia." Accordingly, visits were made to Tahiti, Moorea, Raiatea, Huahine, Taha'a, Borabora, and Maupiti, with particular attention being given to the history and culture of these islands. Then, on their way back to the Bishop Museum, Dr. and Mrs. Handy made short visits to Tonga and to Western Samoa, where they undertook studies of Samoan house building, cooking, and tattooing. When Mead arrived at the Bishop Museum, Handy was completing work on his massive monograph on Polynesian religion, which, when it was published by the Bishop Museum, was described by H. D. Skinner as "a great achievement" and placed "first in merit among general works on Polynesian culture." It was based on three years of library research at Harvard and on his firsthand inquiries in "different island groups of Polynesia" from 1920 onward. In August 1925, at the age of thirty-three, Edward Craighill Handy, now senior ethnologist at the Bishop Museum, possessed a firsthand knowledge of Polynesia, ranging from the Marquesan Islands in the east to the Samoan archipelago in the west, that could not be matched by any other ethnologist then alive.[5]

Margaret Mead was first introduced to Edward and Willowdean Handy at the Bishop Museum on the morning of Friday, August 14, 1925. She had spent the two previous days touring the island of Oahu, first with Dr. Gregory and a geologist from Vienna, who talked "with equal glibness on any subject," and then with Dr. Davis, professor of plant physiology at the University of California, with whom, in a glass-bottomed boat, she had marveled at "coral formations" that looked "like great mourning flowers." These excursions had been arranged because at the time of Mead's arrival in Honolulu, the Handys had been on vacation. At Gregory's request, they had now returned especially to meet the museum's new associate in ethnology. They were, Mead subsequently wrote, "all that was affable." With their experience in Samoa, as well as "their year in the Marquesas," the Handys' "help" would be "invaluable" to her. Realizing this, Mead "played up" her "ignorance" and the Handys' "unique knowledge" with all her "skill." The result was that Dr. Handy agreed to "come back from his vacation a week early" to prepare Mead for her research in Samoa. It was a measure of the importance that those at the Bishop Museum attached to Mead as a student of the renowned Franz Boas and as a research fellow of the National Research Council, of whose Committee on Pacific Investigations Gregory was chairman. On Friday, August 14, Mead was given "a lesson in Samoan" to study for the following Monday. During the week that remained to her in Honolulu, she received instruction for "several hours a day" from Dr. Handy and engaged in discussions with Gregory and Handy about the ethnological research they were hoping she would be able to do as an associate in ethnology of the museum during the course of her stay in American Samoa.[6]

Although Handy's command of Samoan was quite limited, by using Pratt's *Grammar and Dictionary of the Samoan Language*, he was able to assist Mead in comparing Samoan with Marquesan and Tahitian, the Polynesian dialects of which he did have some knowledge. Thus, in Mead's notes of Thursday, August 20, 1925, on the structure of Samoan, there is a comparison between Tahitian and Samoan. This was a serviceable way in which to begin learning Samoan. Even more important, because of her status as a museum associate, Mead was lent a copy of the fourth edition of Pratt's *Grammar and Dictionary of the Samoan Language.* George Pratt had resided in Samoa, mainly at Matautu on the island of Savai'i, for forty years from 1839 to 1879, before retiring to Sydney, Australia. The first edition of his grammar and dictionary appeared in 1862. By the time the third edition was published in 1892, his formidable dictionary contained over 12,000 words and had become an exceptionally valuable source of information on all aspects of Samoan life. The fourth edition of 1911 had been revised and enlarged by J. E. Newell, who by then had himself been a missionary in Samoa for some thirty years. And so, with the flying start she had been given by Handy and with Newell's revised edition of Pratt's *Grammar and Dictionary* in her possession, Mead, with the training in linguistics she had had from Boas, was well equipped to achieve a good working knowledge of the Samoan language.[7]

From New York, in May 1925, in seeking "close affiliation and consultation with the staff of the Bishop Museum," Mead had informed its director that in Samoa during 1925–1926, she would be undertaking "an investigation of the adolescent girl" as "a study in heredity and environment." As it happened, Dr. Handy had studied adolescent behavior during his expedition to the Marquesas Islands. It was thus a topic that Handy discussed with Mead in some detail when he tutored her for several hours each day during the week beginning August 17, 1925, in preparation for her Samoan fieldwork.[8]

It was Mead's view that the Pacific islanders "are part of our romantic tradition," it being "all too easy to conjure up a delightful picture out of a blend of Melville's *Typee*, Stevenson's tales and Gauguin's pictures"—all of these being evocations of the Polynesia of the southern seas. "In the twenties," according to Mead, when she herself was drawn to Polynesia, "there were people who wanted to go to the South Sea Islands as a personal escape from the postwar world, from a dull and empty routine, from the denial of spontaneity, and the trammelling of individual passions." And so, Mead reports, when she announced to other Americans that she was going to Polynesia, "it caused the same breathless stir," as if she were "setting off for heaven"; people would crowd in as if to touch her, while others would move a little away, "as from one already set apart for more than earthly delights."[9]

In the bibliography of the dissertation on Polynesia that she worked on at Columbia University during the years 1924–1925, Mead lists the 1846 edition of Herman Melville's *Marquesas Islands*, which later came to be known as *Typee*. In reading this account of Nukuhiva as it was in 1842, Mead would have come across Melville's instancing of "naked houries" as one of the things that "the very name Marquesas spirits up," as well as his account of how the "wilful, care-killing damsels," danced, flirted, "played all manner of mischievous pranks," and "passed their days in one merry round of thoughtless happiness." In Captain David Porter's *Journal of a Cruise Made to the Pacific Ocean* of 1815, which Mead also studied in 1925, there is an account of how among the Marquesans, unmarried girls "are at liberty to indulge themselves with whom they please."[10]

Even more significant, in *The Native Culture in the Marquesas*, of which she made extensive use in the writing of her doctoral dissertation, Mead studied the extended account given by Handy of the Marquesan *ka'ioi*. The term *ka'ioi*, Handy stated, "was anciently used to designate all males and females from adolescence to the time of settling down with more or less permanent mates to raise families." In his "glossary of Marquesan native terms," he gives "youthful libertines" as the meaning of *ka'ioi*. "During the years of adolescence and early maturity," so Handy claimed, every native "literally ran wild." In his general account of the Marquesan *ka'ioi*, Handy continued:

> During this phase of their life youths and maidens were totally free sexually. An old European resident of the Marquesas has told me that it seems an irresistible instinct with natives of both sexes to run wild for a few years after adolescence, in pursuit of amusement in general, but of the satisfaction of their abundant sexual appetite, in particular. A girl was looked down upon in native society if she did not run wild in this way, to withdraw from the others being thought unnatural and hence something to be ashamed of. Although youths and maids at this period usually lived at home, they had absolute freedom. A mother's pride was greatest and it was a matter of boasting if her daughter had the greatest number of suitors in her train. A party consisting of one girl with ten to twenty youths would sometimes spend the night together in the bush. A favourite pastime was the making of nests in the bush and spending the night in pairs or small groups. Du Petit-Thouars says that some of the young girls did not attain puberty before leaving the paternal roof. Being their own mistresses, they went their own way, abandoned themselves to every caprice, led the most licentious life that can be imagined, until at last each attached herself to one, who having obtained the place of preference in her heart, wished to become her husband.

This then was the vivid impression of the sexual behavior of adolescents in Polynesia, and particularly of female adolescents, that Margaret Mead obtained in 1924 from Handy's account while working on her dissertation in the American Museum of Natural History. In August 1925, it was powerfully reinforced during the course of her personal discussions with Dr. Handy at the Bishop Museum immediately prior to her fieldwork in Western Polynesia.[11]

One of the ruling concepts of the anthropology of the 1920s was that of the "culture area." As Laura Thompson has noted of the 1920s: "Anthropologists divided the world into 'culture areas.' A 'culture area' was defined as a geographic zone in which the cultural behavior of indigenous individuals resembled that of their fellows in contrast to other peoples of the Earth. For example, the culture areas of the Pacific were Polynesia, Melanesia and Micronesia." Handy, in particular, was much given to generalizing about Polynesia at large. In his *History and Culture in the Society Islands*, on which he was also working in 1925, Handy claimed that "certain traits in the *ari'i* culture" of Central Polynesia seemed "to point to early Buddhism which went into

Malaysia in the early centuries of the Christian era." In 1927, having independent means, he traveled with his wife, Willowdean, "in Indo-China, Cambodia, Siam and India in a study of the Asiatic background of Polynesia." For Handy then, in his writings of the 1920s, Polynesia is signally a culture area. In his *Polynesian Religion* there is a far-fetched comparison between the sexual practices of the Marquesans and the Samoans, and he certainly felt justified, when tutoring Mead at the Bishop Museum in August 1925, in instancing the behavior of the female adolescents of the Marquesas Islands, which he had studied in the early 1920s, as an example of the kind of thing Mead would encounter in Samoa. This, furthermore, was given credence by Mead, who fully accepted that in Polynesia there was "a common background of culture" in her dissertation of 1925. What neither Handy nor Mead realized in 1925 was that, as is now known, there are quite major differences between the cultures of Eastern Polynesia, including that of the Marquesas, and those of Western Polynesia, of which the Samoan Islands are a part. These differences were first documented by Edwin Burrows in his monograph of 1938, *Western Polynesia: A Study in Cultural Differentiation*, based in part on research he had undertaken in the early 1930s as an ethnologist of the Bishop Museum. Thus, as Ralph Linton, who was in the Marquesas Islands with Handy in the early 1920s, observed: "In a general description of Polynesia, a number of statements true for most Polynesian localities simply do not apply to Samoa." Unfortunately, Mead did not realize this at all when she began her own studies of Samoan adolescents with quite major preconceptions derived directly from Dr. Edward Craighill Handy of the Bishop Museum.[12]

While Mead was in Honolulu, there were also discussions with Handy and Gregory about the coordinated research on the ethnology of Samoa that was being planned by the Bishop Museum. It was likely, she was told, that Handy would be working on the "religion and cosmology" of Samoa. It was still hoped, however, as had been proposed by Gregory in his letter of June 2, 1925, that Mead would investigate "Samoan family life, birth, marriages, death, care of children, etc." and then have her findings published as a bulletin of the Bishop Museum in the same series as Dr. Handy's *The Native Culture in the Marquesas*. As previously noted, Mead found this prospect, just as she was setting out on her anthropological career, deeply appealing. Moreover, she felt "bound" by her appointment as an associate in ethnology to the staff of a museum that was in the very forefront of Polynesian studies. Ambitious for the future and confident in her ability to work on the problem Boas had set her and, at the same time, to carry out the kind of ethnological inquiry on which her heart was set, she readily agreed to the proposal that Gregory and Handy put to her. As soon as she had sized up her situation in Samoa, she would inform them about the ethnological research she would be able to tackle on behalf of the Bishop Museum during the course of her fieldwork there. She was then furnished, on August 20, 1925, with a document embossed with the crimson seal of the Bernice P. Bishop Museum and signed by Director Herbert E. Gregory certifying that she was an associate in ethnology on its staff, as well as a fellow of the National Research Council, and that the work she would be doing in Samoa was "important in the study of the Polynesian Race."[13]

Her stay in Honolulu, as she reported to Boas, had been "thoroughly pleasant and profitable." Professor Gregory had been "very hospitable and kind." Dr. Handy had given her "several hours a day" preparing her for her fieldwork in Samoa, and she had been lent "a copy of Pratt's dictionary." At the Bishop Museum, she had gone through "the literature on Samoa" that she had not previously seen. She had also made "a great many contacts in Honolulu" that would facilitate her work in Samoa.[14]

On her last night there, she dined at the Moana Hotel, "a great seaside place, built all about a giant banyan tree shading a courtyard, into the open end of which the surf washed." Late on the afternoon of Monday, August 24, 1925, she was bid farewell by Gregory, the Handys, the Frears, and the other friends she had made during her fourteen days in Honolulu. They hung "leis of flowers" around her neck as she boarded the S.S. *Sonoma* of the Oceanic Steamship Company. Then, as the band played "Aloha," the *Sonoma* set course for Samoa and, in Mead's words, "towards a full view of the Southern Cross." Her dream of doing anthropological research in the South Seas was about to be realized.[15]

# 6

# At the U.S. Naval Station, Tutuila, American Samoa

AT DAWN ON JULY 22, 1888, Robert Louis Stevenson watched as the Marquesas Islands "took shape in the attenuating darkness." He later wrote about his feelings then: "The first experience can never be repeated. The first love, the first sunrise, the first South Sea Island are memories apart and touched by a virginity of sense." Thirty-seven years later, Margaret Mead, "remembering Stevenson's rhapsodies," was up at dawn on the S.S. *Sonoma* to experience her "first South Sea island" as it "swam up over the horizon." It was "a cloudy daybreak, with the sun appearing sullenly for only a moment and the surf showing white along the shores of the steep black cliffs" as the *Sonoma* made its way into Pago Pago, "the only landlocked harbor in the South Seas," where "numerous battleships" of the U.S. Pacific Fleet were at anchor, with seaplanes screaming overhead and a band "constantly playing ragtime." It was not a scene to touch anyone's "virginity of sense." As Mead wrote later that day, the presence of so many naval vessels skewed "the whole picture badly."[1]

In the 1920s, Pago Pago, on the island of Tutuila, was the main U.S. naval station in the South Pacific. The U.S. Pacific Fleet, with its four battleships, four cruisers, hospital ship, and numerous destroyers, had arrived the previous day from New Zealand. In 1878, a treaty between the United States and the high chiefs of Tutuila had granted the United States the right to establish "a station for coal and other supplies for the naval and commercial marine of the United States" in Pago Pago Bay. On February 19, 1900, the American president,

William McKinley, signed an executive order placing the island of Tutuila and all the other islands of what is now American Samoa "under
the control of the Department of the Navy for a Naval Station." From
that time onward, and especially after the cession of Tutuila in April
1900 and of Manu'a in July 1904 to the United States, a system of government was established with Samoan chiefs as district governors and
county chiefs and with the commandant of the naval station as the
governor of all the islands of American Samoa. In 1925, when Margaret Mead arrived in Tutuila, the naval station was still "primarily a
supply base." Among other things, it had a coal shed with a capacity
of 4,500 tons and two fuel-oil storage tanks of 55,000 barrel capacity
each, for vessels of the U.S. Navy. Pago Pago Bay occupies the immense crater of an ancient volcano, with its south side open to the
sea. About a mile from this opening, the bay turns sharply to the west,
giving the harbor, in the words of a report of 1926, "the appearance of
the foot of a stocking with the United States Naval Station situated on
the instep, facing north and entirely sheltered from seaward." The inner harbor, which is surrounded by high, sheer-sided mountains, is the
safest to be found anywhere among the South Sea Islands.[2]

In the mid-1920s, the U.S. Naval Station on Tutuila had sixteen officers and an enlisted complement of 147, of whom seventy were
Samoans of the Fita Fita Guard, commanded by a sergeant of the U.S.
Marine Corps. There was a naval radio station that maintained "direct
schedule" with Honolulu, San Francisco, and Washington, D.C. All
government quarters had sewerage, running water, and electric power
from 6 A.M. to midnight. Provisions of all kinds, including meat and
other cold storage supplies, could be purchased from the commissary.
Motion pictures were screened several times a week. There was a
"four-hole, five-green golf course on which nine holes were played"
and three tennis courts. Only white uniforms were worn.[3]

This, then, was the punctilious naval station—a place where, as on
shipboard, the clanging of bells marked the hours and the floor was a
deck—at which Margaret Mead disembarked from the S.S. Sonoma
early on the morning of Monday, August 31, 1925. She found no one to
meet her. In the hustle on the wharf, thronged with Samoans who had
come to see the U.S. Pacific Fleet, she made herself known to Mr. Walters of the Bank of American Samoa. Mr. Walters took her to the only
hotel in Pago Pago, described in a U.S. naval circular of the day as being as good as the patronage warranted. There she left her baggage be-

fore returning to the *Sonoma* for breakfast. Over breakfast, she was "fortunate enough" to meet Lieutenant G. R. Veed and his wife, whose sister she had known at Columbia. They introduced her to naval station life by taking her back to their quarters. From there she was collected by Miss Ellen Hodgson, the chief nurse of the naval station and was taken to "a large and festive lunch" in honor of the nurses of U.S.S. *Relief*, the hospital ship of the American fleet.[4]

Miss Hodgson, a forty-five-year-old Episcopalian from Providence, Rhode Island, had been written to from Washington, D.C., at the request of Rear Admiral E. R. Stitt, the surgeon general of the U.S. Navy, asking that Miss Margaret Mead be given every assistance when she reached Tutuila. Miss Hodgson had been on the wharf when the *Sonoma* docked but had been unable to locate Mead in the milling crowd. From the time they did meet, Ellen Hodgson was to help Mead in innumerable ways, rendering her "the thousand kindnesses so much appreciated by a stranger," giving her the run of facilities at the Training School for Samoan Nurses, of which she was the principal and, free of any charge, the services of G. F. Pepe, a senior Samoan nurse, with "perfect" English, as her "instructor in the native language." Then, after "endless detailed advice on Station etiquette," Ellen Hodgson accompanied Mead to dinner at the residence of Commander Owen J. Mink, the chief medical officer of the U.S. Naval Station, Tutuila, for whom Mead had a letter from the surgeon general of the U.S. Navy. After this dinner party, at which Mrs. Mink "dilated for half an hour" about the pigs of her Samoan "cook boy," Mead remarked that "conversation and social life on a Naval Station demand a Jane Austen to do them justice." Stuffed olives were de rigueur at navy dinner parties, and if the commissary was out of them, "you might as well drown yourself," for substitutions were not possible. Nonetheless, as Mead told Rear Admiral Stitt on her return to the United States, the "co-operation" of the Medical Department of the U.S. Naval Station, Tutuila, was "the backbone" of her work, throughout her stay in Samoa.[5]

This support had come about through the good offices of Mead's husband, Luther, who, after the award of her research fellowship on April 30, 1925, had mentioned to his father, Dr. George Cressman, a country doctor, that Margaret would be working in American Samoa, where the U.S. Navy was in charge. Dr. Cressman at once wrote to Rear Admiral Stitt, who had been his friend at the Medical School of the University of Pennsylvania. In a few days, Stitt replied:

Dear George,
I shall instruct all Navy personnel under my command in Samoa
to do everything possible to facilitate the success of your daugh-
ter-in-law's project.[6]

It was with this cachet that Margaret Mead arrived at the U.S. Naval
Station on Tutuila on August 31, 1925, to have the doors of its Medical Department opened to her by a letter from the surgeon general of
the U.S. Navy. As requested by Rear Admiral Stitt, Commander Owen
Mink, the chief medical officer, did everything in his power to further
Mead's work and make her "residence at the Naval Station enjoy-
able." And from November 1925 onward, it was with Commander
Mink's permission that Mead lived in a U.S. Naval Dispensary while
doing her fieldwork in Manu'a. Rear Admiral Stitt's support was thus
of quite crucial importance. In expressing her "personal indebtedness"
to him for "so generously sponsoring" her research, Mead told Rear
Admiral Stitt that it was through his "foresight and help" that her "investigation in Samoa was made possible."[7]

Mead's close association with Ellen Hodgson and Owen Mink, from
the time of her first arrival in Tutuila, then with Lieutenant and Mrs.
Charles W. Lane, and later with Chief Pharmacist Mate Edward R.
Holt and his family in Manu'a, meant that she was identified, in the
eyes of the Samoans, with the all-powerful U.S. Navy. And as Mead
acknowledged, this identification was greatly strengthened by her association, early in September 1925, with high-ranking officers of the
U.S. Pacific Fleet. On the evening of September 1, 1925, after having
called earlier in the day on the commandant of the naval station, Captain Henry F. Bryan, she went to "a very sumptuous repast" in the Officers' Mess of the cruiser U.S.S. *Marblehead*, after which, with her
"too well bred Bostonian officer escort," she attended the screening on
its quarter deck of *Too Many Kisses*, starring Richard Dix, with the
"gobs" behind her "making lurid comments" and Pago Pago Harbor
"lovely in the moonlight." On September 2, as she was "peacefully
reading a month old *New Republic*" in her hotel overlooking the bay,
she received a quite unexpected visit from the governor's aide-de-
camp, Commander Moore. He had called to convey an invitation from
Admiral Robert E. Coontz, commander in chief of the U.S. Pacific
Fleet, for Miss Mead to attend a dance that was to take place that
evening on Admiral Coontz's flagship, the U.S.S. *Seattle*. "I would be
delighted!" Mead told Commander Moore. It was to be an even more

memorable occasion for Mead than the previous evening. She danced
the first dance with Admiral Coontz and "the last three" with Rear
Admiral Thomas P. Magruder of the cruiser *Richmond*, after which he
took her home "in his own boat." In American Samoa in the 1920s, as
Mead has noted, the Samoans gauged "a visitor's rank" by the rank of
the naval officers with whom he or she associated. Mead's rank after
dancing with Admiral Coontz on his flagship was nonpareil. She could
hardly have refused Admiral Coontz's invitation, nor would she have
wanted to. She was decidedly of the view that there was "nothing to
be gained in Samoa by working in independence of the naval authorities," and she came to believe that American Samoa was "the only
thoroughly decent piece of colonial government which the United
States government can plume itself on." In her letter to Rear Admiral
E. R. Stitt of September 17, 1927, she wrote: "I can say unqualifiedly
that I believe the Samoans are exceedingly fortunate in the naval administration, and that the foresight, tolerance and general interest
with which the government of an alien, primitive and economically
backward people is effected should be a source of pride to every American citizen." It was most certainly a source of pride to Margaret
Mead. Without the help and support of the Medical Department of the
U.S. Naval Station, Tutuila, her research in American Samoa could
not have been accomplished.[8]

On the afternoon of Tuesday, September 1, 1925, on the parade
ground of the naval station, there was a ceremonial welcome to Admiral Coontz by the high chiefs of American Samoa. This afforded Mead
her first opportunity to scrutinize the people she had come to study.
She found the ceremonies decidedly "depressing." Tufele Fa'atoia, the
district governor of Manu'a, who had been educated in Honolulu,
made "a glorious speech" and presented the admiral with the greatest
of Samoan valuables, an 'ie toga, or fine mat, as well as pieces of bark
cloth and shell necklaces and freshly picked and husked coconuts.
Then Mauga, the high chief of Pago Pago, presented his daughter
Sami, a *taupou*. Wearing a *tuiga*, a decorated headdress of human hair
bleached to a russet hue, Sami danced the Samoan *siva*, accompanied
by her retinue, flower-bedecked and in traditional array. But surrounding these performers were hundreds of other "natives." All of them,
Mead wrote when she got back to her hotel, "were in the nondescript
dress which they all wear, the women barefoot and in light shapeless
dresses (some worn over blouses fitted in under the breasts in a most
ungainly fashion), the men in white cotton shirts and *lavalavas*—

cloth caught at the waist with a belt, and falling a little below the knee—of various hideous striped American stuffs." And "to make the scene finally ludicrous," almost all of them "carried black umbrellas."[9]

The hotel in which Mead had been lodged was a large two-story structure at the edge of Pago Pago Bay, famous as the setting for "Rain," Somerset Maugham's macabre short story of 1921. In the story, the brash prostitute Sadie Thompson brings about the downfall of the self-righteous missionary, Alfred Davidson, who, in his disgrace, cuts his throat "from ear to ear," after which Dr. Macphail finds him "lying half in the water and half out" in the nearby bay, the razor "with which the deed was done" still clutched in his right hand. After Ruth Benedict had seen the play based on Maugham's short story in New York on January 4, 1925, she wrote in her diary: "Excellent. I shall remember Sadie in her glory." It was a play that Mead had also seen before she left for Samoa, and she well knew of the lurid events that Somerset Maugham had located in the hotel where she herself was now a guest. On her first and second nights there, she had as fellow occupants the Reverend Savage and his family of the London Missionary Society, who were on their way to Western Samoa. On the morning of Tuesday, September 1, before she attended the afternoon ceremony on the parade ground of the naval station that she found so depressing, the Savages had taken her to the Missionary Rest Home to meet Miss Holder, the headmistress of the Atauloma Boarding School for Girls, sited fifteen miles from Pago Pago, where virginal Samoan girls were trained to become "suitable wives" for Samoan pastors. By the close of her first full day at the U.S. Naval Station, Tutuila, which ended with *Too Many Kisses* on a cruiser of the U.S. Pacific Fleet and with the harbor looking "lovely in the moonlight," Miss Mead was well and truly in the paradisiacal American Samoa of the 1920s.[10]

With the departure of the Savages for Apia, Mead had the so-called Sadie Thompson hotel all to herself. On September 3, she moved to a new room on its first floor, which had "practically a four-sided exposure, opening on two sides with screen doors onto porches and having windows on the two other sides." She had Samoan mats on the floor, a bureau, a table, an "armed chair," a washstand, and a bed. With prints from an *International Studio Magazine* on the walls of her room, with books on her table, and with copies of the *Nation*, the *New Republic*, *Saturday Review*, *American Mercury*, *Dial*, and *Atlantic Magazine* that she was being sent, she felt "very civilized." The hotel was "really very comfortable." Staying there, she decided, was "an excellent scheme," for she could learn "to eat the native food bit by bit sandwiched in between plenty of familiar viands." By the end of her second week, she had eaten "taro, *palusami* (taro leaves cooked with coconut), wild pigeon, octopus soup" and "a raw shell fish" that looked like "a spherical porcupine." She did not, however, much like taro, the staple food of the Samoans. For Mead, it had "the consistency of tough cheese" and was "as tasteless as oatmeal without salt." To stay in the hotel, she had to pay $28 a week. Because the services of her instructor in Samoan were free, she could, she decided, afford to go on living there until she had "a good hold on the language." By September 14, she was thinking in terms of staying on in the hotel for about another three weeks before moving out to a village on the island of Tutuila. She would then, she thought, "spend two and a half weeks" in this village before returning to the hotel for a few days for food, rest, and mail and to write up her results.[11]

On September 3, 1925, three days after her arrival in Pago Pago, Mead began her "lessons in Samoan." She resolved to work for "eight hours a day" on the language she would have to use in her research and to make "no immediate attempt to collect any information." Her instructor, the twenty-nine-year-old Samoan nurse G. F. Pepe, came from "a chiefly family," being a cousin of Tufele, district governor of Manu'a. Having graduated from the Atauloma Boarding School for Girls of the London Missionary Society, where she had been taught to read and write Samoan, Pepe became one of the first pupils of the Training School for Samoan Nurses when it was founded in Pago Pago in 1914 by the U.S. Navy. She later spent two years at the U.S. navy hospital at Mare Island, California, and had "excellent English." For one hour each day, Mead was tutored by Pepe. At first she had Pepe dictate Samoan to her, which she would repeat "with correct pronunciation, phrasing and cadence." Later, she prepared a "series of sentences" in English for translation. Pepe, who was "an intelligent translator," reproduced these sentences in idiomatic Samoan, which Mead, as necessary, would check in the copy of Pratt's *Dictionary and Grammar of the Samoan Language* that she had acquired at the Bishop Museum. The rest of the working day Mead spent "memorizing vocabulary" and in active practice. Her method was to write lists of Samoan words and their English equivalents on postcard-size pieces of paper that she would take with her when she walked about the port of Pago Pago and "tried out Samoan phrases on the children." She had, as she later noted, "by accident, hit on the best way to learn a language, which is to learn as much of it as fast as possible so that each piece of learning reinforces each other piece."

On September 17, after she had "been working on the language" for just two weeks, she wrote her "first report" to Franz Boas. It was type-written on notepaper she had had especially printed with her name and address: "Margaret Mead, Pago Pago, Tutuila, Samoa," and she be-gan the report with "Dear Dr. Boas." She had already acquired, she told him, "a vocabulary of about 500 words" and could "express any type of idea except some so-called subjunctive expressions with very little difficulty." She had, she reported, "talked to ten year old chil-dren for fifteen and twenty minutes at a stretch" and made herself un-derstood. But, unless the conversation of adult Samoans was "specifi-cally directed" toward her, she could not "follow it very carefully." She was "quite confident," however, that she would be able "to han-dle the language well enough for the requirements" of the "problem" that she had come to Samoa to investigate.[12]

Boas's only contribution thus far had been to send Mead "a dreadful German monograph on preadolescence." She began trying to read it during her second week in Pago Pago, but the words in it were "so long and new" that she couldn't find them in the German dictionary she had with her. That same week there was a tea in Mead's honor, at which she was introduced to the wives of the naval officers. She was not impressed. They were "all alike." Only two were "college women." Most of the "ladies of the station," she decided, were "merely pretentious," though they all knew enough to "put rose petals in their finger bowls." There was, however, the wife of Dr. Charles Lane, who was "the most charming woman on the station, mightily spoiled and childless, but with an amount of *savoir-faire* and magnetism" that was "a real life saver." On Wednesday, September 9, when Mead and the Lanes were out motoring, they saw the H.M.S. *Dunedin*, a New Zealand cruiser "of very graceful lines," glide into Pago Pago Bay on an official visit to the naval station. Once again, Mead was invited to a dance aboard ship and then to a dinner party at the house of the U.S. Navy chaplain, Lieutenant Commander William Edell, at which her fellow guests were the commodore of the New Zealand Navy, the captain of the H.M.S. *Dunedin*, and, "dressed in purple silk," the Anglican bishop of Polynesia, who "talked gently about African languages." When the *Dunedin* left, she felt that "all re-ally interesting chances of conversation" had also departed; but then came "Steamer Day," and she was all agog "with fifty-eight letters" strewn over her bed and waiting to be answered.[13]

On Thursday, September 24, after further outings with the Lanes, Mead went on her first major trip beyond the confines of the naval station to the Atauloma Boarding School for Girls of the London Missionary Society. She and the other members of the party were driven to Leone at the western end of Tutuila in cars provided by the naval station. From there, they walked two miles to the historic school, where a "feast" of baked taro, "almost raw pork," and "boiled bananas" was awaiting them. Once again, Mead was not impressed. She found the occasion "tedious." There were "endless speeches," after which the girls of Atauloma sang and danced the Samoan *siva* in their "neat, ill-tailored white muslins which hit their knees in just the wrong place."[14]

She then returned to her study of Samoan at her hotel in Pago Pago, where, when it rained and the clouds hung low over the landlocked bay, she felt "boxed up beside a sullen sea." In Pago Pago, the average rainfall in September is thirteen inches, the average temperature about 81 degrees Fahrenheit.

"It is remarkable how difficult it is to accomplish anything here," she wrote on the evening of Sunday, September 27, 1925, "boxed up" in her hotel room after having been out to dinner. She continued:

> The morning usually has to be broken by at least a fifteen minute rest, for working steadily even at no more elaborate a task than memorizing idioms, one gets almost faint with heat. After lunch, at least a half hour siesta is enjoined upon all. Then I have my lesson and usually some other appointment. If one is to swim, one must start by 4.30, and the afternoon is gone; while the evening consists of only two hours, for 9 o'clock is compulsory bed time except on rare occasions. That decapitation of the evening plays havoc with one's time. It seems treason to read and I can scarcely find the time to write letters, and then, I haven't been putting in an eight hour day at that. If social frivolities are added it becomes impossible, yet the hotel food makes the acceptance of invitations involving meals almost a scientific duty.

She was still fighting a "battle" with taro, and, in particular, with boiled taro. For Mead, when it was served to her "in solitary state," by the hotel cook named Fa'alavelave, whose name was the same as a term that in Samoan refers to anything that seriously interferes with normal life, boiled taro was "so much putty-tasting, soap-textured, grey matter" that rendered "tasteless everything with which it came into contact." Her own name for the cook at whose hands she suffered was Misfortune.[15]

On Thursday, October 1, in furtherance of her study of Samoan, and especially for "practice in hearing translation," she attended the High Court in Fagatogo. Two cases were of particular interest that day. One was of bigamy, by a woman from Western Samoa, and the other that of a girl of fifteen who had "bitten off" the ear of her fifteen-year-old female rival.

A few days later, she set out with Dr. Ryan, of the Department of Public Health, and his wife, on one of the tours of inspection of Samoan villages that were regularly undertaken by officers of the naval station. It was a two-day tour of the villages on the remote northwest coast of Tutuila. It would, Mead hoped, enable her to finally make up her mind whether to "stay on Tutuila or go to Manu'a" to do her fieldwork. At 7 A.M. on Tuesday, October 6, 1925, Dr. and Mrs. Ryan, together with their "cook boy" and two Samoan orderlies, one to act as the party's spokesman and interpreter and the other to carry their baggage and supplies, turned up at Mead's hotel.

Their journey began with "a five mile climb over a steep mountain, gasping and stumbling in the heat of the bush, and tumbling head first down the abrupt descent on the other side" into the village of Fagasā. Oval thatched houses stood on little stone platforms about a foot or two high, with breadfruit trees scattered about and vermilion-leafed cordylines growing everywhere. Here, they were formally welcomed in the house of the highest-ranking chief. Round and open on all sides, its floor was covered with little grey stones. Oblong mats of palm leaf had been spread all around the walls in a triple overlapping circle. Mead, acting as the *taupou*, or ceremonial virgin of the traveling party, sat at the central post in the front of the house, flanked by Dr. and Mrs. Ryan, while the chiefs of Fagasā ranged themselves silently in a circle. The titles of all those present were intoned, and kava was served, Mead being honored with the first cup. Dr. Ryan then distributed gifts, "cigars for the chiefs and chewing gum for the ladies," and there was a discussion of official matters before the party moved on to the next village for a similar sequence of events. Because of the precipitous coast, they had sometimes to travel in open rowboats, to and from which Dr. and Mrs. Ryan and Mead were carried "in the arms of sturdy Samoans." It was arduous in the hot sun, and at one village, Mead "slept peacefully through the wearisome questioning." In the afternoon, they had to walk along the coastal cliffs, "clambering over slippery rocks and hanging to the sides by sheer good fortune," to the village of Poloa, where they spent the night, "arriving very sticky, very thirsty, and very tired, just before sundown." For Mead, who for years "hadn't walked for more than four miles," all this was something of an ordeal. When their tour ended at noon the next day at Leone, after "stops at each village to partake of the endless kava," she was greatly relieved to return to Pago Pago in one of the naval station's Ford cars.[16]

As she noted after she got back to her hotel, she had now "seen the principal social ceremonies of the Samoans, the *ta'alolo* presentation of gifts, the *sivasiva* dance, and the kava ceremony." Behind this "rather nondescript series of acts," there was, she knew, "considerable significance"; an "extensive system of rank and prestige" decided "the place of each individual in the house, the order of the kava ceremony, the type of gift, etc." Yet these were "almost non-apparent," and she had "more sympathy for the transient white man who spoke of a group of half-naked savages living in huts." Such "inward" life as there was, was "well concealed beneath an outer covering of unattractive clothing, rambling dogs and intrusive pigs and chickens. Proceedings were too near the ground for dignity." Her introduction to the realities of Samoan existence on the remote northwestern coast of Tutuila had not been an altogether happy experience. She returned to her hotel to record that it was "much easier to derive aesthetic pleasure" from contemplating "the ideas" underlying Samoan culture than from "looking at the embodiment of these ideas."[17]

This experience also persuaded Mead that there was nowhere on Tutuila where she could effectively do fieldwork on the problem Boas required she solve. Villages such as those that she had just visited, as she informed Boas, were too small. "To find enough adolescents," she would have to spend all her time "climbing mountains or tossing about in the surf in an open boat, both extremely arduous and time consuming activities." There were only two villages on Tutuila that were "really large enough" for her purposes. These were Pago Pago and Leone, both of which were "overrun with missionaries, stores and various intrusive influences." She had, therefore, decided to go to Ta'ū, the main island of Manu'a, sixty-eight miles east of Tutuila, where a naval supply ship went "every three weeks, just before mail day." Ta'ū was the only village, she wrote on October 13, where there were "enough adolescents," which at the same time was "primitive enough" and enabled her to "live with Americans." The "native food," a reference to the taro that she found so very unpalatable, was "too starchy" for her to "live on it" for the six months of the field-work she was intending to do on the behavior of adolescent girls. On Ta'ū, she would be living in the U.S. Naval Dispensary, with "the only white people on the island," yet "close to a Samoan village." This meant that she could be "in and out of the native homes from early in the morning until late at night" but "still have a bed to sleep on, and wholesome food." The food would be "much better than hotel food" because navy people had "canteen privileges." This, for Mead, with her intense dislike of taro, was a quite major enticement. All this had been arranged through Chief Medical Officer Commander Owen Mink, with the approval of Chief Pharmacist Mate Edward Holt and his wife, Ruth, who lived in the U.S. Naval Dispensary on the island of Ta'ū, together with the enlisted man who maintained the radio sta-tion. Ruth Holt, it so happened, was at the naval station in Pago Pago awaiting the birth of her second child. Mead had already gotten to know her, and they planned to go to Ta'ū together on a naval supply ship "sometime in November."[18]

When Mead wrote to Boas on October 11, 1925 (see Appendix), she was "particularly anxious" to have his advice about her decision to live with an American naval family while doing her fieldwork. It was certainly a crucial decision, for it meant that she would be identified with the naval government, toward which there was considerable hos-tility on the island of Ta'ū. Furthermore, it meant she would lose the invaluable advantage of living in close and continuous association with the people she was seeking to understand. "If I lived in a Samoan house with a Samoan family," she told Boas in this same letter,

I might conceivably get into a little more intimate touch with that par-ticular family. But I feel that such advantage as would be reaped would be more than offset by the loss in efficiency due to the food and the nervewracking conditions of living with half a dozen people in the same room, in a house without walls, always sitting on the floor and sleeping in constant expectation of having a pig or chicken thrust itself upon one's notice. This is not an easy climate to work in; I find my efficiency dimin-ished by about one half as it is, and I believe it would be cut in two again if I had to live for weeks on end in a Samoan house. . . . Of course, if I lived in a Samoan household I would have to speak Samoan every minute, and my progress in the language would be considerably acceler-ated. You may feel that it is not right for me to neglect any opportunity to

increase my knowledge of the language and intimacy with the people. If
you do, will you please write to me at once.

Boas's reply of November 7, 1925 (see Appendix), did not reach
Mead until January 4, 1926, by which time she had for eight weeks
been resident at the U.S. Naval Dispensary on Ta'ū, and where, given
Boas's approval, she continued to reside for the rest of her stay of just
over five months. Boas did not at all object to the fact that Mead was
not living in a Samoan household. He knew "from personal experience" how hard it was to "find time for serious work" in a native
house, where there were "constant interruptions of all sorts." As
Ronald and Evelyn Rohner have recorded, in his own fieldwork on the
North Pacific Coast of Canada, Boas "seldom lived in Indian households or communities unless circumstances required him to do so . . .
he typically stayed at a boarding house, hotel or other public accommodation within walking distance of the community where he was
working." Thus, in electing to live in the U.S. Naval Dispensary on
Ta'ū rather than with a Samoan family, Mead was following in Boas's
footsteps. "Great, of course," Boas told her, "will be the satisfaction if
you succeed in getting even a part of what you would like to find, and
I believe that your success would mark a beginning of a new era of
methodological investigation of native tribes." What she would "like
to find," as both Boas and Mead privately knew, was that the behavior
of the adolescent girls of Samoa was culturally determined.[19]

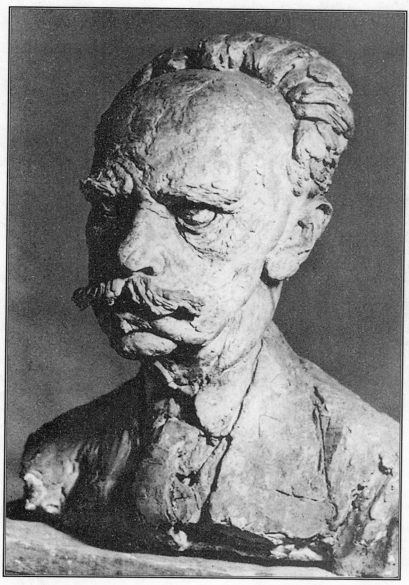

*Portrait bust of Franz Boas by Jacob Epstein, sculpted in New York City in 1927, the year during which Franz Boas stated that he was "completely satisfied" with Margaret Mead's report to the U.S. National Research Council on "the adolescent girl in Samoa" (from* Jacob Epstein, Sculptor, *by Richard Buckle [London: Faber and Faber, 1963]).*

*Ruth Benedict circa 1924
(from Special Collections,
Vassar College Libraries,
Poughkeepsie, New York).*

*Luther Cressman, who
married Margaret Mead
in Buckingham,
Pennsylvania, on
September 3, 1923; a
drawing made in Paris in
1925 (from Margaret
Mead Papers,
Manuscript Division,
Library of Congress,
Washington, D.C.;
courtesy of the Institute
for Intercultural Studies,
Inc., New York).*

*Reo Fortune, who married Margaret Mead in Auckland, New Zealand, on October 8, 1928 (from Alexander Turnbull Library, National Library of New Zealand, Te Puna Mātauranga o Aotearoa, reference number F11647½).*

*Margaret Mead, with Reo Fortune's mother, Hetty (from the Fortune Papers of the Alexander Turnbull Library, National Library of New Zealand, Te Puna Mātauranga o Aotearoa, reference number F121941½).*

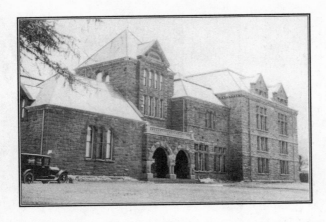

*Bernice P. Bishop Museum, as it was in 1925 when visited by Margaret Mead on her way to Samoa.*

*Herbert E. Gregory, director of the Bernice P. Bishop Museum in 1925; with Edward Craighill Handy, Gregory successfully persuaded Margaret Mead to work while in Samoa on a monograph, an "ethnology of Manu'a," that she was promised would be published by the Bishop Museum.*

*Edward Craighill Handy, senior ethnologist at the Bishop Museum; in August 1925, Handy gave Margaret Mead instruction in preparation for her fieldwork in Samoa.*

The so-called Sadie Thompson Hotel, Pago Pago, Tutuila,
American Samoa, where Margaret Mead lived and worked in 1925
(author's collection).

Admiral Robert E.
Coontz, commander in
chief of the United
States Pacific Fleet, with
whom on September 2,
1925, Margaret Mead
danced the first dance on
his flagship U.S.S. Seattle
(from Nimitz Library,
United States Naval
Academy, Annapolis,
Maryland).

# 7

# Ethnological Research in
# Pago Pago and Vaitogi

W HEN MEAD WROTE TO BOAS on October 11, 1925, she noted
that her "knowledge of the language" was "progressing more
slowly than at first." She was still having "one definite lesson"
each day at the naval station, after which she would "prospect about
for chances of conversation." She had also been taking texts in
Samoan for "several hours a day" and had collected "a good deal of information," which, although it did not bear on the problem she had
come to Samoa to investigate, was "of value ethnologically." Mead, ignoring Boas's repeated instructions to her, had begun this research on
the general ethnology of Samoa on September 30, 1925, just one
month after her arrival in Tutuila, with an inquiry into tattooing.
Some Mormon missionaries she had come to know had found her an
informant named Asuegi. He was an *ali'i*, or titular chief, of the
nearby village of Pago Pago. An elder in the Mormon church, he had
been to a Mormon school and so spoke "a good deal of English." He
was "very intelligent" and "well informed," but "rapacious." Thus,
although he demanded "no pay," he and his "stalwart brothers" always had "something to sell" and marshaled kava bowls, necklaces,
and canoe models before Mead's "obligated eyes." At first, getting information out of Asuegi was "like pulling teeth." He had no objection
to revealing anything but kept his "most ordinary knowledge," so it
seemed to Mead, "in some strange inaccessible spot." He reminded
her of those "old fashioned country wells" that it is necessary to
prime with a bucket of water before anything will issue from the

pump. Drawing on her comparative knowledge of Polynesia, she found Tahitian and Maori custom "excellent priming," as well as "sufficient explanation" for questions about matters that had no parallel in Asuegi's experience and that he was "likely to deem insulting." The first time she talked to him, Mead thought she would "scream with impatience."

*Mead:* When a chief's son is tattooed they build a special house, don't they?
*Asuegi:* No, no special house.
*Mead:* Are you sure they never build a house?
*Asuegi:* Yes. Well, sometimes they build a small house of sticks and leaves. Yes.
*Mead:* Was that house *sā* (sacred)?
*Asuegi:* No, not *sā.*
*Mead:* Could you take food into it?
*Asuegi:* Oh no. *'Ua sā* (That was forbidden).
*Mead:* Smoke in there?
*Asuegi:* Oh no, very *sā.*
*Mead:* Could anybody go into the house who wished?
*Asuegi:* Yes, anybody.
*Mead:* Anybody at all? just anybody?
*Asuegi:* Yes, anybody could go in.
*Mead:* No one was forbidden to go in?
*Asuegi:* No.
*Mead:* Could the boy's sister go in?
*Asuegi:* Oh no. *'Ua sā* (That was forbidden).[1]

That Mead should have begun her ethnological research in Samoa with an inquiry into male tattooing is to be explained by the circumstance that tattooing was one of the "complexes" of Polynesian culture that she had selected for study in her doctoral dissertation. Male tattooing had nothing to do with the "investigation of the adolescent girl" as "a study in heredity and environment" that she had come to Samoa to undertake, and her early concentration on tattooing and allied topics is an indication of her resolve to work on ethnology. Also on September 30, she collected information from Asuegi, in Samoan, about "ceremonies connected with birth." Then, on October 3, she questioned him at length about "funeral customs and treatment of the dead," which was one of the topics in which Edward Craighill Handy was especially interested.[2]

On October 10, three days after her arduous journey along the northwest coast of Tutuila, Mead returned to Leone in a "rattletrap" of a bus packed with Samoans to interview Mrs. Helen Ripley Wilson, who was a friend of the nurse G. F. Pepe, her instructor in Samoan. Mrs. Wilson was a thirty-six-year-old woman of part Samoan and part European descent. She had been educated in Honolulu and for a time had lived at the U.S. Naval Station, Tutuila, as a companion of the wife of Commander W. M. Crose, governor of American Samoa from 1910 to 1913. She had then married an ex-navy man who became a captain in the U.S. Merchant Marine. At Leone, she lived with her Samoan mother, who was from Upolu and who as a girl had been a *taupou*, a ceremonial virgin. For Mead, Helen Ripley Wilson was "a delight." "Intelligent" and an "excellent interpreter," she was still "a Samoan by sympathy" and "thoroughly conversant with Samoan custom."[3]

Mead had gone to Leone specifically to question Mrs. Wilson about the Samoan *taupou* system and the position of girls and women in Samoan society. In Samoa, an *ali'i*, or titular chief of high rank, has the right to confer on one of the sexually mature virginal girls of his family the rank of *taupou*, the girl chosen being usually one of his own daughters. In a Samoan family, daughters possess a special status of respect vis-à-vis their brothers, and so a *taupou* is the apotheosis of the honorific standing of a chiefly family, with her hand in marriage being much sought after by other titular chiefs of rank. A *taupou*, like a titular chief, has an accompanying title unique to the family of which she is a member, and she is given a ceremonial installation in which all the members of the community participate. *Taupou* were to be found in every village in which there were titular chiefs of rank, and their traditional titles were known and respected throughout Samoa.

Mead had taken with her to Leone a list of twenty-five typewritten "Questions to ask Mrs. Wilson." She was correctly informed by Mrs. Wilson that only *ali'i* had the "right to have a *taupou*." A *taupou*, however, belonged to the whole village. As a virgin, the *taupou* was chaperoned, even within her own village, by the wife of a talking chief, or orator, and if she went to another village, her "chaperone" had to go with her. Indeed, "girls even of common families," so Mead was told by Mrs. Wilson, "are never sent from village to village singly, without an older woman." Further, "it was not considered right to send a girl when there were plenty of men around the place." Here, Mead was being accurately informed about the way in which every attempt was made in Samoa to safeguard the virginity not only of the *taupou* but also of the girls of "common families." This safeguarding of virginity in the traditional society of Samoa was to ensure that a male, and particularly a male of rank, could be certain that the female he was marrying was a *virgo intacta* who had not been possessed by any other male, this being regarded as imperative for the maintenance of masculine honor and prestige. Furthermore, this safeguarding of nubile females was associated with the distinctively Samoan custom of the formal testing of virginity at marriage by the manual defloration of the "bride," before witnesses, by a male representative of the "bridegroom." In her notes on Helen Ripley Wilson, Mead described her as having an "accurate knowledge" of and "pride" in the "Samoan people and their customs." Yet after she had been hoaxed in March 1926, Mead was to ignore what she had been told by Helen Ripley Wilson in Leone, only a few months previously, and to give credence to an entirely fictitious "cultural pattern" that provided an answer of the kind that she had originally hoped she would find in Samoa.[4]

At the naval station the next day, Mead wrote to Boas and told him that for "the next five or six weeks" before she left for Ta'ū, she would be dividing her time between the London Missionary Society's Atauloma Boarding School for Girls, where no English was spoken, and the home of Helen Ripley Wilson in Leone, where she could "hear Samoan most of the time." Instead, after interviewing Asuegi once more on the "funeral customs" of the Samoans, she went to live for ten days in the village of Vaitogi, about twelve miles from the naval station, on the exposed southwest coast of Tutuila. Mead had been told about Vaitogi, famous as the village of the turtle and the shark, by Helen Ripley Wilson, who was in the habit of taking American tourists there. Legend had it that an old woman and a child, neglected by other relatives in a time of famine, had thrown themselves into the sea to be transformed into a turtle and a shark. Since then, so it was said, when a chant was sung on a lava outcrop on the rugged coast, one or the other, if not both, of these creatures momentarily appeared. Mrs. Wilson was related through her mother to an *ali'i* of Vaitogi named Ufiti. Ufiti was also one of the eight county chiefs of Tutuila appointed by the naval government. When Mead called on the secretary of native affairs, who was "a civilian appointed by the Navy Department," for a "letter of introduction," she was told that Ufiti was "one of the most intelligent chiefs of the island and one of the few who had remained loyal to the government in the rebellion of four years ago."[5]

This was a reference to the Mau, a Samoan movement of opposition to the naval government of the day. The early 1920s in American Samoa had been, as Governor Bryan put it in a report of 1926, "a period of unrest." This unrest began when the high chief Mauga became dissatisfied with the actions of an American judge of the High Court. Later in 1920, when Lieutenant Commander C. S. Boucher of the U.S. Navy actively supported the Mau, Governor W. J. Terhune, fearing an insurrection, intervened to secure the recall of Boucher and to dismiss Mauga and another high chief from their district governorships. Soon after this, when a court of inquiry had been set up and was on its way to Tutuila on the U.S.S. *Kansas*, Governor Terhune committed suicide with his service revolver. A state of some tension and disaffection continued for the next few years and in 1924, Tauanu'u, Tulifua, and Ti'a, three high-ranking talking chiefs of Ta'ū, where Mead was to do her fieldwork, conferred the august title of Tui Manu'a on Christopher Taliutafa Young, in open defiance of the naval government of American Samoa. Further, the high chief Sotoa, who held the position of acting district governor of Manu'a, participated in the kava ceremony marking the installation of the new Tui Manu'a. These events precipitated a major political crisis. Some fifteen years previously, on the death of Tui Manu'a Eliasara in 1909, Captain J. F. Parker, governor of American Samoa at the time, had proclaimed that from the date of the hoisting of the American flag in Manu'a in 1904, the title of Tui Manu'a had been changed to district governor. This action was taken because "the Tui Manu'a was royal in nature and therefore inadmissible under the constitution of the United States."

In July 1924, when the Samoans of Ta'ū restored their sovereign chieftainship in direct defiance of this ruling, Captain E. S. Kellogg, who had been governor of American Samoa since September 1923, at once dispatched the U.S.S. *Ontario* to Ta'ū to transport the newly installed Tui Manu'a, as well as Tauanu'u, Tulifua Ti'a, and Sotoa to the U.S. Naval Station, Tutuila. On August 7, 1924, they were arraigned before him. Their actions, he told them, "smacked of conspiracy." Sotoa, who was held to be primarily at fault, was suspended from office, and the newly installed Tui Manu'a was detained in Tutuila.

Tauanu'u, Tulifua, and Ti'a remained wholly defiant, telling Governor Kellogg that they were "dissatisfied to the death" with his interference in the affairs of Manu'a. In the judgment of the naval historian Captain J.A.C. Gray, the deposed Tui Manu'a, Christopher Taliutafa Young, became the means by which the Mau of American Samoa "came of age and assumed something of the status of a political party." Alfred F. Judd, president of the Board of Trustees of the Bishop Museum, who visited Manu'a and Tutuila for six weeks early in 1926, reported that the Mau was widespread and that there were few Samoans who did not sympathize with it. This then was the tense political situation at the time of Mead's brief sojourn in American Samoa. Mead, seemingly oblivious of the effect it might have on her research, threw in her lot with the U.S. Navy. For her, the Mau was "an insane procedure fostered by an unstable officer and a scheming carpetbagger." In the seven pages of notes on the Tui Manu'a that she prepared for Dr. Handy, there is no mention at all of the dramatic events of 1924.[6]

In Vaitogi, in contrast to her grueling visits to Poloa and other villages on the northwest coast of Tutuila, Mead was "most perfectly happy." Ufiti's daughter Fa'amotu, who was the *taupou* of Vaitogi and who "spoke a little English," was about the same age as Mead. A special "room" had been prepared at one end of Ufiti's house, with two beds made of sleeping mats from the Tokelau and Ellice Islands. There, as a protective measure against any nocturnal interloper, or *moetotolo*, Fa'amotu and Mead slept together under the same mosquito net. On her arrival in Vaitogi, Mead presented Ufiti and his wife with lengths of cloth, and Fa'amotu with a bottle of perfume. Ufiti, who spoke no English, was a "slender, delicate featured, very handsome man" in his forties, "keenly intelligent and surpassingly kind and gentle." In *Coming of Age in Samoa*, although *not* an inhabitant of Manu'a, Ufiti appears in chapter 4 under the pseudonym of Tui, and the situation of his family is discussed. While Mead was in Vaitogi, "two young chickens" were killed each day. Breadfruit was in season, and there were "mangoes and limes and papayas and a coarse woody pineapple." Early on the morning of Monday, October 26, Ufiti walked several miles to Leone especially to get "tea and coffee and bread." Fa'amotu had been trained in cooking by Helen Ripley Wilson.[7]

One of the typewritten questions that Mead prepared to put to Helen Ripley Wilson in Leone on October 10 concerned the punishment meted out to a *taupou* who was "found not to be a virgin" at time of marriage. This fact is of distinct historical importance, for it shows that before she went to Vaitogi, Mead was fully aware of the unreservedly strict requirement under Samoan custom that any female on whom a *taupou* title is conferred *must be a virgin.* When the twenty-three-year-old Mead arrived at Vaitogi with her "letter of introduction" from the secretary of native affairs of the naval government of American Samoa, she deliberately concealed from Ufiti and his family that she was a married woman. This, she says, was because she knew "too little" about what the "consequences" might be in the "roles" that would be assigned to her. Although she still went by her maiden name, Margaret Mead had by October 1925 been legally married for over two years and was certainly no virgin. Yet when Ufiti conferred on her the title of Sinauala early in her stay, which made her a *taupou* of Vaitogi, Mead voiced no scruple and then happily allowed the people of Vaitogi to acclaim her as a ceremonial virgin. What greatly appealed to her was the adulation given to a *taupou*, who, in Mead's words, enjoyed "the greatest honor" and who on ceremonial occasions was the cynosure of all eyes. For Mead, playing the part of a ceremonial virgin, even though it was quite improper for her as a married woman to do so, was clearly both exciting and gratifying. Thus, in Vaitogi, when an *i'a sa*, or sacred fish, was caught, it was, Mead reported, brought to her "as *taupou* of the village." Again, the chiefs of Vaitogi, according to Mead, were "so tickled" that a visiting American of "high status" was taking "the trouble to learn their ways" that they organized a *ta'alolo*, or ceremonial food offering, for her as a ceremonial virgin of Vaitogi, as well as three separate *fiafia*, or entertainments, at which she had her "first dancing lessons."[8]

It so happened that the members of a *malaga*, or traveling party, consisting of the *ali'i* Fuimaono and two attendant *tulāfale*, or talking chiefs, from Salani on the south coast of Upolu in Western Samoa were staying in Vaitogi at the same time as Mead. They became Mead's companions, and one of the *tulāfale*, named Lolo, who spoke no English, "took it upon himself" to teach Mead the honorific language of the Samoans, and "how to act as a Samoan lady." In this way Mead was taught "the rudiments of the graceful pattern of social relations which is so characteristic of the Samoans" and "learned how to relate to other people in terms of their rank" and "how to reply in terms of the rank" they accorded to her, which, with Mead's connivance, was that of the *taupou*, Sinauala. Most of Mead's stay in Vaitogi was given to this training in "how to manage Samoan etiquette," but she also gave as much time as she could to ethnological inquiry, investigating such things as children's games and methods of fishing and recording that when a shark was caught, its head was given to the "*taupou* and her court."[9]

When the time came for her to leave, she composed a farewell speech that she wrote out in English and then had Liu, Ufiti's nineteen-year-old son, translate into Samoan. This translation, when she repeated it from memory, so touched Ufiti and his family that they wept. It had been a highly successful visit. Indeed, she subsequently described her existence in Vaitogi as "idyllic" and declared that she had never spent "a more peacefully happy and comfortable ten days" in her life. She had certainly not encountered anything at all resembling "the nervewracking conditions" she had conjured up in her letter to Boas to justify her plan to reside, when on Ta'ū, in the U.S. Naval Dispensary. But her experience in Vaitogi did not cause her to change her plan to live, while in Manu'a, not with Samoans but in the U.S. Naval Dispensary "with Americans" who had "canteen privileges."[10]

Mead's last week on the island of Tutuila before leaving for Ta'ū was spent in completing her "formal study" of the Samoan language. On November 3, after having tested her proficiency in Vaitogi, she wrote to Miss Edith Elliott of the National Research Council in Washington, D.C., reporting that she had "mastered the language sufficiently" to make "a definite start" on the problem for which she had been awarded her research fellowship. On her return to her hotel in Pago Pago, she also wrote a letter to Dr. Handy on November 1 (see Appendix). She had been living, she told him, in Vaitogi as its "ceremonial *taupou*." Working in this way "under the shadow of the throne," she told Handy, had been "excellent" for "practice in the language" and the getting of "straight ethnological information."[11]

In her letter to Gregory of June 16, 1925, Mead had stipulated that she would have to wait until she had been "in the field for a couple of months" before she could reach a decision about the ethnological research he had proposed. Two months after her arrival in Tutuila, she was ready to commit herself. On November 1, 1925, ignoring the instructions of her supervisor, Franz Boas, she took the ambitious step of entering into a private agreement with the Bishop Museum to do ethnological research on its behalf during the quite limited time of five to six months she would have available to her in Manu'a for the

investigation of adolescent behavior. She told Handy in her letter of
November 1:

> I shall be able to cover the subjects of birth, childhood and its training,
> games, the simpler domestic arts practised by the girls, marriage, rela-
> tionship system, its tabus and obligations; rank in its relation to the orga-
> nization of the household, and to the ceremonies of birth, marriage and
> death, and the routine of festival and daily life. This leaves untouched,
> mythology (and I haven't taken many folktales in text because conversa-
> tion is so sparse and that was what I needed), tattooing designs, sinnet
> [sennit] designs, weaving (which would be a study of two or three months
> at least), dancing and music and any additional work you might want
> done on the actual construction of houses and canoes. For religion, I can't
> make any promises until I reach Ta'ū.

She also mentioned that she had obtained the names of a number of
"virtuosos" in the art of sinnet lashing and inquired if the Bishop Museum would be interested in paying one of them to make a series of
these lashings for its collection.[12]

Thus, before Mead had set foot in Ta'ū, where she was due under the
terms of her National Research Fellowship in the Biological Sciences
to devote all of her time to the "investigation of the adolescent girl" as
"a study in heredity and environment," she had agreed, in direct defiance of Boas's instructions, to also carry out extensive ethnological research with a view to having it published, under her own name, by the
Bernice P. Bishop Museum. She was obviously confident in her ability
to achieve this and, in the words of Edna St. Vincent Millay's First Fig
of 1920, to burn her candle at both ends and enjoy its "lovely light." It
was, however, a precarious as well as a venturesome undertaking and,
even though Margaret Mead had exceptional abilities, was to have unforeseen and fateful consequences.

# 8

# In Manu'a:
# The First Two Months

ON MONDAY, NOVEMBER 9, 1925, in the company of Ruth Holt and her newly born daughter, Moana, and numerous Samoans, Mead traveled to the island of Ta'ū in a U.S. Navy minesweeper. It was a rough passage, during which she was seasick. When they finally reached Ta'ū, a whaleboat landing schoolchildren capsized when crossing the reef. Ta'ū, a forested, reef-encircled island of fourteen square miles, rises like a huge cone to an elevation of over 3,000 feet. Some seven miles to the west lie the smaller islands of Ofu and Olosega, also volcanic in origin, which together with Ta'ū make up Manu'a. In the mid-1920s, the total population of Manu'a was 2,060. On Ta'ū, there were four different villages. On its west coast were Lumā, Si'ufaga, and Faleasao, with respective populations of 251, 331, and 274, and seven miles away at the northeast corner of the island, Fitiuta, with a population of 346. Olosega had a population of 427, and Ofu, 431. The U.S. Naval Dispensary, where Mead resided with the approval of the chief medical officer, was situated in Lumā, facing west and overlooking a lagoon and coral reef. It was a substantial weatherboard building with a corrugated iron roof. As well as housing the medical dispensary, it provided accommodation, complete with a bathroom, for Chief Pharmacist Mate Edward R. Holt, his wife, Ruth, and their children, Arthur and Moana, as well as for a "young sailor," referred to by Mead as "Sparks," who maintained and operated the radio station within this same building. There was also a Samoan "maid" named Leauala, who made faces behind Edward Holt's back. A

Samoan house built nearby served as a hospital, with a staff of two English-speaking Samoan nurses. There was also a Samoan *fitafita*, or guard, and an official Samoan interpreter. Mead had available to her "half of the back porch of the dispensary-quarters building," which had been divided off by a "bamboo screen." There was room for a single bed, complete with mosquito net, and for two tables to hold her books, papers, and portable typewriter. On one side was the outer wall of the main dispensary building, where Mead put up a picture of Franz Boas, whom she had idolized since 1922. From the other side, she could look out through wire screens, fitted with roll-up blinds of pandanus matting, into the village of Lumā. She thought it "really an excellent arrangement." At night, by opening the screen and pushing back the chairs and tables, she could make a space in which the young people who came to visit her could play their guitars and ukuleles and dance for her.[1]

Edward Holt was a tall, fair man, "intelligent, good-humoured and efficient," as well as "absolutely 150 percent moral and disciplinary." He did "most of the cooking." Breakfast was followed by lunch at noon and a two-hour siesta. Supper was at five, after which Mead would often work late into the night. Within a week of her arrival, her porch room was "crowded from dawn to midnight with all and sundry," and she found the "consistent need to be endlessly affable, enthusiastic and gay, an awful strain," even though the people of Ta'ū were "most lovable." During her second week, she suffered "a really bad attack" of tonsillitis and was ordered to bed by Edward Holt. On Thanksgiving Day, which in 1925 fell on November 26, she was still convalescing, writing letters, and reading the *New Republic* and the *Nation*, while the Holts talked about "how inexplicable it was for a white man to go native."[2]

Three days later, on Sunday, November 29, in a typewritten letter of four foolscap pages, Mead wrote her first report from Manu'a to Franz Boas. She felt "amply justified," she told him, in her decision "to live in a white household." "Natives of all ages and sexes and ranks" drifted on and off her porch "in a casual fashion," which would be out of the question if she were "living in a native house." This fact, she reckoned, more than compensated for "the slight loss in linguistic practice." She had to lock the door to keep the adolescents out and "yawn prodigiously to get rid of them at midnight."

The people of Ta'ū were all adherents of the London Missionary Society, and even the oldest people on the island had "almost all always

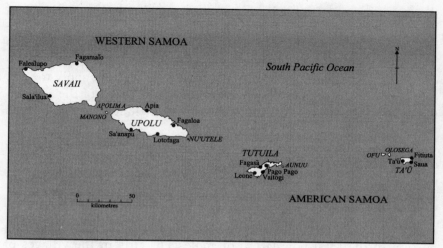

*The Samoan Archipelago, showing the island of Tutuila
and the islands of Manu'a: Ta'ū, Ofu, and Olosega,
where Margaret Mead worked in 1925–1926*

been Christian." The young people, both children and adolescents, attended a school conducted by the pastor of their village, at which they were taught "to read and write in Samoan and to read the Bible." This Christian school was held between 7:30 A.M. and 9 A.M. and between 3 P.M. and 4:30 P.M. In addition, there was the government school, with "quite rigorous truancy regulations" that were "strictly enforced by the native judicial authorities." At this government school, the teachers were "supposed to teach in English." It was held each weekday from 9 A.M. to 3 P.M., with a break of one hour at midday. These schools, as far as Mead was concerned, imposed a "definite limitation" on what she hoped to accomplish, restricting her access to the adolescent girls she was proposing to study to a few hours each day. Furthermore, fifteen of the adolescent girls of Lumā, Si'ufaga, and Faleasao lived in the household of the Samoan pastor of their village, where their lives, including their "physical chastity," Mead reported, were "very strictly supervised." This religious institution was one of the "ideals" by which the conduct of an adolescent girl was curbed by the community in which she lived. The other was the traditional *taupou* system of Samoa. Formerly, all the unmarried girls slept with the widows of the village, in "the same house" as the *taupou*, and "constituted a sort of court." This group, known to the Samoans as the *aualuma*, was by 1925 no longer fully active, but the concept of the *taupou* was, Mead reported, "still vividly alive." The "central requirement" for a *taupou* was that "she should be a virgin." She was "severely watched" and "chaperoned everywhere she went." However, this chaperoning, so Mead informed Boas, did not apply to "the other girls of the village," for whom there were "none of the requirements of modesty, dignity and chastity" that held for the *taupou*, the "village virgin."[3]

This was a quite mistaken assertion and the expression of a preconception that Mead had manifestly brought with her to Manu'a. On her own evidence, in this same letter to Boas, "physical chastity" was an explicit requirement for the fifteen adolescent girls in Ta'ū in November 1925, who were "very strictly supervised" in the household of the pastor of their village and who thus made up a quite significant proportion of the total population of adolescent girls in the villages of Lumā, Si'ufaga, and Faleasao. Of the pastor in whose household these girls lived, Mead stated: "He virtually adopts them." This was an accurate assessment, for in 1925, a Samoan pastor, or *faifeau*, stood in a strict relationship to the entire community by which he had been appointed, and he and his wife were, by formal agreement, in loco parentis to the virginal adolescent girls entrusted to their care. Again, the house of a pastor, he being a man of God, was held to be a sanctuary that no *moetotolo*, or surreptitious rapist, would dare to enter. In the account she gave to Boas in her letter of November 29, Mead was also departing, in respect of "the other girls of the village," from what she had been told by Helen Ripley Wilson in Leone on October 10, 1925. Furthermore, her supposition that the requirement of virginity applied only to the *taupou* was proven wrong in the course of an interview she conducted soon afterward on December 16 with To'aga, the wife of Sotoa, the high chief of Lumā. Thus, as Mead's notes on this interview with To'aga record: "In the marriage of the *taupou* the tokens of virginity are taken by the boy's *tulāfale*, or talking chief. In the marriage of an ordinary girl the ceremony takes place in the house, only the family and the boy's friends are present and some older man, chosen by the boy, performs the ceremony."

It was this account of the general requirement of virginity among "ordinary" girls as well as the *taupou* that Mead followed in her report of January 6, 1926, to the National Research Council, so correcting the error contained in her letter to Boas of November 29, 1925. Because it would have to be dispatched at the beginning of January 1926, Mead's report to the National Research Council would, she told Boas, cover "only a month's work." She had made *no systematic investigation of sexual behavior*, and any discussion of "sex and religious matters" would, she said, have to wait for her "obtaining greater linguistic practice." No one, she bemoaned, had ever learned the Samoan language "in less than eighteen months." She would, she informed Boas, probably ask for reappointment to her research fellowship, but she considered the granting of such reappointment "exceedingly doubtful," as she would have "so little" that was "tangible" to report.[4]

One week later, when Mead wrote to her husband, Luther Cressman, who was traveling in Europe, she was still in a state of considerable anxiety about what the future might hold for her. She had "not heard a word" from Pliny Goddard and was "very much afraid" that she had not got the "job" at the American Museum of Natural History, which she had been as good as promised before she set out for Samoa. The alternative, if she were to be "assured of a good living" from August 1926 onward, was to apply as she had originally intended for an extension of her research fellowship for another year. If granted, this would enable her to continue her fieldwork in Manu'a far beyond the six months she had planned. However, she thought she had no very strong case for fellowship renewal, and even if she applied, the results would not be known until after the Board of National Research Fellowships in the Biological Sciences met in April 1926. In these perplexing and uncertain circumstances, she told her husband on December 6, 1925, that she had decided to adhere to her scheme to "leave Samoa on an Oceanic Steamship Boat," probably the S.S. *Ventura*, on "the 31st. of May, or the first of June," so that she could meet him in Marseilles in the spring as they had planned. To adhere to this itinerary and make sure of connecting with the S.S. *Ventura* in Pago Pago, Mead would have to leave Ta'ū by about mid-May. Thus, from December 6, 1925, onward, she would have only about five months in Manu'a in which to complete her study of adolescent girls and to carry out the ethnological research that she had agreed to undertake for the Bishop Museum. This was a demanding schedule even for the most dedicated of researchers.[5]

When it was known that she was going to Samoa, Mead's father had generously offered to give her "the money for a trip around the world." The form that this trip might take was very much in Mead's mind throughout her stay in Manu'a. When, soon after her arrival on Ta'ū, a "young Fitiuta chief" offered to accompany her, she told him that she had to go alone so that she could "boast about it when she got back." On December 6, 1925, in the naval dispensary at Ta'ū, she formulated alternative plans for her itinerary after she departed Sydney. These she sent both to Luther and to her father. The first plan was for her to meet Luther in Aden, after which, en route to France, there could be "excursions into Egypt or French Africa." Her second plan was to meet Luther in Bombay, whence they would "go into India" before continuing on to Europe. Her third and most ambitious plan was to travel "around the east coast of Australia, by way of Dutch New Guinea, the Moluccas, Borneo and the Philippines to Hong Kong." From Hong Kong, there could be a "six day trip" to Japan before traveling to France by way of the Malay Peninsula, Sumatra, Siam, Calcutta, and Madras, or by way of Singapore, Colombo, and Aden. She would not, she noted, want to embark on this third itinerary unless Luther could meet her in Hong Kong. Thus, from the beginning of her stay in the U.S. Naval Dispensary at Ta'ū, there was the lure of France and the other exotic places that she hoped she might visit as soon as her research in Samoa had been completed to her satisfaction.[6]

Although by December 6, 1925, Mead had "heard not a word" from Pliny Goddard, he had not been idle. Before Clark Wissler, the museum's curator of anthropology, left for Australia on September 12, Goddard had discussed with him Boas's suggestion that Mead might be employed by the American Museum of Natural History. On October 31, Goddard wrote to George H. Sherwood, acting director of the museum, recommending that Margaret Mead be appointed assistant curator of ethnology, with a salary of $2,000 a year. At a special meeting of the Board of Trustees held on Wednesday, December 23, 1925, in the offices of J. P. Morgan at 23 Wall Street, Mead's appointment as assistant curator of ethnology on the scientific staff of the American Museum of Natural History was formally approved. Mead was at once notified by cable. The news of the appointment that she had so hoped for would have reached the radio station of the naval dispensary at Ta'ū on December 24, or soon thereafter. There was no one there other than herself who understood what this appointment meant to her, and there was "no way to celebrate." She "just walked along the beach alone" suffused with feeling and thinking about what her future would now be like.

She at once decided to abandon entirely the plan she had toyed with a month earlier of applying for reappointment to her research fellowship and extending her fieldwork in Manu'a beyond just five or so months. On December 3, Edith Elliott, secretary of the Board of National Research Fellowships in the Biological Sciences, had written to Mead informing her that in 1926, the board would be meeting at the end not of April, but of February, and that any application she was proposing to make for an extension of her fellowship should reach Washington, D.C., by Monday, February 22, 1926. Although Mead did not receive this letter in Ta'ū until January 7, 1926, it announced a deadline that she could, had she so wished, readily have met. The previous day, in the letter that accompanied her report of January 6 to Dr. Frank R. Lillie, chairman of the Board of National Research Fellowships in the Biological Sciences, she had written, "I am not asking for reappointment as I think that my problem can be satisfactorily completed within the year that I have allotted to it. I expect to remain in Samoa until early in June."

By January 6, 1926, then, knowing that she would be returning to a secure and congenial job at the American Museum of Natural History, she was intent on completing her fieldwork in Samoa well within the twelve months of her fellowship, which had begun on August 1, 1925. The prospect of extending her research in Manu'a by successfully applying for an extension to her research fellowship had been abandoned. Thus, despite the arrival of notification of the possibility of extension *before* her letter to Frank Lillie had been dispatched, she made no alteration to her plan to sail from Samoa for Sydney on "the 31st of May or the first of June," as announced in her letter to Luther Cressman of December 6, 1925. Further, realizing that on her return to New York she would be employed by the American Museum of Natural History as an ethnologist, her time during the remainder of her stay in Manu'a was increasingly given to ethnological inquiry, even though this involved neglecting for substantial periods addressing the problem for which her research fellowship had been awarded.[7]

This ethnological inquiry had begun well before Mead received word of her appointment as an assistant curator of ethnology. As is apparent from her letter to Handy of November 1, 1925, she arrived in Ta'ū with the fully formed intention of completing her ethnology of Manu'a. Indeed, during her first few weeks at Lumā, she was already thinking of making visits of "a strictly ethnological nature" to Fitiuta, as well as to Ofu and Olosega. Again, during November and December 1925, while conducting a detailed survey of Lumā, Si'ufaga, and Faleasao, she actively engaged in a good deal of ethnological inquiry.

Her two principal informants were Tufele Fa'atoia of Si'ufaga and To'aga of Lumā. Fa'atoia had received, at the expense of the naval government, "an American education" for six years at the Hilo Boarding School in Honolulu and had then served as an assistant teacher at the government high school in Pago Pago. He delighted in singing "the latest Broadway hit" while strumming on his ukulele, was "very sophisticated," and spoke fluent English. In 1925, on the death of his father, Fa'atoia succeeded to the high ranking *ali'i* title of Tufele and, after the dismissal of Sotoa, was appointed district governor of Manu'a in his place. Although his title came from Fitiuta, Tufele Fa'atoia's place of residence was in Si'ufaga, only a few minutes' walk from the naval dispensary, and there he would always offer Dr. Mead, as she was known to him, "his hand and an armchair."

To'aga, Mead's other main ethnological informant, was the wife of Sotoa, the former acting district governor of Manu'a. She lived in Lumā, close by the naval dispensary. Her father was the son of an Englishman named Young who had married into the "royal" family of the Tui Manu'a during the second half of the nineteenth century. She was "the widow of a Pharmacist Mate of the U.S. Navy," from whom she had inherited $10,000, and had a child, a boy of five, who was the illegitimate son of another navy man. Because of her rank and wealth, To'aga had "great influence and prestige," but she disdained "the circumlocutions of Samoan politeness" and spoke "excellent Navy slang." Mead was thus also able to converse with To'aga in English. In November and December 1925, she interviewed To'aga on the *taupou* of Ta'ū, on crime and punishment, birth customs, childhood, marriage, and rank; Tufele was interviewed on feasts, the *fono*, the carpenter's guild, and the ownership of land and property. Other informants during this same period were interviewed on forbidden degrees of marriage, birth defects, and the *'aumāga*, a grouping consisting of the untitled men of a village. Thus, from the outset of her stay on the island of Ta'ū, Mead gave much of her time to the study of the ethnology of Manu'a.[8]

On December 7, 1925, Handy responded enthusiastically to the letter in which Mead had listed the subjects on which she would be able to do ethnological research. He wished that the Bishop Museum had "a hydroplane" so that he could, now and then, "run down and spend a weekend" at Ta'ū. He eagerly accepted Mead's "excellent idea" to have a Samoan expert in the art of braiding make a set of "sinnet [sennit] lashing patterns" for the Bishop Museum. He hoped that she would be able to learn as much as possible about the Tui Manu'a, the principal sacred "king" of ancient Samoa, and to "work out for Samoa," as he was doing for the Society Islands, "a definition of culture traits belonging to *ali'i* on the one hand and to commoners on the other." To assist Mead in her ethnological inquiries in American Samoa, he sent to her from the archives of the Bishop Museum copies of manuscripts that had been collected by William Churchill when he was living in Samoa at the end of the nineteenth century. These manuscripts, comprising 145 sheets of genealogies and four loose-leaf binders of *fa'alupega*, or honorific titles, in order of precedence, for both Tutuila and Manu'a, reached Mead in Ta'ū on December 21. She began working through them on January 6, 1926, immediately after completing her report to the National Research Council and made extensive use of them during the course of her wide-ranging ethnological research in Manu'a before returning them to the Bishop Museum by mail early in May 1926.[9]

Mead began work on her report to the National Research Council, sitting in the naval dispensary and gazing out on the surf on the morning of New Year's Day, 1926, which had dawned "wet and ominous." Within a few hours, Lumā and the other villages of Ta'ū were being devastated by one of the tropical hurricanes that from time to time strike Samoa during the wet season. At first, when the hurricane blew from the east, Lumā was to some extent protected by the escarpment immediately behind it. But when the eye of the storm had moved westward toward nightfall and the full force of the hurricane came from the open sea, the naval dispensary was in imminent danger of destruction. Edward Holt's response was to have the radio operator and a visiting sanitary inspector hack a hole in the side of the dispensary's massive cement water tank. When the water had drained away, Mead was lowered into the "pitch dark" interior to receive first the two-month-old Moana and then the two-year-old Arthur. After the others had entered the tank, they all crouched by the light of a candle, listening to the tin roof of the dispensary "coming off very noisily," to trees "slapping and banging," and to the "surf roaring like thunder." When they emerged the next morning, "general desolation" reigned. Half of the dispensary building was uninhabitable; its roof was off, its porches down, and its radio smashed. Further, as Mead informed Handy, the hurricane had "razed 75 percent of the houses in Ta'ū to the ground, ruined the crops and the copra, and generally disorganized native society." When news of the hurricane, which had also seriously damaged buildings of the U.S. Naval Station, Tutuila, appeared in the New York newspapers, Boas, apprehensive about Mead's plight, had Ruth Benedict send a cable to Ta'ū "asking for a reply." Mead responded on January 10 with the one word: "Well." This, literally, was the case. She had survived the hurricane unscathed and with great aplomb. She had succeeded in protecting her books, papers, and typewriter from the elements. A new roof was being put on her room. Nonetheless, her work had been very seriously affected, as the people she wanted to study were all fully occupied rehabilitating their villages in the aftermath of the hurricane.[10]

She wrote her report to the National Research Council in "a couple of days" immediately after the hurricane, under most trying conditions. Understandably, it was a brief report of just over six typewritten pages. As she explained in a prefatory note, it was based on "only five weeks of actual work" in Manu'a, which was "a period too short to justify even tentative conclusions." These five weeks had been entirely taken up, in addition to research on "some of the aspects of Samoan culture" that were being studied "in cooperation with the B. P. Bishop Museum," in "a detailed personnel study of the entire population of the three villages, Lumā, Si'ufaga and Faleasao." During the course of this "personnel study," she reported having collected "information as to sex; approximate age; rank; marital state, past and present; number of living children; order of birth in relation to living siblings (in the case of younger people only); occupation; foreign contacts; amount of education (of younger people); functions in village political organization; defects and abnormalities; and relationship to every other member of the household." This information "provided a thorough background for understanding the place of each girl in the structure of her community." Mead proposed concentrating her investigation, *when it did begin*, upon "three aspects of the life of the adolescent girl." These three aspects were, first, "problems" of the adolescent girl's "relation to her household, her age group and her community in terms of conformity and divergence of behavior, of rebellion or submission or indifference"; second, "problems of sex," under which would be included "all affectional relationships such as friendship, devotion to an older individual of the same sex, etc."; and, third, "an inquiry into the development of religious interests or intellectual interests of any sort."[11]

As this report of January 6, 1926, to the National Research Council establishes, all of Mead's time up to this juncture of her fieldwork had been given either to her "detailed personnel study" of Lumā, Si'ufaga, and Faleasao or to ethnological research. Thus, although only four months remained to her in Manu'a, she had *still to begin* sustained work on "the investigation of the adolescent girl" as "a study in heredity and environment" and had, since her arrival on Ta'ū on November 9, 1925, made *no systematic study of the sexual behavior of the adolescent girls of Manu'a.*

The other principal interest of Mead's report of January 6, 1926, lies in the statements it contains about premarital sexual behavior, despite the fact that, on her own admission, she had made no systematic investigation of this topic. In her report, Mead quite correctly stated that "the whole emphasis" of the Protestant Church of the London Missionary Society, which in 1925 was "very heavily entrenched all over Samoa," was on "physical chastity." And she also correctly reported as concerned the traditional nuptial system of Samoa that at the marriage of "girls of lesser rank," as well as at that of the *taupou,* a "representative of the bridegroom" was "permitted to test the virginity of the bride." As these two statements clearly indicate, Samoa in the 1920s, in contrast to some other parts of Polynesia, had a society in which the virginity of nubile females was of preeminent and vital concern. Yet in this same report, Mead unaccountably and quite inconsistently asserted that there was also in Manu'a "an extensive tolerance of premarital sex relations." As Mead, on her own testimony, had *not* by January 6, 1926, engaged in *any systematic investigation* of the sexual behavior of the adolescent girls of Manu'a, this statement, like the premature assertion in her letter to Boas of November 29, 1925, was manifestly the expression of a major preconception that stemmed from what she had been told about the premarital promiscuity present in other Polynesian societies, like that of the Marquesans, as described by Edward Craighill Handy. It was a preconception that was to loom large during the whole of her stay in Manu'a and to contribute in a pivotal way to her being hoaxed in March 1926.[12]

On January 4, 1926, when Mead was working on her report to the National Research Council, Franz Boas was writing in the capacity of her supervisor to the Board of National Research Fellowships in the Biological Sciences. He had concluded from Dr. Mead's letters that she had made "a very excellent start" and felt that he and the board could be "fully satisfied" with the work she had done. In another letter written on that same day, he informed Mead that, knowing of her appointment at the American Museum of Natural History, he had not made any application to the National Research Council on her behalf for an extension of her research fellowship. Boas was thus quite content to let Mead complete her "investigation of the adolescent girl" in Manu'a within a period of six months or less and did not enjoin her to extend her research beyond this quite brief period. When Boas's letter reached Mead in Ta'ū in February, she thanked him warmly for having anticipated her wishes.[13]

# 9

# In Manu'a:
# After the Hurricane

A S SOON AS SHE HAD COMPLETED HER REPORT to the National Research Council, Mead wrote an urgent letter to Boas. In
the "explanatory note" attached to her report, she had emphasized
that it covered a period of fieldwork "too short to justify even tentative conclusions." She reiterated this point in her letter to Boas of January 5, 1926 (see Appendix), saying of her report that it "made absolutely no showing in conclusions at all." With only just over four
months remaining to her in Manu'a, this had become a matter of serious concern. Added to this, she was "very much at sea" about another
vital issue. "What I need most," she told Boas, "is advice as to the
method of presentation of results when I finally get them." In her letter to Boas of July 19, 1925, she had told him: "I am afraid I shall never
get properly weaned from asking your advice." "I ought," she continued in her letter of January 5, "to be able to marshall an array of facts
from which another would be able to draw independent conclusions.
And I don't see how in the world I can do that."

Two possibilities had occurred to her, but they both seemed "inadequate." The first possibility was to present the material in a "semi-
statistical fashion," though, given the nature of the material she
would be collecting, she could not see "how any sort of statistical
technique would be of value." The second possibility was to "use case
histories." The problem here was how to do this effectively. "Facts"
that possessed significance in one case but were "mere bagatelles of
externality in another" would, she thought, have to be included in

each case history, or "they would not be comparable." Finally, she put to Boas the crucial question: "If I simply write conclusions and use my cases as illustrative material will it be acceptable?"

Hoping that she might get an answer in time for it to be of use to her while she was still in Manu'a, she dispatched her letter of January 5 by airmail with a request to Boas that he should "dash off an airmail answer" that she might get in March. This Boas did. His immediate reply of February 15 (see Appendix) reached Mead in the U.S.S. *Tanager*, the same ship on which she returned to Ta'ū during the third week of March 1926, after her visit to Ofu and Olosega with Fa'apua'a and Fofoa. It was a reply that decisively determined the way in which *Coming of Age in Samoa* was written.[1]

For Mead, who had *yet to begin* sustained research on the adolescent girls she had selected for study, the weeks following the hurricane of New Year's Day 1926 were enormously difficult. Everyone was "busy rehabilitating the village." "Informants" were "not to be had for love or money," so she had to spend her time wandering about, "sometimes engaging in useful activity and sometimes merely sitting on the floor and looking on." It was extremely frustrating. Furthermore, as she had reported on December 11, 1925, on the island of Ta'ū she experienced a "most peculiar sensation" from even a few hours in a native house, "a different taste in the mouth, a sense of heavy, almost sickly heat, a feeling as if one's skin were going to float off, in thin gossamer layers in the near future; and a curious buzzing inside one's head, mostly from the strain of listening." She did not know exactly what was responsible for this; possibly it was "the food and sitting cross-legged, and the flies."[2]

On January 16, she gave further expression to her feelings in a dejected handwritten letter to Boas. "It is very sad," her letter began, "that anyone as willing to take advice as I am should be so far beyond the reach of it. Life here is one long battle with my conscience as to whether I'm working correctly and whether I'm working hard enough. I remember your saying to me 'You will have to waste a great deal of time,' but I wonder if you guessed how much." In the afternoon, she would be going fishing on the reef with two young men, Falepogisa and Vimotu. The "ethnological gain" would "probably be nil." However, Falepogisa was "an excellent informant" on the ethnology of Manu'a. She had interviewed him the previous day about house building. It was, she wrote, "a curious scene" to see Falepogisa and Vimotu and "half a dozen other boys, clad only in *lavalavas* with hibiscus behind their ears or a graceful fillet of leaves on their heads," sitting on the floor of her room, "tremendously at ease amid its various sophistications and privacies," as they musingly turned "the pages of a *Dial* or a *Mercury* with an air of detached tolerance." She had, she told Boas, been giving the girls she was studying "individual intelligence tests," though for "motives unconnected with usual test purposes." They came to her room at the U.S. Naval Dispensary and had somehow to be kept occupied. The tests provided "an extremely harmless subject for village conversation" and obscured somewhat the prying nature of her questions. They were also "an excellent excuse" for getting the girls alone, which hitherto had been difficult, as they seldom called in groups of "under three." She was also trying "to make as detailed a study as possible of the social organization and all its various minute variations." She supposed that all of her research, in its broadest aspect, might be subsumed under the heading of "the individual's reaction to the culture," with the description of the culture as a necessary side issue. "But thru it all," she confessed to Boas in harrowing terms, "I have no idea whether I am doing the right thing or not, or how valuable my results will be. It all weighs rather heavily on my mind. Is it worth the expenditure of so much money? Will you be dreadfully disappointed in me? . . . Oh, I hope I won't disappoint you in this year's work."[3]

Mead's deeply despondent mood was also in part due to the fact that life had become much more complicated at the naval dispensary. Because the crops of Manu'a had been so extensively damaged by the hurricane, Lieutenant Commander William Edell, the chaplain of the U.S. Naval Station, Tutuila, had been sent to Ta'ū to take charge of the distribution of emergency food supplies. Lieutenant Commander Edell's presence in the naval dispensary at Lumā, as well as that of "another sailor," made "a large, ill-assorted, uneasy household." On Saturday, January 23, Chaplain Edell ordered Edward Holt and the two other naval ratings on Ta'ū to parade in dress uniform and salute him as their superior officer. Then, as Mead described it, when inspecting the dispensary, he "objected pompously to the baby's clothes on the line." Also, although according to Mead there were three people on Ta'ū who spoke "much better English" than she spoke Samoan, because she was residing in a naval establishment, Lieutenant Commander Edell had her "do most of his interpreting for him." This included such tasks as translating into Samoan official letters to the high chief of the off-lying island of Olosega. When this happened, Mead would have Fatuloa, the official Samoan interpreter at the naval dispensary, go over her translation. When Fatuloa found "only three mistakes" in one of her translations, she felt "quite puffed up." Mead was also called on to act as an interpreter when Lieutenant Commander Edell "held court over a land case." She was, she remarked, "properly nervous." But that she was able to act as an interpreter in a case involving chiefs is evidence that by the end of January 1926, she had become reasonably competent in Samoan. Mead had been unexpectedly called on after an objection by one of the disputants to Tufele's acting as interpreter. It was an uproarious hearing, during which District Governor Tufele, who was drunk, "sassed" the judge. According to Mead, he was suspended from office "for six months."[4]

Mead had brought with her to the island of Ta'ū a letter of introduction from Duke Kahanamoku, the champion Hawaiian swimmer and Olympic Games hero, as well as a picture of a statue of him to present to his "ceremonial brother," Tufele Fa'atoia. Tufele, "a famous athlete" himself, had gotten to know Duke Kahanamoku in Honolulu. Mead soon became friendly with Tufele, who was a young man "of great force and resourcefulness." From November 1925 onward, she was a frequent visitor at Tufele's house at Si'ufaga, which in 1929 the English painter Aletta Lewis stayed in and described as "vast and austere, like some simple cathedral translated into wood," with its thatched roof and floor of "immaculately white" pebbles.

When on November 28, 1925, Mead interviewed her other principal informant, To'aga, about the *taupou* of Ta'ū, she was told that with the abolition of the Tui Manu'a title by the naval government of American Samoa, there were only five other high ranking *ali'i* whose families had the right to have a *taupou*. And further, of these five, only Tufele Fa'atoia had exercised his right to confer his family's *taupou* title of Laulauga on one of his young female relatives. She was a beautiful and accomplished young woman named Fa'amū, who, as Samoan custom required, was a *teine muli*, or virgin. Christened Fa'amū after her birth on April 30, 1901, in the remote settlement of Fitiuta, she was installed early in 1925 as Laulauga, the *taupou* of Tufele Fa'atoia, the newly appointed district governor of Manu'a. Fa'amū had thus become the highest-ranking young woman in all Manu'a. Yet, with the sardonic sense of humor that Samoans have in these matters, she was soon given the nickname of Fa'apua'a, which literally means "like a pig," an arrestingly paradoxical recognition of her incomparable

beauty and poise, as well as a wry comment on her possible rivals, for
it is also a tag that carries the connotation of "she compared with
whom all others are pigs." Although her family lived in Fitiuta, much
of Fa'apua'a's time was spent in Tufele's house at Si'ufaga, and it was
there, in December 1925, that Mead first became friendly with her. In
the fourth chapter of *Coming of Age in Samoa*, Fa'apua'a Fa'amū is
given the pseudonym of Pana, and Tufele Fa'atoia appears as Malae.[5]

Eleven letters from Fa'apua'a to Mead, all of them in Samoan, have
survived in the collections of the Manuscript Division of the Library of
Congress. The first of them was written on January 6, in Fitiuta, after
Fa'apua'a had returned there from Si'ufaga, where she had been on the
day of the great hurricane of January 1, 1926. It is formally addressed:
*"Mo Lana Afioga a Makerita"* (For Her Highness Margaret), this being
recognition, by Fa'apua'a, of Margaret Mead's high rank, both as the
holder of a Samoan *taupou* title and as an expatriate American who had
the support of the all-powerful U.S. Navy. But the letter itself is
couched in the most affectionate terms. It begins: *"Si o'u alofa"* (My
loved one); and ends: *"O alofa mo 'oe"* (Love to you). It inquires how
Makerita, who is again called *"lau afioga"* (your highness), had fared in
the hurricane, and it was sent by hand, with the gift of a pineapple.

According to Fa'apua'a, when she traveled from Fitiuta to Tufele's
house at Si'ufaga, she would usually call on Mead at the naval dispensary with, as is customary in Samoa, a gift of food. During such visits,
she and Makerita would sometimes have a meal together. However,
during one of her visits to the naval dispensary, when Mead began to
question her about the chiefly titles and ceremonies of Fitiuta, Fa'a-
pua'a claimed in 1988 to have then pleaded ignorance, to have told
Makerita she should visit Fitiuta (as Mead subsequently did) for discussions with Poumele, an *ali'i* who knew all about such things. Their
relationship gradually became sufficiently friendly for Fa'apua'a to feel
she could call on Mead for small material favors. Thus, on February 9,
1926, Mead recorded, in one of her bulletins, that Fa'apua'a had written to her "from Fitiuta" for "powder and soap." By early in 1926,
then, Fa'apua'a Fa'amū and Margaret Mead, both of them twenty-four
years old and both of them with *taupou* titles, had become close
friends. It was to become the principal friendship into which Mead entered while in Manu'a and was to have, because of Mead's insufficient
understanding of the mischievously jocular ways of the Samoans, the
most discrepant of anthropological outcomes.[6]

Toward the end of January 1926, a *malaga,* or traveling party, arrived in Ta'ū from the island of Upolu in Western Samoa. Its most important member was Talala, the widow of Tufele Timiali, the mother of Tufele Fa'atoia, and the holder of a chiefly title in her own right. She had returned to Ta'ū, where she had once lived, accompanied by her entourage of talking chiefs and "several ladies of her age and experience" from Mulivai, on the south coast of Upolu, for the birth of her son's first child. Soon after the visitors had settled in Tufele's "great guest house" in Si'ufaga, Mead called on Talala, "bearing a gift of four yards of old rose calico," to tell her, using the honorific language appropriate to someone of Talala's rank, why she had come to Samoa. So "pleased and flattered" was Talala by this action that she announced her intention of conferring on Mead a *taupou* title that was hers to bestow, from the district of Tuamasaga in Western Samoa. This was an honor that Mead could with ease have politely declined. She was well aware, as she recorded in her letter to Boas of November 29, 1925, that "the central requirement for the *taupou* was that she should be a virgin." It was, therefore, inadmissible under Samoan custom for her, as a married woman, to have the title of a *taupou* formally conferred upon her. Yet although she was dealing with one of the most sacrosanct institutions of the Samoan people, she had accepted the position in Vaitogi three months earlier, and once again, she did not demur. On January 26, 1926, she allowed herself to be installed as the *taupou* of Tufele Fa'atoia's mother, Talala.[7]

The kava ceremony that formally sanctioned her installation as a *taupou* with the title of Fua i le Lagi, was held at high noon, an honor, Mead recorded, "reserved for a half a dozen high chiefs." She was then obliged, in accordance with Samoan custom, to make presentations to all of the talking chiefs present; and by February 14 there was, according to Mead, "not a day" on which Talala, as her "chief," did not send "half a dozen times for something, salmon or ink or stamps." In her bulletin of January 26, 1926, Mead described herself as being "caught in the toils of high rank again." In fact, by failing to make it known that she was a married woman, she was engaging of her own volition in a masquerade that had little or no significance for her research on adolescent girls. Yet even though she found it "very elaborate and time-consuming," it was a masquerade that was obviously deeply gratifying. As in Vaitogi, she was greatly excited at being the center of chiefly attention. At the end of her bulletin of January 26, she identified herself as the holder of two different *taupou* titles, Sinauala and

Fua i le Lagi. Her new title, Fua i le Lagi, which means Flower in the Heaven, was, she thought "very nice." Her "chief gain," she considered, was that when she went to Fitiuta to do ethnology, she would be received as Talala's *taupou* and there would be "the most splendid entertainment." Added to which, she had been told that when she got to Fitiuta, which was "the stronghold of original custom" and "a very polite place," she was going to be given "another high *taupou* name." As this account indicates, by January 26, 1926, Mead had become far more interested in the ethnology she was planning to do in Fitiuta and in the recognition she would receive there as a ceremonial virgin than in her work on adolescent girls with which, as she had confessed to Boas in her letter of January 16, she was having so much difficulty. The course of her research during the ten weeks or so that remained to her in Manu'a had been set.[8]

As soon as her informants had recovered from the effects of the hurricane, Mead resumed her general ethnological inquiries. Thus, on January 23, she interviewed Tufele about the making of sennit; on January 24, To'aga was questioned about funeral ceremonies and ghosts; on January 29, Tufele was again interviewed, this time about rank; and on February 2, she discussed the kava ceremony of the Tui Manu'a with Asi of Faleasao. Her problem was, as she noted on February 9, that when she used "real informants" and sat down with them and asked questions "by the hour," she could not pay them once and for all. Her informants, both "noble and common," all preferred "endless little favors." Thus, during the previous fortnight, she had given away to various informants "some 100 envelopes and sheets of paper, dozens of cigarettes, boxes of matches, onions in threes, needles, thread, ink, pencils, carbon paper to trace embroidery designs and scissors." It was an endless problem, with "perhaps a dozen people" coming "within fifteen minutes," and took up much of her valuable time.[9]

However, when on Saturday, February 13, there was a lull during heavy rain, and "no children came," she grasped the opportunity of "taking stock" of the information she had collected. It relieved her mind "immensely" to find that after all the time it had taken "to learn the language," she had "a sizable amount of material to show" for the three months she had been in Manu'a. The following Monday, she wrote to Boas. "I have," she informed him, "been taking stock of the amount of material I have accumulated and I think I can now report that my work is going nicely. I have finished, with the exception of a few gaps which I have to await the opportunity to fill up, a study of the domestic industries, and of all others in which girls and women participate." In addition, she had completed "a study of rank and its peculiar aspects" for the three villages of Lumā, Si'ufaga, and Faleasao, as well as "a study of the ceremonialism surrounding the various crises, of age classes, division of labor, the relationship system and its implications, ownership of property and its ramifications," and "of the degree in which women participate in the knowledge of the community and in the various activities of her social status and her specialized skills." Much of this "study" was primarily concerned with the ethnology of Manu'a, which Mead was working on "for the Bishop Museum," but in part, it also provided background information for her research on adolescent girls.[10]

For her study of adolescent girls, Mead had, by mid-February 1926, a total of sixty-six individuals, "26 between 8 and 12 years old; 10 between 12 and puberty; and 30 between puberty and about 20 years of age." For these sixty-six individuals, she would, she told Boas on February 15, 1926, have "at the end of next month"—that is, by the end of March 1926—the following information:

> Approx. age, rank, and birthplace of parent, make-up of household, order of birth, amount of schooling in government and pastor's school, amount of foreign experience, health and physical defect, date when puberty was attained; regularity, pain, amount of disability during menstruation; extent to which girl has participated in various crises, as birth, death, miscarriages, etc.; the extent to which she participated in a knowledge of the current superstitions, taboos, sanctities, paraphernalia of rank and status; what are her specific ambitions in the way of choice of husband, number of children, etc.; her training in etiquette, her skill in all of the domestic industries; her general personality traits, intelligence, as measured by observation and by a series of short, well-standardized intelligence tests; her friendships and allegiances within the household, and her general status in her age group.

It was a catalogue intended to reassure Boas after her despairing letter of a month earlier. It was also a formidable amount of information to collect for no fewer than sixty-six individuals living in three different villages. And if it was to be accomplished within the next six weeks, it would call for sustained research throughout the whole of this period.[11]

When all this information had been collected, by the end of March 1926, as Mead hoped, there would still remain "for special investigation" the "sexual life" of the adolescent girl, as well as "any philosophical conflicts" that might be evinced. These topics, Mead observed, were "the most difficult to get at" and required "the greatest facility in the language and the longest intimacy." She was, for these substantial reasons, deferring systematic research on the "sexual life" of the adolescent girl and on "any philosophical conflicts" until April 1926, the last month of her stay on Ta'ū, even though, as she mentioned to Boas, she had "a good deal" of material on both subjects already.[12]

When she wrote to Boas on February 15, 1926, Mead had for some time been recording preliminary information in a special loose-leaf folder on the sexual and other behavior of the adolescent girls she was studying. However, the quality of this information, which was fragmentary and in some cases merely hearsay, was not sufficiently reliable or complete to permit the delineation of any cultural pattern of the kind that Mead was seeking. It was for this reason that she was planning to undertake a "special investigation" of the "sexual life" of the adolescent girl beginning in April 1926. In her report of January 6, 1926, written before she had made any systematic investigation of sexual behavior, she had recorded her personal belief that in Manu'a there was, as elsewhere in Polynesia, as she knew from her discussions with Edward Craighill Handy, "an extensive tolerance of premarital sex relations." And in her letter to Boas of February 15, 1926, although she still had to undertake her "special investigation" of this aspect of Samoan behavior and so had *no reliable information* on which she could draw, she again recorded the preconception that she had manifestly brought with her to Samoa—that there was, in Manu'a, "great promiscuity between puberty and marriage." If, so Mead assured Boas on February 15, 1926, "nothing untoward" occurred in the "next two months"—that is, by about mid-April 1926, when her planned "special investigation" of the sexual behavior of female adolescents would be well advanced—she thought she would be able to complete her work on adolescent girls "fairly satisfactorily." It still seemed to her, however, that she had "terrifically little on paper."[13]

On February 18, 1926, just three days after Mead had written to Boas concerning the mass of information about adolescent girls that she was intending to collect during the ensuing six weeks, there arrived at Lumā a major research expedition from the Bishop Museum. Its leader was the malacologist Dr. C. Montague Cooke Jr., who, in August 1925, had each morning driven Mead the five miles from the Frears' town house in Honolulu to the Bishop Museum while dis-

coursing on the evolution of snails in the Pacific region. Dr. Cooke
was accompanied by Theodore T. Dranga, the Bishop Museum's col-
lector of marine and land shells, and by Alfred F. Judd, the president of
its Board of Trustees. Although Judd had an interest in ethnology, the
primary purpose of the Cooke expedition was "to obtain a knowledge
of the distribution (both lateral and altitudinal) of land snails on the island of Ta'ū and elsewhere in American Samoa." In this endeavor, it
was successful. From February 15 to April 2, 1926, "nearly 40,000
specimens were collected on the islands of Ta'ū, Ofu and Tutuila,"
with "the known species inhabiting these islands" being "about doubled." As Cooke and Dranga wished to collect land snails at the eastern end of the island of Ta'ū and as Judd wanted to visit the remote
settlement of Fitiuta, Tufele Fa'atoia, the district governor of Manu'a,
organized a special *malaga* to visit the village of which he was one of
the high chiefs. The *malaga* also included his mother, Talala, who was
eager to return to Fitiuta, where she had once lived, with her retinue
from Western Samoa.[14]

This, despite the mass of information she was due to collect on her
adolescent girls by the end of March 1926, was, Mead felt, "too good a
chance to miss." A visit to Fitiuta, which had the reputation of being
"the proudest, most complex and the most ancient" of polities, was
something of which she had long dreamed. In particular, it was imperative for the completion of her ethnology of Manu'a, to be published
by the Bishop Museum, on which, in contravention of Boas's instructions to her, she had been devoting a great deal of her attention since
her arrival in Ta'ū in November 1925. Abandoning work on her adolescent girls, all of whom lived in the villages of Lumā, Si'ufaga, and
Faleasao at the western end of Ta'ū island, she joined Dr. Montague
Cooke, Alfred Judd, and the others on their seven-mile journey to Fitiuta to give all of her time for the next ten days to ethnological research. The investigation of heredity and environment in relation to
adolescent behavior, for which she had been granted a National Research Fellowship in the Biological Sciences, was, because of her ever-
deepening involvement with the Bishop Museum, being put in real
jeopardy.[15]

# 10

# In Fitiuta:
# "A Gold Mine, Ethnologically"

ALTHOUGH IT HAD NOTHING TO DO with her study for Franz Boas on heredity and environment in relation to adolescence, Mead had planned, from the time of her first arrival in Manu'a, to visit Fitiuta for research "of a strictly ethnological nature" for the Bishop Museum. She had, however, deliberately "procrastinated" until she had acquired a sufficiently "fluent command" of Samoan. By February 1926, even though she had been living in the U.S. Naval Dispensary with other Americans, she had become proficient enough in Samoan to act as an interpreter at a court held by Lieutenant Commander Edell and at an "emergency case" for Edward Holt, when "both nurses were at the other end of the village." She thus felt ready by February 20, 1926, to tackle the ethnological research that she wanted to do in Fitiuta. Once there, she only "tried an interpreter once," when she used a native nurse to communicate with an old midwife named Fa'agi. Thereafter, except in her conversations with the Samoan schoolteacher, Andrew Napoleon, who spoke fluent English, she "gave up attempting interpreters and worked on everything from religion to medicines without them."[1]

Getting to Fitiuta, which was seven miles from the naval dispensary by a rough foot track, was something of an ordeal for visiting Americans. According to Mead, the sanitary inspectors and other government officials who "had to make the trip dreaded it, articulating for a week before, and came back to be nursed and sympathized with for a week afterwards." Mead found the trail "awful" with "miles of mud,"

of a kind she had only previously seen "in barn yards," with "sharp de-
scents into little canyons full of rocks" and "miles along a lava coast,"
where the sand was "a dark red black" and there was "no shade."
However, when she finally got there, she found Fitiuta "charming."
Its houses, all of them traditional in construction, were spread out
along either side of a "high stone road" overgrown by grass and moss
and ran the entire length of the settlement. Nowhere else in American
Samoa was "the flavor of native courtesy" so well preserved.[2]

Because the *malaga* was such an important one, including visitors
from Upolu as well as Tufele's mother, Talala, the first three days were
"consumed by ceremonies." In these ceremonies, Mead had the status
of a visiting *taupou*. At the major rituals, first when the *malaga* presented its kava and then when the chiefs of Fitiuta came with theirs,
Mead was given especial recognition as the holder of the *taupou* title
Fua i le Lagi, which she had accepted from Talala knowing that this
would happen when she visited Fitiuta. With the kava rituals concluded, she presented a "case of salmon" to the chiefs of Fitiuta. They
reciprocated with a traditional presentation of food, first with a freshly
picked and husked coconut, pierced and ready for drinking, and then
with chickens and fish, land crabs, octopus, pork, breadfruit, and taro,
all steaming from the oven. In the evening, there was another kava ritual and another presentation of food. Then Mead, as the *taupou* of the
*malaga*, danced before the assembled chiefs of Fitiuta, "in native
dress," with scarlet cordyline leaves tied around her wrists and ankles
and coconut oil smeared over her arms and shoulders. To mark this
performance by a visiting *taupou*, presents of bark cloth, soap, and to-
bacco were distributed. Finally, after the chiefs of the village had dispersed, Mead as a *taupou* had to meet, banter, and play cards with the
untitled men of Fitiuta at one end of the guest house while the girls of
the household made up beds and hung mosquito nets at the other end.
On the second day, the wives of the chiefs of Fitiuta came to do
"homage" to Mead and the others of the *malaga*. Dressed in their
gayest garments, with necklaces and wreaths of flowers, they sat "in
state around the circular guest house, at the posts where their hus-
bands had the right to sit," and there was another lengthy kava ceremony, followed by much singing and dancing.[3]

Mead wrote on her return to Lumā:

> All this ceremonial took up a great deal of time but it was worth it for the
> first hand knowledge it gave me of the workings of a *malaga*, and also it

established my position and popularity, so that I could get informants—
high chiefs whom I could not have bought. To try to buy information in
Polynesia would be fatal, they are too ready liars. But now Poumele,
huge, indolent, unbelievably wise, with his close-cropped black hair just
white at the tips, so that his lion's head looked as if it had been touched
by a September frost, would sit and talk to me by the hour, immensely
proud of the speed with which he understood my peculiar questions, and
the amount of detail with which he could answer them.

At other times, half a dozen or so chiefs would gather in the guest
house where Mead was staying to discuss traditional "judicial procedure" and other such matters. A Samoan house, she discovered, was
"an excellent place for ethnology." This is because its floor is covered
with "small stones of all sizes and descriptions," and an informant
"simply put them in rows as chiefs, raises them aloft as cups, or piles
them ceremonially as food." In this way, as soon as the welcoming
ceremonies were over, Mead, with the command of Samoan she had
achieved, was able to work productively on the ethnology of Manu'a,
to which all of her time was now being given. Instead of accompanying the members of the Bishop Museum expedition when they left on
February 24 with the shells they had collected, she stayed on for another six days to "do ethnology" and to converse with the young
Samoan schoolteacher Andrew Napoleon.[4]

Andrew Napoleon was born in 1904 to a leading Roman Catholic
family of the village of Leone on the island of Tutuila. In 1862, his
grandfather, who later became the holder of the Tuiteleleapaga title,
had welcomed to Leone the first Roman Catholic missionaries to visit
Tutuila. He subsequently visited France, and on his return to Leone,
Napoleon came to be accepted as a name for sons of the Tuiteleleapaga
family. From 1921 onward, when he graduated from the eighth grade
of the Marist Brothers' School at Leone at age seventeen, Andrew
Napoleon, as he was known, was employed in various capacities by
the naval government of American Samoa. This continued until 1951,
when he assisted in the transfer of the administration of American
Samoa from the U.S. Navy to the U.S. Department of the Interior. After being given the high-ranking *ali'i* title of his family, he became
known as Napoleone A. Tuiteleleapaga and practiced as an attorney at
law in Pago Pago. He died in Leone on December 25, 1988. In February
1926 when Mead arrived in Fitiuta as Talala's *taupou*, Fua i le Lagi,
young Andrew Napoleon, who was already married, was one of the
schoolteachers at the public school in Fitiuta that had been estab-

lished there by the naval government of American Samoa in 1922. In her introduction to Napoleone A. Tuiteleleapaga's book of 1980, *Samoa Yesterday, Today, and Tomorrow*, which she was sent a typescript copy of in January 1976, Margaret Mead gives an account of her meeting with Andrew Napoleon, or Napo, as she called him, in Fitiuta in 1926. She had come to Fitiuta, she said, "bearing a native title, and accompanied by all the protocol and etiquette of the ceremonial journey of a Samoan titled princess." On the second evening of her visit, as she sat in the great guest house of Tufele Fa'atoia, Napo, a slim, handsome youth slipped into a space beside her. His first words, as Mead remembered them over fifty years later, were: "*Talofa, teine papālagi mānaia*" (Hello, beautiful white girl). He then told her that he had heard that "*a taupou*" (which Mead describes as "a virgin girl, usually the daughter of the highest chief of the village") was visiting Fitiuta but that he had not realized until he saw her that she was an American and not a Samoan. Thereafter, as Mead put it: "Throughout my stay in Fitiuta where I danced for my hosts and they, in return, provided me with wise men and women to school me further in their customs, Napo would appear, quietly, unofficiously, to give me background material on the attitudes of Samoan young men."[5]

An indication of the nature of this "background material" is contained in thirty-six pages of Mead's field notebook number 4, in which, in February 1926, she recorded in English a range of statements on Samoan sexual behavior from the twenty-two-year-old Andrew Napoleon. As is apparent from Napoleon's letter to Mead of April 7, 1926, he had an excellent command of English. Mead made use of some of the information on Samoan sexual behavior that she obtained from Andrew Napoleon in *Coming of Age in Samoa*. For example, on page 31 of notebook number 4, Mead recorded Napoleon's statement that he "didn't know of impotence in any case nor of frigidity." This statement is in no sense evidence that impotence and frigidity do not, in some cases, occur among Samoans, as they certainly do. However, this opinion of Napoleon's, based on the obviously very limited experience of a twenty-two-year-old Roman Catholic schoolteacher, found its way into *Coming of Age in Samoa*, where on page 228 of the first edition of 1928, Mead asserts, so establishing, without revealing the questionable source of her information, one of the "patterns" of Samoan culture: that in Samoa, there is "a cultural atmosphere in which frigidity and psychic impotence do not occur and in which a satisfactory sex adjustment in marriage can always be established."

Again, Napoleon's statement that in Manu'a people had intercourse "several times in one night" and that he knew of "fifteen times in one night," which Mead recorded on page 23 of her notebook number 4, is the insecure base for her laughable assertion on page 151 of *Coming of Age in Samoa* that among Samoans "the capacity for intercourse only once in a night is counted as senility." However, nowhere in the information recorded by Mead in Fituta in February 1926 is there any kind of warrant at all for her assertion on page 157 of *Coming of Age in Samoa* that "to live as a girl with many lovers for as long as possible" was one of the "uniform and satisfying ambitions" of adolescent girls.[6]

Chapter 10 of the book by Napoleone A. Tuiteleleapaga, which Mead, in her introduction to the book, describes as "a treasury of astute comments on Samoan custom and culture," is entitled "The Role of the Woman." In it, Napoleone states (on p. 43), of *all* Samoan girls and *not* just the *taupou*:

> After she has reached puberty, her girlhood and womanhood periods are guarded very closely; everywhere she goes she is escorted by her mother, older married sisters, or the family old ladies. Her brothers, because of the brother-sister taboo, would not dare to go near her, but keep an alert ear-eye watch to assure her safety, so that she can keep her virginity until she gets married.

Again, on page 63 of his chapter on marriage, Napoleone writes: "Brothers and other male relatives did everything to protect their virgin female relatives. As a result of this custom, women up to the age of twenty-five years, kept their virginity to the time of their marriage, hence the custom of *fa'amāsei'au* (defloration of the virgin bride)."[7]

It was to this custom that prime attention was given in the information that Andrew Napoleon gave to Mead, at her request, when they conversed together in Fituta. Thus, Mead's notebook number 4 begins with Napoleon's account of ritual defloration at marriage. In this ritual, as Mead's own notes of February 1926 record, the talking chief of the bridegroom, having wrapped his first and second fingers in a piece of white bark cloth or, if that was unavailable, white trade cloth, would rupture the bride's hymen. The cloth stained with hymeneal blood was then, with a great shout, held up "for all to see." When it was known that the bride was a virgin, drums were beaten, objects broken, guns fired off, and there was feasting and dancing. If a girl was not a virgin, so Napoleon stated, it was for her to confess this in advance to the officiating talking chief, for if the ritual were performed and the bride proved "not to be a virgin," then all the old women of her family would "beat and berate her."

Napoleon's account of February 1926 made it plain, furthermore, that this custom applied not only to the *taupou*, but to "ordinary marriages" as well. His account also made very clear that with their ritual of public defloration at marriage—a ritual that traditionally applied to "ordinary marriage" as well as to that of the *taupou*—the Samoans were much preoccupied with female virginity. In addition, this information fully confirmed all that Mead had been told by Helen Ripley Wilson in Leone on October 10, 1925, and by To'aga, the wife of Sotoa, the high chief of Lumā, on December 16, 1925. From these and the other accounts that had been given to Mead, Samoa, though a part of Polynesia, was obviously very different indeed from the Marquesas Islands, where, according to Edward Craighill Handy, "youths and maids were totally free sexually" and "literally ran wild."

Yet for Mead, the task of comprehending a system radically different from the Marquesas Islands was to prove insuperable. When she returned to her research headquarters at the naval dispensary early in March 1926, if she had only been able to free herself from the notions about premarital promiscuity among Polynesians that she had obtained from her reading of Herman Melville and Edward Craighill Handy, then she could have used the information she already had from Helen Wilson, To'aga, and Andrew Napoleon, the information she needed for an accurate understanding of the sexual mores of the Samoans. However, absorbed as she still was with completing her ethnology of Manu'a, this understanding was to elude her, and after she had been hoaxed, she returned to the United States to depict Samoa as a place where there was "great premarital freedom." In later life, Mead remarked of her research in Samoa that it was "crazy" that she "got a culture" that made the "point" that Boas wanted made "so clearly." In truth, in no respect did the culture make such a point. Of one thing there can be no doubt: Samoa was very far from being a place where there was "free love-making" before marriage, as Mead mistakenly supposed in coming to her facile solution to the problem Boas had required her to investigate.[8]

When Mead arrived in Fitiuta she had, because of the ethnological advantages she thought would accrue, deliberately assumed the role of a *taupou*, using the title of Fua i le Lagi that had been conferred on her by Tufele Fa'atoia's mother, Talala. "There are," she wrote when she got back to the naval dispensary in Lumā, "two ways in which a girl of high birth can come out in Samoa. Her father, or chiefly relative, may make her a *taupou* on which occasion there is much ceremony, feasting and dancing, or, she may be taken on a *malaga*. I have had the chance to watch every detail of both of these at first hand." To which she added: "But I haven't merely watched these procedures, I've been them." Playing the role of *taupou* appealed to her immensely. It could not, she considered, "have worked out better," for in Fitiuta, where she got all her "richest ethnology," she had "rank to burn" and could "order the whole village about." Indeed, on her last night there, in "a grand assembly of all chiefs," she was made a *taupou* of Fitiuta itself, this being her third unwarranted *taupou* title. On this occasion, having arrived in Fitiuta with the *taupou* title of Fua i le Lagi, she was in no position to reveal that she was, in fact, a married woman and therefore ineligible under Samoan custom to hold any *taupou* title. The title conferred on her in Fitiuta was that of Iliganoa, which was in the gift of Poumele, the *ali'i* who had been her principal informant in matters ethnological. At her installation as Iliganoa, the oration was made by Lapui, "the best talking chief in Manu'a," and when Mead's kava was announced, the young man who ritually presented it to her held it "aloft in both hands and circled and circled the house" in the manner prescribed for those of the highest rank. It was an experience she found deeply gratifying. As she told Boas in her last letter to him before leaving Manu'a: "It's been such fun being able to talk the language and make speeches, being the center of genuine ceremonies, rather than merely a strictly scientific onlooker." Polynesia, with orders "to be as one of them," Mead reported, was "very pleasant work."[9]

As soon as she got back to the naval dispensary at Ta'ū on March 3, 1926, Mead at once wrote to her father, thanking him for his "gorgeous present" of her "trip around the world." She had received a cable informing her that her employment at the American Museum of Natural History was to begin in September rather than at the beginning of August 1926. This meant that she could have an extended holiday in Europe with her husband, Luther, and attend the Twenty-Second International Congress of Americanists in Rome with Ruth Benedict before returning to New York. In these changed circumstances, she thought it would be best to travel directly "from Sydney to Aden, with no side stops, and see as much of Europe as possible." Luther had written inquiring whether she would prefer to "spend a week at a little village on Lake Como," or "go up thru the Chateaux country to Paris." After having been in Samoa since the beginning of September 1925, she was ready by March 1926, so she said, for "a good three months' rest—five weeks on the water and the rest in Europe."[10]

After her ten days of ethnological inquiry in Fitiuta, Mead was feeling "very happy and confident," with "a sense of work well done." Because Fitiuta had proved to be "a gold mine, ethnologically," she was hoping to go back there for "a great farewell feast" and also, if possible, to spend "a week or so" on the islands of Ofu and Olosega to do research that would enable her to complete her ethnology of Manu'a for the Bishop Museum. The hurricane of January 1, 1926, had destroyed the buildings of the government school at Ta'ū. However, by the beginning of March 1926, a new building consisting of four classrooms and a central assembly room had been built at the northern end of Lumā. When Mead returned from Fitiuta, the Manu'a District School, as it was called, was open again from 9 A.M. to 3 P.M.; as mentioned earlier, the pastor's school was open from 7:30 A.M. to 9 A.M. and from 3 P.M. to 4:30 P.M. Consequently, as Mead noted on March 7, it was "practically impossible" for her to get hold of the girls she was supposed to be studying. Before she went to Fitiuta to "do ethnology," she had been told that the government school would be opening again at the beginning of March. This meant that the final ten days of February were her last opportunity for sustained work with her adolescent girls. However, so strong was Mead's desire to do ethnological research for the Bishop Museum that, even while knowing this, she had nonetheless abandoned her research on these girls and had gone to Fitiuta. As a result, when she returned early in March 1926 to the naval dispensary at the western end of the island of Ta'ū, where all of the girls she was studying lived, she had made virtually no progress in the collecting of data on her sample of sixty-six girls. Nor, as events unfolded, did she ever complete the collection of this information. In particular, she had not yet begun her "special investigation" of the "sexual life" of these girls, which she had told Boas she would be starting on in April 1926.[11]

In terms of her plan of December 6, 1925, Mead had about eight weeks left to her in Manu'a by March 7, 1926. Because the U.S. Navy supply vessel ran "so irregularly" between Lumā and Pago Pago, she estimated that she would have to spend several weeks in Tutuila if she were to make sure of embarking for Sydney on the S.S. *Ventura* on May 31, 1926. Thus, with only some eight weeks remaining to her in

Manu'a and with the opening of the government school having made it "practically impossible" for her to get hold of the girls she was studying, her investigation of the adolescent girl as a study in heredity and environment—to which she had been instructed both by the Board of National Research Fellowships in the Biological Sciences and by Franz Boas to devote all of her time—was without question the research to which all of her energies needed to be given. Yet the very next day, March 8, 1926, when a whaleboat by chance arrived at Lumā from the off-lying island of Ofu, Mead, "lured by thoughts of ethnological gain," at once hired it to take her there. Her aim was to complete the ethnology of Manu'a, which had become her principal research interest. Her plan was to spend ten days or so on the islands of Ofu and Olosega, doing ethnological research, before returning to Lumā in the third week of March in the navy's U.S.S. *Tanager*. Once again, Mead was completely abandoning research on her adolescent girls, none of whom could be contacted from Ofu or Olosega, but she took with her, as companions and informants, Tufele's *taupou*, Fa'apua'a, with whom she had become very friendly, as well as Fa'apua'a's close friend, Fofoa, who also came from Fitiuta. With Mead still having to investigate systematically the sexual behavior of the adolescent girls she was studying and with the time available to her being so limited, the stage was set for an extraordinary happening: a prank that was to completely hoax the twenty-four-year-old Margaret Mead and that was, through her, to mislead virtually the entire anthropological profession, as well as countless others in the educated Western world.[12]

# 11

# The Ides of March

EAD'S MAIN REASON FOR GOING to the remote islands of Ofu and Olosega, as she stated it to Boas, was to "round out" the ethnology of Manu'a that she was writing "for the Bishop Museum." This was the first direct indication she gave Boas of the depth of her involvement with ethnological inquiry at the expense of the research she had been appointed to undertake in Manu'a as a national research fellow in the biological sciences. Boas was, moreover, being informed of a fait accompli. Before Mead's letter reached him, her research in Manu'a was at an end and she had set out for the south of France.

In 1931, in a letter to Ralph Linton, Mead wrote of her Bishop Museum monograph on Manu'a, published in 1930 as *Social Organization of Manu'a*, that "from the standpoint of my fellowship grant and my instructors some of it represents an ethnological fling." Again, in her introduction of 1968 to the second edition of *Social Organization of Manu'a*, she confessed that because she had been "explicitly instructed by Professor Boas to resist the temptation to do standard ethnography," the "specific ethnographic materials" in this monograph had been "almost boot-legged." This is a considerable understatement. In 1968, Mead stated that Fitiuta, as well as Ofu and Olosega, were places "where I abandoned my interest in children and socially unimportant adolescents and concentrated on adults of high rank and superior knowledge." This abandonment of research on adolescent girls to "do ethnology" had begun with Mead's visit to Fitiuta, which had commenced on February 20, 1926. This was just five days after she had written the letter to Boas in which she listed the information she was due to collect on sixty-six girls by the end of March 1926, after which their "sexual life" would still remain "for special investigation." This was also Mead's situation on March 8, 1926, when she once again abandoned her very far from completed research on the adolescent girls of Lumā, Si'ufaga, and Faleasao to devote ten days to the ethnological study of the islands of Ofu and Olosega "for the Bishop Museum."

During these ten days, entirely removed from all contact with the girls she was supposed to be studying, there was no way in which Mead could, by direct investigation, advance her knowledge of their sexual or other behavior. All that she could possibly do during these ten days was to discuss these things with her two companions from the island of Ta'ū, Fa'apua'a and Fofoa. Of the two, Fa'apua'a was by far the better known to Mead. She had gotten to know Fa'apua'a first in the household of Tufele Fa'atoia at Si'ufaga, and then in Fitiuta, where Fa'apua'a's father, Logoleo, was one of her principal ethnological informants. By March 1926, according to Fa'apua'a, she had become Mead's "very closest Samoan friend." Mead knew Fofoa rather less well, although she had seen a good deal of her in Fitiuta, where Fofoa was the adopted daughter of Mead's other principal informant, Poumele. Fa'apua'a and Fofoa, who had grown up together and had long been very close friends, were of about the same age as Mead. During her ethnological research on Ofu and Olosega, while acting as her advisers, attendants, and informants, they became, as Mead recorded, her "merry companions."[1]

Although Mead's main reason for going to Ofu and Olosega was to "round out" her ethnology of Manu'a, she had also become disenchanted with life in the naval dispensary at Ta'ū. She was longing, she told Boas, "to escape from that tiny island and the society of the tiny white colony on it." As already noted, when she returned to the dispensary from Fitiuta on March 3, the government school had reopened after being closed for two months. This meant that the girls she was studying were "much too excited to manage" as well as "inaccessible except for about two hours a day." This made further detailed research on these girls, dispersed as they were in three different villages, "practically impossible." Furthermore, hearing the gong of the government school and seeing the pupils with their "slate pencils" had made her peculiarly homesick, "never just collectively for America" but rather "homesick for New York or for the farm or for bathtubs or beefsteak." In this mood, she was "lured" away from the dispensary not only by "thoughts of ethnological gain" but also by the circumstance that her friends Dr. Charles Lane and his wife,

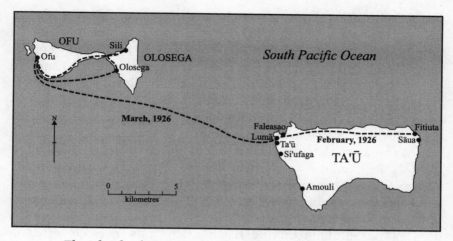

*The islands of Manu'a, showing Margaret Mead's research
headquarters of 1925–1926 at Lumā on the island of Ta'ū and
her ethnological excursions to Fitiuta in February 1926 and to Ofu and
Olosega in March 1926 in the company of Fa'apua'a and Fofoa*

whose "*savoir-faire*" and personal "magnetism" had been "a life-
saver" for Mead when she was living in Pago Pago, were "temporarily
stationed" on Ofu.[2]

On Monday, March 8, accompanied by Fa'apua'a and Fofoa, Mead
set out for the island of Ofu, under a "broiling sun" in a fifteen-foot
whaleboat, manned by nine Samoan oarsmen. Fa'apua'a and Fofoa
were desperately seasick. Mead, with her head resting on a burlap bag
of canned goods, her "ear on a tin of salmon" and her "temple on a can
of prunes," enjoyed the "three hour pull in the open sea." The Samoan
oarsmen chanted as they rowed through the ocean swell. For a time, a
downpour blotted out all landmarks. Then there was "an hour of thin
rain," with the "portals of the sun set all about the horizon." By the
time they reached Ofu, it was dark. Parts of Ofu and Olosega had suffered even more heavily than Ta'ū from the hurricane of New Year's
Day, 1926, and at the time of Mead's visit, there was a severe crop
shortage. Many of the inhabitants had nothing to eat but *masi*, the traditional famine food of Samoa, consisting of breadfruit fermented in a
pit and smelling in Mead's nostrils "worse than Limburger cheese."
This, from time to time, was supplemented by emergency rations of
rice and tinned fish issued by the naval government. Throughout her
stay of ten days, Mead had to provide provisions from the local U.S.

Navy Commissary, both for herself and her "court," as she called it, made up of Fa'apua'a and Fofoa. Fortunately, there was a bakery on Ofu, and "for a whole ten days," she "revelled in yeast bread." Both at the beginning and end of the day, there were her friends, the Lanes, to call on and go bathing with at sunset in Ofu's beautiful lagoon.[3]

On March 9, 1926, when a reception was held in the guest house of Misa, the "high chief of Ofu," with whom they were staying, Mead sat before the assembled chiefs dressed "not as a white girl, but in the fine woven mat skirt, the broad white bark cloth sash, the tight bodice of a Samoan, with ankles, wrists, neck and hair wreathed with leaves and flowers," and then performed as a ceremonial virgin, with Fa'apua'a and Fofoa dancing on either side of her. Thus, on Ofo and Olosega, as in Fitiuta, Mead took on the persona of a visiting *taupou*. The title she used was her third *taupou* title, Iliganoa, which had been conferred on her a week or so previously in Fitiuta. Using this title while she was on Ofu and Olosega and playing the part of a ceremonial virgin was, according to Fa'apua'a, something that very greatly appealed to Mead. She was accompanied everywhere she went by both Fa'apua'a and Fofoa, who acted as her advisers and attendants, making "all the speeches" and "accepting and dispersing gifts," as well as performing the menial tasks of preparing Mead's meals and washing her clothes. It was, according to Mead, "all much pleasanter than having a real servant." It was, however, an equivocal situation, with Fa'apua'a, a genuine ceremonial virgin and the lawful holder of the *taupou* title of a high chief of Fitiuta, waiting on a visiting American, slightly younger than herself, who was using a *taupou* name to which, as a married woman, she was not entitled and which was lower in rank than Fa'apua'a's own *taupou* title of Laulauga. Yet Mead, identified as she was with the U.S. Navy, was, in effect, a member of the governing elite from America and so was able to behave as she did, living, as she put it, "like a visiting young village princess." In particular, at the U.S. Navy Commissary, Mead had access to resources quite beyond the reach of either Fa'apua'a or Fofoa. Subordinate though they were to their American benefactor, Fa'apua'a and Fofoa were, nonetheless, thoroughly enjoying themselves. They were having a holiday together with all expenses paid. When they went to wash Mead's clothes, they would always take along the ukuleles they had brought with them. In the mornings, before getting up, they would sing songs together.[4]

In Samoa in the 1920s, it was unusual for unescorted females to travel about together. The arrival in Ofu village of three young women, one of them an American with a Samoan taupou title, aroused intense interest. On the second night of their stay, Mead, Fa'apua'a, and Fofoa were ceremonially courted by the 'aumāga of Ofu, made up entirely of untitled men, most of them unmarried. On such occasions, which are called 'aiavā, there is much speech making, singing, and dancing, with first one side performing and then the other. There is also, during 'aiavā of this kind, a great deal of light-hearted banter, frequently involving sexual innuendoes and allusions. Fa'apua'a recollected that during their meeting with the 'aumāga of Ofu, she and Fofoa joked with Mead, asking if there was a young man she especially fancied and that when Mead jokingly replied that indeed there was, they bantered with her about the choice she had made. According to Fa'apua'a, it was when they were on the island of Olosega, the day following this formal but agreeably titillating encounter with the high-spirited young men of Ofu, that Mead, with whom they had already begun to joke about erotic matters, first began to question them concerning the sexual behavior of the girls of Manu'a.

On Thursday, March 11, 1926, accompanied by Fa'apua'a and Fofoa, Mead was taken in a U.S. Navy boat from Ofu village to the main settlement on the south coast of the island of Olosega. This settlement, which also goes by the name of Olosega, had been devastated by the hurricane of January 1, 1926. Its people were stricken with shame at being unable to welcome their visitors in traditional Samoan style. For Mead, however, who was intent on ethnological research, the visit went well. She found "a most excellently old and wise man," the Tui Olosega, from whom by the next day she had gotten all the information she wanted. With this accomplished, she set out on foot, accompanied by Fa'apua'a and Fofoa, for Sili, the only other village on the island of Olosega. A small village of only eighty-six inhabitants, "tucked in under a tremendous cliff," Sili had largely escaped the hurricane. This made it much easier for Mead to collect the ethnological information she was after. In the evening, there was a feast of roast pork, after which Mead was regaled with "anecdotes" of "the days of cannibalism," and a "gaunt and pitiful mad man," who believed he was the high chief Tufele, sang and danced for her.[5]

The next day, accompanied by Fa'apua'a and Fofoa, Mead walked all the way back to Ofu village. It was an experience she described as "sheer delight." From the western tip of the island of Olosega, they were ferried one at a time by outrigger canoe to the eastern end of the

island of Ofu. From there, the three of them made their way along the
southern coast of Ofu back to the village in which they had been staying earlier. It was, as Mead described it, "a long walk skirting the sea,
at places racing the tide or leaping between high waves from one wet
rock to another, but mostly following an easy trail, under a weak,
complacent sun." According to Fa'apua'a, it was when she and Fofoa
were with Mead on the islands of Olosega and Ofu that she began to
question them. During the first four days of their visit Mead had been
preoccupied with ceremonies at Ofu, with calling on Dr. and Mrs.
Lane, and with intensive ethnological inquiry. Thus, Saturday, March
13, was the first day on which Mead, when alone with Fa'apua'a and
Fofoa during the hours of their "long walk" together, had any opportunity to question them at length about the sexual behavior of Samoan
girls, about which she was due to begin a firsthand investigation in
April. According to Fa'apua'a, Mead first mentioned sexual behavior
late on the evenings of their visit to the island of Olosega, when they
were lying in their mosquito nets, and had then closely questioned
them during the course of their long walk together from Sili to Ofu
village. This journey, as Mead recorded in the last bulletin she dispatched from Samoa, took place on Saturday, March 13, 1926.[6]

Since writing to Boas on February 15 about the research she intended to do on her sixty-six girls, virtually all of Mead's time, except
for bulletin and letter writing, had been given to ethnological research,
first in Fitiuta and then on Ofu and Olosega, locations far removed
from the villages of Lumā, Si'ufaga, and Faleasao, where all of these
girls lived. Indeed, by Saturday, March 13, 60 percent of the time that
Mead had allowed for the collection of the mass of information listed
in her letter to Boas of February 15 had passed without her making any
progress at all. And there still remained to tackle, in April 1926, her
"special investigation" of the sexual behavior of Samoan girls, when
she would be systematically investigating this topic for the first time.
There was an immense amount still to be done—and very little time
left in which to do it. Thus, by March 13, 1926, the "investigation of
the adolescent girl" as "a study in heredity and environment," which
she was in Samoa to undertake at the express wish and under the direct supervision of Professor Franz Boas, was in a state of crisis. It was
a crisis that had been created because, in Mead's own words, she had
"abandoned" her interest in "socially unimportant adolescents" for almost a month in order to do quite unrelated research for her projected
monograph on the ethnology of Manu'a. It was in this impasse that

Mead, who by this time was reasonably fluent in Samoan, turned to the questioning of her traveling companions about sexual behavior, hoping that in this way she could make up for lost time and, if at all possible, reach a solution to the research problem Boas had assigned her.

It was on Saturday, March 13, 1926, then, when alone with Fa'apua'a and Fofoa for some hours, that Mead grasped the opportunity to question them. According to Fa'apua'a, Mead put to Fofoa and herself the preposterous proposition (so it seemed to them) that despite the great emphasis on virginity in the traditional *taupou* system of Samoa and within the Christian church to which all Manu'ans were adherents at that time, unmarried Samoan girls were, in secret, sexually promiscuous. In so doing, Mead must have been seeking to substantiate the baseless claim in her report of January 6, 1926, made before she had done any research on the subject, that in Manu'a there was "an extensive tolerance of premarital sex relationships." It was a claim prompted by her preconceptions about Polynesian sexuality derived from Melville, Handy, and others, which she had repeated in her letter to Boas of February 15, 1926, when she wrote of "great promiscuity between puberty and marriage," while noting that the sexual behavior of the girls she was studying was something she had yet to investigate systematically. If only she could obtain from Fa'apua'a and Fofoa a clear confirmation concerning the premarital promiscuity that she supposed existed in Manu'a, she thought she would then have established a cultural pattern that would allow her to reach what she so desperately needed: an acceptable solution to the problem Boas required her to investigate under the terms of her research fellowship.[7]

In Samoa, as Albert Wendt has noted, it is not acceptable, in ordinary conversation, "to discuss sexual matters publicly." And so, in their embarrassment at Mead's brashness, Fa'apua'a and Fofoa, having conspiratorially pinched one another, blandly agreed with all she had suggested to them, telling her with due embellishment that they, like other young women and adolescent girls, regularly spent their nights with members of the opposite sex. In so doing, they were, as a prank, engaging in what Tim O'Meara has termed "recreational lying," which he accurately calls "one of the main forms of entertainment" among Samoans. It is also a custom that is very much a part of Samoan culture.[8]

Called *ula, tausua, taufa'alili,* or *taufa'ase'e* (depending on the intentions of the perpetrators), "recreational lying," as O'Meara has noted, "happens continually" in Samoa, with "all ages" engaging in it; people tell you stories, "especially about sex," try to get you to believe them, and then "sort of chuckle inside." As this account of O'Meara's indicates, the "recreational lying" that is so common among Samoans is a form of behavior in which, in the words of Curtis MacDougall, "a deliberately concocted untruth" is made to "masquerade" as the truth, this being MacDougall's definition of a hoax. In the *Shorter Oxford English Dictionary*, a hoax is defined as "a humorous or mischievous deception with which the credulity of the victim is imposed upon," with the term *hoax* being derived from the Latin *iocus*, meaning a joke or jest. This definition also holds for the Samoan behavior of "recreational lying." The terms that Samoans commonly use to describe or refer to this behavior clearly demonstrate that we are dealing with a form of joking behavior. Thus, whereas *ula* (the term that Galea'i Poumele used in his conversation with Fa'apua'a on November 13, 1987) means "to make fun of someone," *tausua* (the term that Fa'apua'a used in her interviews with Unasa L. F. Va'a) means "to joke"; *taufa'alili* (another term used by Fa'apua'a on November 13, 1987) means "to cause someone to shake with laughter," and the meaning of *taufa'ase'e* is "to deceive in a joking way (lit., to cause someone to lose her footing)." *Taufa'ase'e* behavior is thus a culturally ordained form of joking behavior, quite different in its intention from outright lying. It was, moreover, very much a part of the Samoan culture of Manu'a in the mid-1920s. In Fitiuta, in February 1926, Mead commented in her field notes on the way in which Samoan youths, when ragging one another about sex, "delight in giving false names, in puns and hyperboles."[9]

This, then, was the quintessentially Samoan response that Fa'apua'a and Fofoa fell back on when Mead advanced what was to them the ludicrous notion that despite the traditional emphasis on virginity in the *fa'aSāmoa* and within the Christian church, the adolescent girls of Manu'a were, in fact, sexually promiscuous. As Fa'apua'a remarked to Galea'i Poumele, secretary of Samoan affairs of American Samoa, when he interviewed her in Fitiuta on November 13, 1987: "As you know, Samoan girls are terrific liars when it comes to joking, but Margaret accepted our trumped-up stories as though they were true."[10]

Her acceptance of these stories would have been all the readier since a hoax is much more easily perpetrated when it plays to a listener's preconceptions. That Mead did in fact accept these stories and that it was on Ofu that she allowed herself to be taken in by her "merry companions" is shown by the five-page letter she wrote to Boas in Ofu village on Sunday, March 14, 1926 (see Appendix), the day immediately after her fateful questioning of Fa'apua'a and Fofoa. In evidential terms, this letter is the "smoking gun" that provides explicit corroboration of what had happened the previous day. As for why it happened, the answer to this is the self-induced crisis in Mead's Samoan research project. By March 14, 1926, she was desperately in need of two things: a convincing solution to the "problem" she had been sent to Samoa to investigate and at the same time a convincing justification for Boas of the great amount of time that she had been giving to ethnological work. These objectives she was able to attain, as though by magic, by her use of the wholly false information she had been given by Fa'apua'a and Fofoa on the previous day. It is not at all surprising, therefore, that her handwritten letter ends by hoping that she has provided "the sort of thing" Boas wanted and that he will "be pleased" with her results.

It should be noted that Mead's use of the information provided by Fa'apua'a and Fofoa was perfectly sincere, for a hoaxed individual is quite oblivious of what it is that has happened. Indeed, all of Mead's attitudes in respect of Samoa from mid-March 1926 onward must be assessed in the light of this fundamental psychological fact. Her letter to Boas dated Ofu, March 14, 1926, her book *Coming of Age in Samoa* of 1928, and everything she subsequently wrote on Samoa was written in a complete lack of awareness that she had, on Saturday, March 13, 1926, been comprehensively hoaxed about the sexual mores of the Samoans. Further, as Gordon Stein has noted in the introduction to his *Encyclopedia of Hoaxes*, a "hoax only ends when it is definitively exposed to the public as a hoax." Thus, Margaret Mead died without ever knowing that she had been grossly misinformed by her "merry companions." Fa'apua'a's testimony about how she and Fofoa had, as a prank, hoaxed Margaret Mead on the island of Ofu in March 1926 first became public knowledge in Fitiuta in American Samoa on November 13, 1987, almost nine years after Margaret Mead's death in New York on November 15, 1978.[11]

According to Fa'apua'a, she and Fofoa colluded in telling Mead what they did because of their embarrassment at her insistent questioning on the forbidden topic of sexuality. They were enjoying themselves like true Samoans at the expense of a visiting American. They had no idea that Mead was an anthropologist, who, having taken their untruths and hyperbole to be facts, would put them in a book. If only

Mead had challenged them, Fa'apua'a commented, they would at once have admitted that they were only joking. But Mead never did. And so, Fa'apua'a thought no more of what had happened until many years later, when, having been told by Galea'i Poumele of the wildly inaccurate account of Samoan sexual behavior in *Coming of Age in Samoa*, she realized that Mead had believed every word of their outlandish stories.

Having satisfied herself from her questioning of Fa'apua'a and Fofoa that the Samoans, like other Polynesians, were indeed sexually promiscuous and that they were without "the neuroses accompanying sex in American civilization" and having also concluded, to her satisfaction, that there was no significant stress from rebelliousness or from "religious and philosophic development," Mead went jubilantly on in her letter to Boas of March 14 to declare that the "sum total" of her evidence was that

> adolescence is a period of sudden development; of stress, only in relation to sex—and, where the community recognizes this and does not attempt to curb it, there is no conflict at all between the adolescent and the community, except such as arises from the conflict of personalities within the household (and this is immediately remedied, as I have shown, by the change to another relationship group) and the occasional delinquent— any age from 8 to 50—who arouses the ire of the community.[12]

This quite major conclusion of Mead's rests on the mistaken supposition, derived from Fa'apua'a and Fofoa, that Samoa is a place where "the community" does not attempt to "curb" the sexual activity of adolescents. With this established, so Mead thought, she had successfully identified a fundamental pattern of Samoan culture. In his farewell letter to Mead of July 14, 1925, Franz Boas had given emphasis to "the pressure of the general pattern of culture" on the individual, and Mead, like Boas and Benedict, was convinced that cultural patterns "set the mold" into which "human nature" flows. In Benedict's words, "It is in every case a matter of social patterning, of that which cultural recognition has singled out and standardized." And once a cultural pattern had been identified, the behaviors that did not accord with it were judged to be no more than "exceptions" or "deviations." Thus, in her account in the *American Anthropologist* of how she had proceeded in Samoa, Mead explicitly stated that she "used the deviant individuals to delineate the pattern." This, then, was the way in which Mead proceeded on the island of Ofu in March 1926. She had been led to believe that in Samoa, as in the Marquesas Islands and elsewhere in Polynesia, "the community" did not attempt to "curb" the sexual activity of adolescents. With this identified as the "cultural pattern" that determined adolescent behavior in Samoa, she could dismiss as mere exceptions the instances she had previously recorded that were not in conformity with this primarily important cultural pattern. That Mead proceeded in this doctrinaire way is evidence of the quite extraordinary extent to which she was in the grip of the cultural determinism of her mentors, Franz Boas and Ruth Benedict. According to this ideology, as Mead herself put it, the behavior of the adolescent girls of Manu'a was "relentlessly shaped and molded" by the "patterns" of their culture, and in particular, as she claimed in her letter to Boas of March 14, 1926, by the pattern that in Samoa the community did not attempt to "curb" the sexual activity of adolescents.[13]

Yet as Mead's own field notes and reports clearly demonstrate, in Manu'a in 1926, quite major restrictions were, in fact, placed on the sexual activity of adolescents. In Fitiuta, in February 1926, Andrew Napoleon had told Mead at length of the traditional Samoan practice of testing the virginity of females, whatever their rank, by ritual defloration at time of marriage, and he had indicated how highly valued female virginity was. This major custom Mead had accurately described in her report to the National Research Council of January 6, 1926, on the basis of information she had received on December 16, 1925, from Toaga, the wife of Sotoa, the high chief of Lumā. In this same report, Mead also recorded that the "whole emphasis" of the Protestant Church in Samoa, of which all the inhabitants of Manu'a were adherents, was on "physical chastity." Further, throughout Manu'a, it was the custom for adolescent girls to be sequestered in the household of the village pastor, where they were, in Mead's words, "very strictly supervised and their virginity vigilantly safeguarded." On Mead's own reckoning, in her field notes and in Coming of Age in Samoa, more than one-half the adolescent girls she studied in Manu'a were, at the time of her research, still teine muli, or virgins. Mead's claim, in her letter to Boas of March 14, 1926, that "sex begins with puberty in most cases," is—even on her own evidence—manifestly untrue.[14]

Furthermore, Mead's claims, made after she had been hoaxed, that after marriage, there was in Manu'a "a good deal" of promiscuous intercourse and that "many adulteries . . . hardly threaten the continuity of established relationships" were similarly at odds with what she had previously been told by her Samoan informants about the seriousness of adultery in Samoan society. In Vaitogi, in October 1925, she had recorded Ufiti's statement that it was traditional in Samoa for adultery to be punished "with slavery," or "*tu'i le paepae,*" which involved the confiscation of all the adulterer's possessions, the razing to the ground of his house, and the killing of his pigs. In Lumā, on November 28, 1925, she had recorded the testimony of To'aga that "in the case of adultery the man will flee to the bush and if the husband kills him there will be no blood revenge, because he has the right to kill him; sometimes he will kill the wife too." In the 1920s, under the Regulations and Orders of the Naval Government of American Samoa, adultery by any Samoan was a criminal offense punishable by a fine of "not more than one hundred dollars" or imprisonment for "not more than twelve months, or both," as well as being a sin for which adulterers were expelled from the church. Yet, ignoring these realities and what she had been clearly told by Ufiti and To'aga, Mead relied instead on the supposed cultural pattern she had derived from the untruths and hyperbole of Fa'apua'a and Fofoa to inform Boas that in Manu'a there was "fairly promiscuous intercourse" before marriage and "a good deal" of it "after marriage" as well.[15]

What Mead achieved in her letter to Boas of March 14 is breathtaking. While letting him know of the ethnology of Manu'a on which she was working "for the Bishop Museum," she at the same time assuaged him with an apparent solution to a long-standing and vexing problem, which for Boas was gratifying in the extreme. During her trip to Ofu, she had virtually completed her ethnology of Manu'a and, with the ready assistance of Fa'apua'a and Fofoa, had solved the problem Boas had designed for her; the excursion, so it seemed to her, had been a singular success. It was an extraordinary denouement, and on her last night in Ofu, secure in her false belief that there was "great premarital freedom" in Samoa, Mead dreamed that her fun-loving informant, Fa'apua'a, who was in fact a *taupou* and a virgin, had "had twins." Fa'apua'a and Fofoa, as Mead recorded in her bulletin of March 24, 1926, were each presented with "three new dresses," a happening that Fa'apua'a still appreciatively remembered when questioned in 1993.[16]

Mead and her "merry companions" returned to the naval dispensary at Ta'ū together with Dr. and Mrs. Lane on Thursday, March 18, on the U.S.S. *Tanager*. In the mail brought by *Tanager* was Boas's reply of February 15 (see Appendix) to Mead's letter of January 5, in which she had sought his advice by airmail on the "presentation" of the "results" of her research on adolescence. Boas was "anxious" to answer Mead's questions as well as he could. "I am very decidedly of the opinion," Boas told her, "that a statistical treatment of such an intricate behavior as the one you are studying, will not have very much meaning, and that the characterization of a selected number of cases must necessarily be the material with which you have to operate." To which he added: "I am under the impression that you have to follow somewhat the method that is used by medical men in their analysis of individual cases on which is built up the general picture of the pathological courses that they want to describe."[17]

As Mead told Boas in reply, this was exactly the advice she "needed." In her letter of January 5, she had asked Boas: "If I simply write conclusions and use my cases as illustrative material will it be acceptable?" Boas had answered this momentous question in the affirmative, granting her the option to "simply write conclusions" and to use "cases" as "illustrative material." This approval transformed Mead's appreciation of her situation. From her questioning of Fa'apua'a and Fofoa, she had identified, she was convinced, the cultural pattern that determined adolescent sexual behavior in Samoa. And with this achieved, there was, she felt, no need for further detailed investigation.[18]

Boas's letter approving this course of action reached Mead on March 18, 1926. So completely was Mead in the grip of her luminous insight that less than twenty-four hours later, on March 19, she wrote to Boas again (see Appendix) from the U.S. Naval Dispensary on Ta'ū, still in an elated state at the turn events had taken. Convinced that she had hit upon a cultural pattern that had effectively solved the problem Boas had set her, she had decided, on the spur of the moment, even though it meant the total cancellation of the "special investigation" of the sexual behavior of her adolescent girls, which she was due to undertake during April 1926, to "finish up" her fieldwork some four weeks sooner than previously planned. This, she rationalized, in her hurried note to Boas, was because of "the increasing difficulty of living in Manu'a with too many people quartered at the Dispensary" for her to stay there and because of "a famine in native foods." She would be leaving Manu'a in time to connect with an earlier passage of the S.S. *Sonoma* from Pago Pago to Sydney. She would, she promised Boas, get her results "pretty thoroughly worked up" during her six-week voyage to Marseilles.[19]

In her "plan of research" submitted to the Board of National Research Fellowships in the Biological Sciences in February 1925, Mead had written of spending "a year in actual fieldwork in Samoa." In Samoa, in her report to the National Research Council of January 6, 1926, she proposed five months "of intensive study" of the adolescent girl, in addition to the four weeks of inquiry she had completed in 1925, meaning a total of six months of fieldwork in Manu'a. To achieve this, she would have had to continue her research in Manu'a until early in June 1926, when she would have been entitled to "six weeks' vacation." But now, she was intent on leaving Manu'a and heading for the south of France just as soon as she possibly could. The "blue honey of the Mediterranean," as F. Scott Fitzgerald called it, was beckoning. By terminating her fieldwork in Manu'a after only five months, she could sail from American Samoa for Australia on May 10. This would enable her to embark on a P. and O. liner in Sydney on May 19 and reach Marseilles on June 25 for a protracted holiday in France, England, and Italy. She would then, at the end of September, attend the Twenty-Second International Congress of Americanists in Rome with her confidante, Ruth Benedict, before returning to New York early in October, to begin her work as an assistant curator of ethnology at the American Museum of Natural History. It was an alluring prospect. As she noted in her bulletin of March 24, 1926, written after a severe attack of tonsillitis that Dr. Lane had been treating for her, she would devote the time that was left to her in Ta'ū to patching such "holes" in her ethnology of Manu'a as "the width of a basket, the height of a post, the name of a feast, how they burn scars, what you really do call your mother's brother, and how many fires there were at a death feast."[20]

Cutting short the fieldwork on her Boas assignment in this abrupt way and her involvement in even further ethnological inquiry meant that *no systematic, firsthand investigation of the sexual behavior of her sample of adolescent girls was ever to be undertaken.* Instead, Margaret Mead's account of adolescent sexual behavior in *Coming of Age in Samoa* and elsewhere was based on what she had been told by Fa'apua'a and Fofoa, supplemented by other such inquiries that she had previously made.

Luther Cressman has recounted how when she was a graduate student of anthropology at Columbia University and when Melville Herskovits would show, with chapter and verse, that a conclusion of hers was untenable, Mead's defense would always be, "If it isn't, it ought to be," to which she would add, "Well, what's so bad about that?" She was also much given to the having of hunches. For example, in her letter to Ruth Benedict of March 21, 1933, from Tchambuli, she wrote: "I've had a tremendous spurt of energy and I've gotten the key to this culture from my angle—got it yesterday during hours of sitting on the floor in a house of mourning. Now it is straight sailing ahead, just a matter of working out all the ramifications of my hunch."[21]

Mead had gotten her hunch for the solution of the problem that had brought her to Samoa from her questioning of Fa'apua'a and Fofoa on the island of Ofu. At her prompting, they had told her exactly what she was wanting to hear and had given her a solution to the problem Boas had set her of the very kind for which she was hoping. It was, she felt sure, just the kind of solution that Boas "wanted" and would readily accept. Everything depended on Boas. If Boas, her official supervisor, were to accept her solution, all would be well. "I shall not be entirely at ease," she told him, "until I have laid my work in your hands." It made her very happy, she said, to realize that she would soon be back with him again.[22]

By the first week of April 1926, when she should have been conducting the "special investigation" of the sexual behavior of her adolescent girls, which if it had been conscientiously carried out would have decisively refuted the counterfeit "facts" on which Mead's "solution" to Boas's "problem" was based, her days were "simply a procession of ceremonial farewells." With "so little left to do," there was even time, as she mentioned on April 7, 1926, in a letter to her grandmother, for her to write a short story about the faraway valley in rural Pennsylvania where she herself had come of age. It was a story entitled "The Conscientious Myth Maker."[23]

*The islands of Ofu and Olosega, viewed from Lumā on the island of Ta'ū, the site of Mead's fieldwork in 1925–1926. These three islands are known collectively as Manu'a (photo by Derek Freeman, 1967).*

*An aerial photo of part of the south coast of the island of Tutuila, American Samoa, taken during the visit of the U.S. Pacific Fleet in August 1925. Vaitogi, the village where Margaret Mead lived in October 1925 and again in April–May 1926, is in the foreground.*

*The village of Lumā on the island of Ta'ū, Manu'a, American Samoa, site of the U.S. Naval Dispensary, Margaret Mead's research head-quarters from November 1925 to April 1926 (photo by Derek Freeman, 1967).*

*High Chief Tufele Fa'atoia, district governor of Manu'a in 1925 (photo from William L. Calnon,* Seeing the South Sea Islands *[New York, 1926], p. 116).*

*The U.S. Naval Dispensary, Lumā, Ta'ū, Manu'a, American Samoa, as it was in 1967 (photo by Derek Freeman).*

The island of Ofu, Manu'a, American Samoa, where Margaret Mead was
hoaxed on March 13, 1926, by her Samoan traveling companions, Fa'apua'a
and Fofoa (photo by Donald Sloan, **The Shadow Catcher** [New York, 1940]).

A Samoan taupou, or
ceremonial virgin, circa
1924 (photo by Frances
Hubbard Flaherty).

*Margaret Mead in Manu'a in 1926, dressed as a taupou, or ceremonial virgin (from Margaret Mead Papers, Manuscript Division, Library of Congress, Washington, D.C.; courtesy of the Institute for Intercultural Studies, Inc., New York).*

*Fa'apua'a Fa'amū of Fitiuta, Ta'ū, Manu'a, American Samoa, who on November 13, 1987, in a sworn statement to the secretary of Samoan affairs in the government of American Samoa, confessed that in March 1926 on the island of Ofu, she and her friend Fofoa had hoaxed Margaret Mead when she questioned them about the sexual behavior of Samoan adolescent girls (photo by Larry Gartenstein, 1989).*

Dust jacket of the first edition of Coming of Age in Samoa, *1928*
*(from Margaret Mead Papers, Manuscript Division, Library of*
*Congress, Washington, D.C.; courtesy of the Institute for*
*Intercultural Studies, Inc., New York).*

# 12

# Mead's Samoan
# Fieldwork in Retrospect

EAD'S LETTER OF MARCH 14, which announced that her investigation of the problem Boas had assigned to her was "practically completed," reached Franz Boas at Columbia University in New York City on the morning of Tuesday, April 20, 1926. On January 4, 1926, in a letter to the Board of National Research Fellowships in the Biological Sciences, Boas had noted, in his role as Mead's supervisor, that the "principal object" of her investigation in Samoa was "to attempt to determine how far the behavior of an adolescent girl is determined by the cultural environment." On January 6, in her report to the National Research Council about her fieldwork in Manu'a, Mead had made "absolutely no showing in conclusions at all," as she confessed to Boas. Yet just over two months later, in her letter to Boas of March 14, she claimed that because at puberty there was no "curb" on the expression of sexuality, adolescence in Samoa was without "stress." This was an impossibly brief period in which to have completed the systematic research on which these sweeping generalizations could be validly based—especially when, for over half of this period, Mead had not been investigating the behavior of adolescent girls at all but instead had been researching the ethnology of Manu'a for the Bishop Museum.

Boas, however, had no knowledge of this, nor did he know of the singular fashion in which, on the island of Ofu, Mead had suddenly acquired from Fa'apua'a and Fofoa the information on which her characterization of Samoan adolescence was based. Boas's reply, his last com-

149

munication to Mead in Samoa, was written by hand within a few hours of receiving her letter of March 14. It began, effusively, "My dear Flower of Heaven," a reference to the *taupou* title that had been conferred on Mead in Si'ufaga on January 26, 1926. That salutation set the tone for what followed. Boas was more than pleased at Mead's sweeping conclusion. "I am glad you were able," he told her, "to do so well with your difficult problem that you feel able to state your results so succinctly." On March 28, 1926, Boas had written to Elsie Clews Parsons: "Margaret Mead sends encouraging reports. I believe she is getting a good deal that will clinch the point that fundamental individual natures depend upon cultural setting more than upon heredity or innate characteristics." This is a clear indication of the kind of clinching of the nature-nurture controversy that Franz Boas very much hoped would result from Margaret Mead's Samoan research. And in February 1927, on his return from a visit to Germany, when he made a formal assessment as Mead's supervisor of her official report to the National Science Council, he was, as Mead reported on March 4, 1927, "completely satisfied." It was a report in which she concluded that "human nature," far from being "fixed," was "relentlessly shaped and molded" by cultural "patterns." This was sweet music to Boas's ears, and at no stage did he question the conclusion that was implicit in Mead's letter of March 14, 1926, and explicit in her report to the National Research Council: that adolescent behavior is wholly determined by the "cultural environment." As Mead had sensed on March 14, 1926, her sweeping conclusion was very much "the sort of thing" that Papa Franz "wanted." She had become his "Flower of Heaven."[1]

Boas's letter of April 20 (see Appendix) reached Mead in Pago Pago by the Oceanic Steamship Company's S.S. *Sonoma*, on which she finally sailed from Samoa for Australia on May 10, 1926. Boas had also written to her two months earlier, on February 24, 1926, after reading her report to the National Research Council and corresponding with the secretary of the Board of National Research Fellowships in the Biological Sciences about Mead's fieldwork in Manu'a. "It is of course quite obvious," he had told her in the February letter, "that under the present conditions you ought to continue your work in the field as long as possible." However, before this instruction from her supervisor had reached her, Mead had prematurely ended her work in the field. Exultant at the outcome of her excursion to Ofu and Olosega and having decided, after a stay of little more than five months, to leave Manu'a to vacation in France, she had already left her research headquarters in the U.S. Naval Dispensary at Lumā and was on her way back to Vaitogi on the island of Tutuila, there to await the arrival of the S.S. *Sonoma,* which would carry her to Sydney.

How had Mead's months in Manu'a been spent? In particular, considering her deep involvement with research on the ethnology of Manu'a for the Bishop Museum, how much time had she actually given to the study of adolescent girls? And was this study conducted by methods likely to lead to results of an empirically reliable kind?[2]

Mead arrived in Manu'a late on the afternoon of Monday, November 9, 1925, after just over two months spent studying the Samoan language on the island of Tutuila. During the remainder of that month, she had spent some days confined to bed with tonsillitis, and as her report to Boas of November 29 records, she had done no more than size up the local situation and plan a "detailed personnel study" of the villages of Lumā, Si'ufaga, and Faleasao, in which all the girls she was proposing to study lived. This "personnel study," which was intended to provide "a thorough background for understanding the place of each girl studied in the structure of her community," was completed by the end of December 1925. Against this background, as Mead noted in her report of January 6, 1926, "more than fifty girls" were to be "individually studied." She had been ready to embark on these individual studies at the beginning of 1926, only to have her inquiries severely disrupted by a destructive hurricane, in the unsettled aftermath of which she could do no effective research on her adolescent girls for three weeks. After having her research "terribly complicated" in this way, Mead had continued to work for just over a month at the U.S. Naval Dispensary at Lumā, until her ethnological excursions, first to Fitiuta and then to Ofu and Olosega, began on February 20. After returning from Ofu to the western end of the island of Ta'ū, where all of the girls she was studying lived, Mead suddenly decided on March 19, believing she had successfully solved her research problem, to cut short her research by about a month and leave Manu'a early in April 1926 for the south of France. By April 7, her days had become "simply a procession of ceremonial farewells and presentation of gifts," she informed Boas. This means that Mead's fieldwork in Manu'a lasted for only twenty-one weeks.[3]

Mead gave over one-third of this time, as her records show, to the ethnological research on which she had covertly agreed to work, as agreed in her letter of November 1, 1926, to Edward Craighill Handy of the Bishop Museum. On ten different days of December 1925 and

January and February 1926, she interviewed To'aga, Tufele, and others on purely ethnological topics. Following the hurricane of January 1, 1926, when informants were "not be had for love or money," she was forced to devote some "two weeks" to "the ethnology of activity." Her ethnological excursions, first to Fitiuta and then to Ofu and Olosega, took almost one month, including travel. After her return to the naval dispensary at Lumā, there were still holes to patch, as she put it on March 24, in her ethnology of Manu'a as well as some "collecting" to be done "for the Bishop Museum." In sum, then, Mead devoted about two months, or more than one-third of the total time available to her for fieldwork in Manu'a, to research on ethnology that had virtually no bearing on the problem for which her National Research Fellowship in the Biological Sciences had been awarded. With this major involvement in ethnological inquiry, only about thirteen weeks remained for other research.[4]

A significant amount of Mead's time was also given to the writing of bulletins and the like. When she was in Manu'a, letters from the United States and elsewhere would descend on her, she reported, "in intermittent downpours, sometimes seventy or eighty at a time." Dealing with these "downpours" was something of a strain, even for bystanders. Quite early in her stay in Manu'a, on December 5, 1925, she was feelingly exhorted to "discontinue letter writing" by the radio operator at the naval dispensary, whose "conscience" had become "restless" at her "dutifulness." Her main recourse in dealing with her numerous correspondents was a series of bulletins, the originals of which were sent to the United States for copying and distribution to "family and friends." During her stay in Manu'a, seven of these bulletins, totaling twenty-four single-spaced, typewritten pages, were completed. Further, in addition to her report of January 6, 1926, to the National Research Council and other official correspondence, she also wrote ten letters, totaling twenty-five pages, to Franz Boas; ten, totaling twenty-four pages, to her paternal grandmother; and six, totaling twelve pages, to Edward Craighill Handy, as well as a yet undisclosed number of letters to Ruth Benedict. On "boat day," when a navy supply vessel arrived at Ta'ū to deliver and collect letters and the like, the whole day, according to Mead, was taken up in dealing with her mail. There were at least seven of these boat days during her stay, and in all, two weeks or more of Mead's time was taken up by her very extensive correspondence.[5]

When this time is added to her two bouts of tonsillitis, one in November 1925 and the other in March 1926, by both of which she was, on medical orders, confined to bed, about ten weeks are left during which research on the adolescent girls of Lumā, Si'ufaga, and Faleasao could have been carried out. Further, these weeks include the first seven weeks of Mead's stay in Manu'a, during which, after a settling-in period of three weeks, her energies were given to a "detailed personnel study" of all 856 inhabitants and 100 households of the villages of Lumā, Si'ufaga, and Faleasao. During this survey of December 1925 of the three different villages, some three weeks of Mead's time were given to the collection of preliminary information on the "more than fifty girls" that by early January 1926 had been identified for individual study. When the three weeks of her village census of December 1925 are added to the three weeks of her settling-in period, during which no research on adolescents was undertaken, it is evident that in all, a total of not more than four or five weeks could have been spent in the actual "investigation of the adolescent girl" as "a study in heredity and environment."

Such information as Mead was able to obtain on the adolescent girls of Lumā, Si'ufaga, and Faleasao during this time was collected intermittently during the months of December 1925 and January, February, and March 1926. Further, given her major involvement in ethnological inquiry from February 20 onward and because of the disruption of some three weeks caused by the hurricane of New Year's Day, the only period available to Mead for sustained research on the adolescent girls of Lumā, Si'ufaga, and Faleasao was between the third week of January and the third week of February 1926. During this period, aside from the ceremony at Si'ufaga on January 26, when she was given the *taupou* title of "Flower of Heaven," the funeral of a pregnant woman at Faleasao during which she witnessed an autopsy to remove the fetus for burial beside its mother, and a daylong excursion to the fishing settlement of Amouli, there were no other major interruptions.

It was mainly during this period of some four weeks, then, that Mead collected most of her information on individual girls, recording it in English in a special loose-leaf folder. It was recorded piecemeal, as opportunity offered, sometimes from the girl herself and sometimes as hearsay from other informants. There are brief entries for most of the twenty-five fully adolescent girls listed in table 1 of *Coming of Age in Samoa*. Most entries consist of a string of adjectives in which Mead characterizes the appearance and personality of individual girls. Thus, the entry for girl number 4, Sona, begins: "Ugly crony, self-assertive, dishonest, efficient, plausible, ambitious; says boys don't like her because she can't *tafao* (i.e. stroll about); wants to live all her life with girls." That for number 10, Tulipa, contains the information: "Uncomely, but subtly attractive; excellent dancer, sloe-eyed, good sense of humor, sly . . . Is now living in the house of *faifeau* (i.e. Pastor); says she likes it. Almost blind. Only fourteen—seems much older—looks old . . . Too young to have any real sex interests." That for number 24, Leta, reads in part: "A very dull, giggly, apologetic, unattractive little slavey. Lives in the household of Solomona (the Pastor of Faleasao). Doesn't go to school. Was raped at the age of eight. Only case of rape on Taʻū, there is another in Olosega." The entry for number 27, Mina, describes her thus: "Stolid, stupid, honest, reliable, good-natured, lazy. Not given to quarrelling or gossiping. Doesn't want to be a Church member at present. (Suspected of having a lover)." As these entries indicate, the information on the adolescent girls of Lumā, Siʻufaga, and Faleasao in Mead's loose-leaf folder is highly unsystematic and anecdotal. Furthermore, and most important, it does not contain information that reveals any cultural pattern pertaining to sexual behavior of the kind that Mead was both expecting and hoping to find. Thus, from the entries in Mead's loose-leaf folder, it was certainly not possible by February 20, 1926, when Mead abandoned her investigation of adolescent behavior to carry out ethnological research, first in Fitiuta and then on Ofu and Olosega, to discern any cultural pattern of the kind required for a solution to the research problem that Boas had set her. Nor would any extension of the arbitrary and equivocal information contained in Mead's loose-leaf notebook have provided her with the kind of solution she was seeking. With little time left to her, she was in a major quandary.[6]

It was in this state of chronic uncertainty that Mead took recourse in questioning Faʻapuaʻa and Fofoa about the sexual behavior of adolescents in a determined attempt to discover a cultural pattern that, from her hearsay knowledge of the Marquesans and other Polynesians, she felt sure must also exist in Manuʻa. What she was told by Faʻapuaʻa and Fofoa in jest was a travesty of the facts of Samoan existence, conspicuously at odds with what she had been told by various other informants such as Toʻaga and Andrew Napoleon, but it did provide her with an apparent "pattern" in terms of which a solution could be found that would be acceptable to Boas. What transpired on the island of Ofu on March 13, 1926, was thus very much the outcome of the adventitious way in which Mead had carried out her inquiries in the aftermath of the hurricane, and in particular, it was the result of the great amount of time she had given, at the instigation of Gregory and Handy, to collecting information on the ethnology of Manu'a for publication by the Bishop Museum. This major and illicit involvement with the Bishop Museum was a crucially important determinant of the fateful course of Mead's Samoan research.

As has been discussed already, Mead developed a passionate desire to conduct ethnological research in fall 1924, after participating in the Ninety-Second Meeting of the British Association for the Advancement of Science in Toronto, when the idea of having a people of her own, preferably in the South Seas and, if at all possible, in the remote Tuamotu Islands, became "a driving force" in her life. But she abandoned this coveted objective at the insistence of Papa Franz and then, in order to get to the South Seas at all, reluctantly agreed to work on a project entirely of Boas's devising—the problem of "heredity and environment" in relation to adolescence, which, as she later confessed, she "didn't even want to study."[7]

The directive she received from the National Research Council and her supervisor, Franz Boas, was that she should give *all of her time* to this demanding problem and strictly avoid any involvement in ethnological research while in Samoa. However, her intense desire to try her hand at ethnology led her to succumb to the enticing proposal put to her by the renowned Bernice P. Bishop Museum, six weeks before she was due to sail for Samoa. Mead therefore accepted Dr. Gregory's offer of an associateship in ethnology and provisionally agreed to write an ethnology of Samoa for publication as a monograph of the Bishop Museum, without having consulted either Franz Boas or the National Research Council. During her visit to Honolulu in August 1925, she was insistently encouraged by both Gregory and Handy to work on ethnology. And publication of her own monograph was an irresistible inducement for the ambitious young Margaret Mead. On November 1, 1925, after she had been in Samoa for just two months, she entered into a secret agreement with the Bishop Museum to work on an ethnology of Manu'a, as had been proposed by Gregory and Handy. This agreement with the Bishop Museum, it is important to note, was entered into in advance of Mead's arrival in Manu'a and before she could form any clear idea of how much time would be needed to solve the problem Boas had set her. It was an active assertion of her personal in-

terest in "doing ethnology" and in having a monograph of her own
published by the Bernice P. Bishop Museum.[8]

On November 15, 1925, six days after her arrival, Mead wrote to
Boas from the U.S. Naval Dispensary on the island of Ta'ū: "I have
gotten settled in Manu'a and find it admirably suited to all my purposes." With the dispatch of her letter of November 1, 1925, to Edward Craighill Handy, Mead's "purposes" prominently included the
carrying out of extensive ethnological research for the Bishop Museum. Although well aware what Boas's instructions to her were,
Mead said nothing of this to her official supervisor. Thus, there is no
mention at all of her agreement with the Bishop Museum in Mead's
letter to Boas of November 15, 1925.[9]

Yet within a few days of her arrival on the island of Ta'ū, Mead was
considering a visit of three weeks to the islands of Ofu and Olosega,
which are clearly visible from the U.S. Naval Dispensary at Lumā
where she had taken up residence. This can only have been for ethnological inquiry, for none of the adolescent girls she was proposing to
study lived on these off-lying islands. Thus, from the very outset of
her fieldwork in Manu'a, Mead was giving attention to two quite separate research projects: one of them her "investigation of the adolescent
girl" as "a study in heredity and environment," at the behest of Franz
Boas, and the other an ethnology of Manu'a "for the Bishop Museum."
Further, of these two projects, each of them highly demanding in its
own way, it was by ethnological research, as her bulletins show, that
she was really fascinated. It was research of the kind in which she had,
in the fall of 1924, become passionately interested while studying the
ethnology of Polynesia as a whole in her aerie in the tower of the
American Museum of Natural History. In Manu'a this interest, having
been reinforced by Gregory and Handy of the Bishop Museum, became
so strong that she was led during her five months there, even though it
directly contravened the instructions she had been given by Boas and
the National Research Council, to give more and more of her time to
purely ethnological research. This process, which is observable from
the outset of Mead's research in Manu'a, quickened late in December
1925, after she had been appointed assistant curator in ethnology at
the American Museum of Natural History. Edward Craighill Handy
was among the first to congratulate her. With this appointment, her
professional career, it seemed to her, would definitely be in the field of
ethnology, and from February 20, 1926, onward, virtually all of her

time was given to the gathering of information for the ethnology of Manu'a that she was determined to complete "for the Bishop Museum" to ensure her professional future. By proceeding in this self-willed way, with very little time left to her in Manu'a and with her insurmountably difficult research on adolescent behavior still substantially incomplete, she was seriously risking, as she had apprehensively conjectured in her letter to Boas of January 16, 1926, that he might have cause to be "dreadfully disappointed" in her Samoan research. The completion of her ethnology of Manu'a, in addition to the thorough investigation of the behavior of sixty-six Samoan girls, as outlined in her letter to Boas of February 15, 1926, was a task beyond even Margaret Mead's phenomenal energy and ambition. Thus, during the last weeks of her fieldwork in Manu'a, in devoting almost all of her time to ethnology, Mead was ostentatiously burning her candle at both ends in the audacious spirit of Edna St. Vincent Millay's First Fig, of which she had been so fond when at Barnard College.[10]

By abandoning research on her adolescent girls for the second time, as she did when she set out for Ofu and Olosega on March 8, 1926, Mead was ensuring that her ethnology of Manu'a for the Bishop Museum would be successfully finished. But with the collection of data on some sixty-six girls, as laid out in her letter to Boas of February 15, still far from completed, no solution to the research problem was in sight. And so at the end of the second week of March 1926, with only a brief period left to her in Manu'a, Mead was faced by the imminent prospect of failure if she could not, by some expedient, swiftly arrive at a plausible solution to the problem of heredity and environment in relation to adolescence, with which she had made very little progress since her arrival in Manu'a and had entirely neglected for the previous month or so. It was a juncture at which her "fear of failure," of which she subsequently wrote to Boas, had become intense. The course she followed in this impasse, with all of the girls she was supposed to be studying quite out of contact on another island, was to interrogate insistently her twenty-four-year-old companions, Fa'apua'a and Fofoa. And then, not realizing that she had been hoaxed, she constructed a cultural pattern that in her letter of March 14, 1926, she presented to Boas as a plenary solution to the "difficult problem" he had sent her to Samoa to investigate. With this achieved, her "haunting fear" of failure and of "completely disappointing" Boas was at an end. She had defiantly burnt her candle at both ends, and, so it must have seemed to her, with a "lovely light," for in a little over a month, she had as good as completed an ethnology of all of the islands of Manu'a and, in the space of a couple of days, had seemingly solved the hitherto intractable problem of her research for Boas. In her elation at this propitious turn of events, Mead felt justified in terminating her inquiries in Manu'a about a month earlier than she had planned and in heading for the south of France.[11]

As soon as she returned from Ofu to her research headquarters in the naval dispensary at Lumā, Mead wrote to Handy at the Bishop Museum informing him of the remarkable progress she had made and seeking advice about the monograph she would, as a result, be submitting to the Bishop Museum for publication. Mead received his reply of April 30, 1926, just as she was leaving Samoa. Handy had consulted Gregory and asked that she prepare a general ethnology of Manu'a, because for the Bishop Museum's "work in Polynesia as a whole," it was "clear-cut descriptive accounts" that were wanted. Mead assured Handy that she would begin writing such an account as soon as she had completed her report on "the adolescent girl in Samoa" for the National Research Council.[12]

A few days before embarking on her ethnological excursions to Fitiuta, Ofu, and Olosega, Mead had told Boas in her letter of February 15 that in the continuation of her "particular study" of the adolescent girl in Samoa, she would, at the end of March 1926, be undertaking a "special investigation" of "sexual life and any philosophical conflicts." This special investigation was vitally important for any empirically based solution to the problem Mead was working on, and in February 1926, she thought it imperative because of the scant information on sexual behavior in her loose-leaf folder. By March 14, however, she had obtained adequate evidence, so she believed, that in Samoa there was at puberty no "curb" on sexual activity, and back on the island of Ta'ū on March 19, she judged the special investigation to be no longer necessary. She had, she firmly believed, successfully identified the cultural pattern that determined adolescent behavior in Samoa. This was wholly in accord with what seemed "so obvious" to her at this stage of her anthropological career—"that a culture shapes the lives of those who live in it"—and, having defined what she believed to be the Samoan pattern she felt her work had been completed "satisfactorily." Thus, the sexual behavior of the adolescent girls she had selected for study was *never systematically investigated* by Mead.

Instead, in framing generalizations about "many years of casual love-making," she relied on the cultural pattern derived from Fa'apua'a and Fofoa, which she had first formulated in her letter to Boas, written on the island of Ofu on March 14, 1926.[13]

There also no longer seemed to be any need to collect all of the information on the sixty-six-girl sample she had identified for study in her letter to Boas of February 15. Her planned research on these girls was therefore allowed to lapse. Consequently, most of the information that she assured Boas she would be collecting before her departure from Manu'a is not given in the table (which is for only fifty girls) that appears in *Coming of Age in Samoa*. Again, although in her letter to Boas of February 15 Mead's plan was to collect a wide range of information on thirty girls "between puberty and twenty years of age," this plan, with the curtailing of her fieldwork by about a month, was also abandoned, and in *Coming of Age in Samoa* partial information on only twenty-five girls in this age group is provided.[14]

With Boas having agreed that she could "simply write conclusions" and use "cases as illustrative material," Mead's remaining days in the field were mainly spent in dealing with "all the holes" there were "to patch" in her ethnology of Manu'a, although there are additional entries, dated March 21 and March 23, for individual girls in her loose-leaf folder. In a mere twenty-one weeks, she had established to her own satisfaction the epoch-making conclusion that adolescent behavior could be explained in cultural terms, and in addition, by an extraordinarily determined application of her energies, she had also gathered, as she had promised Edward Craighill Handy she would, "the ethnological material" for a comprehensive monograph on Manu'a.

On the face of it, this was a remarkable amount to have accomplished in just five months, especially with her fieldwork during this time having been "terribly complicated by a severe hurricane." This was certainly Mead's own view. In her last letter to Boas, written on April 7, 1926, just before she left Manu'a, she told him: "I am finishing up my stay in the field with a good taste in my mouth." In another letter of April 7, 1926, in reporting the satisfactory completion of her research in Manu'a, she wrote: "I am leaving here with a very clear conscience." A few months earlier, in her letter to Boas of January 5, 1926, about the presentation of her results when she finally got them, Mead had written: "Ideally, no reader should have to trust my word for anything, except of course in as much as he trusted my honesty and averagely intelligent observation." In her letter to Boas of January 16, 1926, she reported that her life in Manu'a was "one long battle" with her "conscience" as to whether she was "working correctly" and "hard enough." She had gone to Samoa completely convinced that "anthropology was all good, hard science based on fieldwork." She had been brought up "to believe that the only thing was to add to the sum of accurate information in the world." In the judgment of Professor William F. Ogburn, she had been "wonderfully well trained along the lines of precision and accuracy." As these statements and all of the other available evidence indicate, Mead's research in Manu'a was carried out in conscientious good faith. She was, it is evident, utterly oblivious of having been hoaxed.[15]

That this happened should occasion no great surprise. As Russell Bernard has noted, "it is not unheard of for informants to lie to anthropologists." Indeed, in the judgment of Bernard and his fellow investigators, "on average about half of what informants report is probably inaccurate in some way." Boas himself was once taken in by a Comox Indian woman. Hoaxing then, as Gordon Stein documented in his *Encyclopedia of Hoaxes*, is an ubiquitous phenomenon in human societies, both ancient and modern. A hoax is "a test of how gullible people are" and is thus a way of comparing one's own gullibility with that of others. Accordingly, as Stein noted, "we all like to fool people" and, in some societies, notably including those of Polynesia, the fooling of others, and especially of interlopers, has long been commonplace. William Bligh, in reporting that in Tahiti on November 12, 1788, he was told of an island where there were "large animals . . . with eight legs," remarked that his informants were "so much addicted to that species of wit which we call humbug, that it is frequently difficult to discover whether they are in jest or earnest." Another revealing example is the hoaxing of a "natural philosopher" of the French Enlightenment, Jacques de Labillardière, of the expedition of 1791–1794 led by D'Entrecasteaux in search of La Perouse. When in Tonga, de Labillardière set about the recording of native numerals, which he single-mindedly continued until he reached 1,000,000,000,000,000! He then communicated his findings to the Academy of Sciences in Paris, quite unaware that the numerous Tongan phrases he had recorded beyond 1,000 were for the most part gross obscenities.[16]

If only Mead had arranged to live with a Samoan family in Manu'a, as she easily could have done, she would have known from direct observation just how false were the conclusions set out in her letter to Boas of March 14, 1926. However, because of the comforts that she felt she could not do without, she chose to reside with fellow Americans in the U.S. Naval Dispensary at Lumā, where, cut off from the realities of Samoan existence, she relied for the most part on informants who came to visit her there. And so, lacking the experience of protracted residence in a Samoan family that is vital to any genuine knowledge of Samoan behavior and values, she was quite unable to appraise the tall tales of Fa'apua'a and Fofoa for what they were.

During recent years, research on the papers of Mead, Boas, and others dating from the 1920s, supplemented by detailed questioning of Fa'apua'a Fa'amū, has revealed crucially significant new information about Margaret Mead's Samoan fieldwork of 1925–1926. It is now known that the conclusions Mead reached in *Coming of Age in Samoa* are essentially a restatement of two dominating preconceptions that she took with her to Samoa. The first of these preconceptions was a passionate belief in "the phenomenon of social pressure and its absolute determination in shaping the individuals within its bounds," which she had derived from Boas, Benedict, and Ogburn when she was their student in New York. The second of her major preconceptions was the mistaken conviction, gained, in the main, from Edward Craighill Handy of the Bishop Museum, that adolescent promiscuity was a pervasive cultural pattern in island Polynesia. It was by these two beguiling preconceptions, as the relevant documents show, that Margaret Mead's brief research in Manu'a was principally informed. And in her intense desire to please Boas, she quite failed to realize how deeply her "starting assumptions" affected the way she went about looking for and interpreting the data she collected. As Colin Tudge has observed, "whether you are a scientist or not, it is all too easy to fit whatever you see into a story that is already inside your own head."[17]

From this fundamentally flawed fieldwork, in her room high in the tower of the American Museum of Natural History in New York, Mead constructed her misinformed account of "free love-making" in Samoa. In his foreword to her book of 1928, Franz Boas declared her account to be the result of a "painstaking investigation." And so, with this stamp of approval from "the most eminent anthropologist in

America," Margaret Mead's *Coming of Age in Samoa*, from the late 1920s onward, came to be quite generally accepted by American anthropologists as a resplendent proof of Boasian culturalism.[18]

That the "youthful jollity" and "wanton wiles" of two high-spirited young Samoan women could have led to such an outcome is one of the more bemusing marvels of twentieth-century anthropology.[19]

# 13

# From Pago Pago to New York: Via Paris, London, and Rome

IN NOVEMBER 1925, MEAD HAD INITIALLY THOUGHT that living in the U.S. Naval Dispensary on Ta'ū was "really an excellent arrangement," but by March 1926, less than four months later, her attitude had changed, and as she confessed to Boas, she very much wanted to escape from the society of the dispensary's "tiny white colony." In her letter to Boas of April 7, 1926, she avowed that Polynesia, with her orders "to be as one of them," was "very pleasant work," and she went on to record that all the "unpleasantness" had been extraneous: "The heat, the few uncongenial white people, the canned food, the various minor ailments" had all "kept the year from being an unalloyed delight," especially when these "physical discomforts" were added to her "fear of failure." The main reason she had given to Boas on March 19, 1926, for leaving Manu'a much earlier than originally planned was "the increasing difficulty" of living there "with too many people quartered at the Dispensary." Samoa, she announced in a letter written on her last day in the no longer idyllic dispensary, would be a "pleasant paradise" if only "there were no dull white people and mosquitoes." Having her research headquarters in the naval dispensary rather than in a Samoan household had had disadvantages, it is evident, of more than just a methodological kind. Nonetheless, disenchanted as she had been with some of the naval personnel with whom she had had to live, "the Samoan part" she had "loved quite thoroughly." On April 15, 1926, her last day in the dispensary, as she gazed through one of its windows at "palm leaves hanging in a hundred separate attitudes of languid loveliness," she realized with a pang that in a few weeks there would be "no more palms" and "no more lithe brown bodies, passing and repassing, silhouettes against the sunset."[1]

On their return to Ta'ū from Ofu on March 18, Fa'apua'a and Fofoa, who had become Mead's closest Samoan friends, stayed for several nights at Tufele's house at Si'ufaga before returning to their own homes in Fitiuta. From Fitiuta, between March 25 and April 17, Fa'apua'a sent to Mead no fewer than nine separate letters, all of which Mead took back with her to America. Written in Samoan and carried by hand from Fitiuta to the naval dispensary at Lumā by various villagers, each of these letters is addressed to Iliganoa, the *taupou* title that Mead had been given in Fitiuta. They are all couched in the most affectionate terms. They provide abundant evidence of the loving relationship that existed between Fa'apua'a Fa'amū and Margaret Mead and show that the prank to which Fa'apua'a and Fofoa resorted when questioned by Mead about adolescent sexual behavior was not perpetrated out of any malice toward her, being no more than the kind of facetious response that Samoan custom condones in such a situation. If only Mead had spent more time in the company of Samoans in their own families and less with the "dull" and "uncongenial" compatriots with whom she lived in the U.S. Naval Dispensary, she would have been in a position to recognize this.[2]

In her letter of March 25, Fa'apua'a expressed sorrow at the illness that had overtaken Mead on her return from Ofu. She also sent to Mead a gift of bark cloth, while asking in return for tinned salmon and soap, of which she was in need. Then, in a letter dated April 17, as already recounted, Fa'apua'a wrote to Makerita of how she constantly remembered her "love" (*alofa*) during the "many" days (*aso e tele*) they had gone about together and asked her American friend not to forget their "good companionship" (*masaniga lelei*) that she herself would "always remember" (*manatua pea*).[3]

These heartfelt words and Fa'apua'a's action in traveling to Pago Pago to be with Mead before she sailed for Australia are clear evidence of the amicable relationship that existed between the two young women. It is also evidence that substantiates Fa'apua'a's claim that she and Fofoa in their "recreational lying" on the island of Ofu were merely joking. In a last letter written in Fitiuta on March 4, 1927, sent to Mead at the American Museum of Natural History in New York,

Fa'apua'a informed her that Fofoa had given birth to a son. This son was Galea'i Poumele, who became a high chief of Fitiuta and the secretary of Samoan affairs in American Samoa, the same man who interviewed Fa'apua'a on November 13, 1987, about her association and that of his mother, Fofoa, with Margaret Mead during their fateful excursion to Ofu and Olosega.

On April 6, 1926, Mead had written from Ta'ū to Ufiti's daughter, Fa'amotu, with whom she had become friendly during her visit to Vaitogi the previous October, asking if she could stay with Ufiti's family while awaiting the arrival of the S.S. *Sonoma* from Honolulu. Delighted at this prospect, Fa'amotu suggested to Mead that she should come to Vaitogi on Monday, April 19, after spending two days in Pago Pago. Mead had to call on Mr. B. F. Kneubuhl, the local agent of the Oceanic Steamship Company in Pago Pago, to finalize the reservation she had made on March 24, when she had sent him from Ta'ū a deposit of $25 on "a first class, one way ticket from Pago Pago to Sydney" in the name of "Dr. Margaret Mead." Mead's last letter from the naval dispensary, whence she had been "particularly anxious to be gone" since her return there from Ofu, was written on Thursday, April 15, 1926. The next day she was back at the naval station on the island of Tutuila, on her way to Vaitogi.[4]

In Vaitogi, Mead was welcomed as though she "had been away for many years" and had "the sensation of returning home from a long voyage." She suddenly realized how "home sick" she had been and how "starved for affection" while living with other Americans in the naval dispensary on Ta'ū. Most of her time in Vaitogi was spent with Ufiti's daughter Fa'amotu, to whom later in 1926 she sent a wedding dress from the Galerie Lafayette in Paris, only to be told that Fa'amotu's fiancé had "married someone else." However, on February 23, 1929, Fa'amotu did marry Robert Lee Smith of the U.S. Navy, and, having changed her name to Sylvia, settled in San Diego. On May 26, 1931, she wrote to Mead in fluent American English, enclosing a number of snapshots taken on a trip to Los Angeles to see the movie studios and hoping that Mead would not be unhappy at seeing how Americanized her Samoan "sister" had become.[5]

By the time she had been back in Vaitogi for a week, one part of Mead's homesickness had been assuaged. This, however, made her all the more aware of "a far more fierce longing," a longing for conversation and for contact with people of her own kind, people who had read the same books and who would understand her allusions, people who would understand her work, people who could help her understand what she had been doing and who would give her some perspective on whether she had "actually done" what she had "been sent out to do."[6]

In her letter to Boas of April 7, Mead had told him that she planned, before embarking for Sydney, "to visit every village on Tutuila and make a special study of the variations in rank." However, nothing came of this plan. She went on living in Vaitogi until she traveled back to the port of Pago Pago to board the S.S. *Sonoma*. In her autobiography, Mead wrote of returning to Tutuila from Manu'a in June 1926 and, in the introduction to the 1969 edition of *Social Organization of Manu'a*, of leaving Samoa "in July 1926." In fact, the S.S. *Sonoma* sailed from Pago Pago for Sydney on Monday, May 10, 1926, by which time Mead had been in American Samoa not for "nine months" of fieldwork, as she later claimed, but for eight months and ten days, with a full three months of this time having been spent not in fieldwork in Manu'a but on the island of Tutuila either in learning Samoan or in transit.[7]

During the six-day voyage to Sydney, the S.S. *Sonoma* encountered an exceptionally severe storm, with waves breaking over the decks and passengers going down "like ninepins, deathly ill." Mead herself was not seasick. She was met in Sydney by members of her husband's "Australian clan," their arms "full of flowers from their own gardens." After two "very comfortable days" that included "a real bath tub and a beef steak" and being taken to hear both "the Don Cossacks and the Vatican choir," she boarded "the P. and O. luxury liner, the S.S. *Chitral*," en route to Marseilles for the long-awaited reunion there with her husband, Luther Cressman, who had been traveling in Europe while his wife was in Manu'a.[8]

By a happenstance that was to affect Mead's life profoundly while she was writing about her research in Samoa, a fellow passenger on the *Chitral* was a twenty-three-year-old postgraduate student of psychology from Victoria University College of Wellington, New Zealand, who was on his way to the University of Cambridge. His name was Reo Fortune. Even before the *Chitral* left Sydney, Margaret Mead and Reo Fortune had discovered their common interests. Seeing them talking together "so eagerly," the *Chitral's* chief steward offered them a table to themselves, where for the next five to six weeks they would discuss the psychological and anthropological issues that the two of them found so engaging. The "fierce longing" for intellectual conversation that Mead had felt on escaping from the company of the "dull white people" at the U.S. Naval Dispensary at Ta'ū was to be fully assuaged. The two of them, according to Mead, were in states of "profound excitement." Mead, having at twenty-four been appointed assistant curator of ethnology on the "scientific staff" of the American Museum of Natural History, was on her way to attend the Twenty-Second International Congress of Americanists in Rome. The Bernice P. Bishop Museum, of which she was an associate in ethnology, had agreed to publish her ethnology of Manu'a. In addition, she was convinced that she had collected evidence in Manu'a to prove that adolescent behavior was to be explained in cultural terms. With these accomplishments to her credit, and as one who had completed her doctorate at Columbia University under the renowned Franz Boas, she enormously impressed Reo Fortune. During the voyage of the *Chitral*, he became a sounding board for the ideas Mead was to develop in *Coming of Age in Samoa*. She felt more convinced than ever of her conclusion about adolescence.[9]

Fortune's particular interest was in the psychology of dreaming, and "quite early in the voyage," Mead began to record her dreams for him. In South Australia, they went ashore to the library of the University of Adelaide to read the article on anthropology that Bronislaw Malinowski had written for the latest edition of the *Encyclopedia Britannica*. So "enthralled" did they become with each other, fitting all that each of them had learned "into a new approach to the study of primitive peoples," that they sometimes had to be "shooed away" from their table by "impatient waiters." They would then spend the evening "at the very bow of the ship where the spray came in and the sea sometimes seemed to be on fire." In this way their days were spent, lost in the depths of anthropology—and of themselves.[10]

When she wrote to her grandmother from Port Sudan on June 18, 1926, with her arrival in France only a week away, it seemed "incredible" to Mead that she had "been at sea over five weeks—lost to time and place—as remote as the great porpoises who gambol ever in the mid-Pacific." She was not, because of the heat of the Red Sea, "doing any work at all." All that she had done during the amaranthine voyage was, she said, to index her field notes, write a short story, work on the psychology of dreams, learn to play chess, and watch the sea. This, she insisted, was all that had been "possible." She and Reo Fortune had not, according to Mead, been "having an affair," but by the time the S.S. *Chitral* reached Marseilles on June 25, they were very much in love with one another. This was especially so in the case of Reo Fortune, who had "almost succeeded" in persuading Mead to voyage on with him to England, only to be left on the *Chitral*, unrequited, at their table for two. But Mead had given him her address in Paris, where he was determined to make contact with her again just as soon as he possibly could.[11]

Having booked "a large, sunny hotel room," Luther Cressman was on the pier at Marseilles when the *Chitral* tied up. Mead, "very crestfallen and completely without enthusiasm," was among the last to disembark. Back in their hotel room, she sat on the knees of her husband, who found himself thinking of the words of her letter of August 1925 from San Francisco: "I'll not leave you unless I find someone I love more." "Well," she told him, "I met someone aboard ship I love that way and I want to marry him." She was very much on edge during the troubled days that followed, "in a state of extreme emotional tension," not knowing what the future would bring.[12]

Louise Rosenblatt, Mead's roommate at Barnard College, was due to join them after a year at the University of Grenoble. When she did arrive they tried their best "to enjoy the Roman ruins" and "the old cities of Nimes, Arles and Avignon." Then, in medieval Carcassonne, so Mead recorded in her autobiography, she "rechose Luther," although Cressman, in his autobiography, stated he was wholly "unaware" of this having happened. Certainly, it was by no means the romantic holiday that Luther Cressman had planned and for which Mead had been longing, when having cut short her fieldwork in Manu'a by about a month, she wrote on April 7, 1926, of "racing about France and Italy under Luther's frantic guidance."[13]

When they got to Paris, there was, as Mead was expecting, a letter from Reo Fortune announcing his imminent arrival. At this, Luther Cressman agreed to absent himself. When he returned, supposing the visit to be over, he caught a glimpse of his wife and Reo Fortune "in a close embrace." Cressman kept this knowledge entirely to himself, though having been offered a lectureship at the College of the City of New York, he at once brought forward the date of his return to the United States. Louise Rosenblatt and Mead were at the Gare St. Lazare to see him off to Cherbourg to board the *George Washington*. In tears, Margaret once again implored Luther to tell her "what to do." He remained adamant. He had, he told her, given her "a choice and freedom," and she must make her "own decision." As he sprang onto the bottom step of the departing train, he called: "Take care of her, Louise, take care of her"—and was gone. He was taking with him for safe storage in New York all of Mead's field notes and other papers from Samoa, which already seemed a world away.[14]

On July 13, about a week before Luther Cressman left for New York, Mead wrote to Boas from Paris (see Appendix). In her letter of April 7 from Manu'a, she had told Boas that she would try to have her research "worked up and typewritten" by the time she reached Europe. In the event, something very different had happened, and a situation, still quite unresolved, had developed of which Boas knew nothing. In his letter of April 20, he had wished the "Flower of Heaven," as he called her, "a pleasant time in Europe," after "all the hardships" of Samoa. In thanking Boas for this letter, in particular for having taken "precious time to write it by hand," she disingenuously told him in her letter of July 13 from Paris: "I was seasick the whole trip and utterly incapable of doing any consecutive work on shipboard." "I find now," she continued, "that I am still very, very tired, and I'm just beginning to realize how strenuous this year has been, coming as it did right on top of my year at Columbia." "I fear," she continued, "that if I am to adequately discharge my duties next year and write up my fieldwork also, I shall have to give these two months in Europe to rather thorough relaxation."[15]

After her tearful parting with her husband, Mead stayed on in Paris for a reunion with Ruth Benedict, with whom there was an immense amount to be discussed. Ruth Benedict, it so happened, had had "an unhappy summer" and was "deeply depressed." Sitting with Mead in a Parisian churchyard, she remarked "with passionate repudiation in her voice" as she looked toward the Gothic towers of Notre Dame, "Isn't it unbearable that that is all about nothing?" And the following month while waiting for Mead, who was in England, to accompany her to Rome, she wrote in her journal, while in St. Paul sur Nice:

> I know to the bottom of my subconscious that no combination of circumstances, no love, no well-being will ever give me what I want. But death will. Passion is a turn-coat, but death will endure always; life is a bundle of fetters or it isn't worth living and for all our dreaming of freedom, only death can give it to us. Life must always be demeaning itself, but death comes with dignity we don't have even to deserve. We all know these things, but in me it's bred a passionate conviction that death is better than life.[16]

Mead, in England, where there had been further meetings with the ardent Reo Fortune, was in rather better spirits. Ruth Benedict, she told her grandmother, in a letter written in London on August 26, had met "many English people," when traveling with her husband earlier in the summer of 1926, and was "immensely depressed by England." Mead, in marked contrast, felt herself to be living in an England that was "ageless" and was "immensely on tiptoe about it." Oblivious of time, she had spent hours in the British Museum studying its "beautiful" Polynesian collection. She had been to Westminster Bridge to be reminded of how the poet William Cowper, after having attempted unsuccessfully to commit suicide, had written in one of his Olney Hymns of 1779, "God moves in a mysterious way, His wonders to perform." "In Hyde Park, on Rotten Row" she had seen a guardsman "all in scarlet and with a black plush hat, walking with a girl in French blue." She would, she said, be in London for only a week before leaving to travel in Italy where she was to represent the American Museum of Natural History at the Twenty-Second International Congress of Americanists.[17]

Before attending the congress in Rome, which would be in session from September 23 to September 30, 1926, Mead met up again with her mentor and confidante, Ruth Benedict. The two of them were in one another's company until they returned to New York together on October 11. During this time, there was full opportunity for Mead to discuss with Benedict her conclusions about the sexual mores of the Samoans, as well as her major conclusion about the cultural determination of adolescent behavior. As is known from her subsequently published statements, these were conclusions to which Benedict gave unquestioning credence. Benedict's influence during the weeks immediately before Mead began writing what was to become *Coming of Age in Samoa* was then unwaveringly in support of all that her much-loved former student had done and was intending to do.

From Rome, where Benito Mussolini received the International Congress of Americanists with "a blast of trumpets, a ruffle of drums and all the uniforms of the middle ages," Mead and Benedict returned by train to France to embark for New York. Reo Fortune, though he would not finally succeed until they met again in Berlin in June 1927, was there to try to persuade Mead to terminate her marriage to Luther Cressman and become his wife. Despite his experiences in Marseilles and Paris, Luther Cressman was on the pier on October 11, 1926, when Margaret Mead reached New York, a full six months after ending her fieldwork in Manu'a—months during which she had attained her goal of traveling around the world and during which her private life had been thrown into emotional turmoil. Luther had found "a nice apartment" at 610 West 115 Street, between Broadway and Riverside Drive. It was close to Columbia and had "convenient transportation" to both the American Museum of Natural History and the College of the City of New York. Deeply uncertain as to what the future might hold, Margaret Mead took up residence there and at once plunged into writing her report to the National Research Council on her investigation in Samoa of the adolescent girl as "a study in heredity and environment."[18]

# 14

# *Coming of Age in Samoa* and Boasian Culturalism

G ETTING BACK" TO NEW YORK ON OCTOBER 11, 1926, after "four glorious months in Europe" was, as Mead confided to Stella Jones of the Bishop Museum, a "dreadful strain." At first, "it was very hard to get to work" at nine and to be there "until five every day." By October 29, however, she was "getting along beautifully."[1]

Gladys Reichard, who some years earlier had taken over from Franz Boas at Barnard College, was in Germany on a John Simon Guggenheim Memorial Fellowship, doing research on Melanesian design. Thus, during the academic year of 1926–1927, Ruth Benedict became instructor in anthropology at Barnard, with Margaret Mead as her assistant. By October 29, Mead had done her "first teaching" and had "gotten over" her "first fears" on that front. On October 25, "wearing the aura of her year in the 'romantic' Pacific isles," she presented a lecture, "Rank in Samoa," to a joint meeting of the New York Academy of Sciences and the American Ethnological Society. She had also written "six chapters" of her report to the National Research Council. She had been able to make this flying start because of the detailed discussions she had had with Ruth Benedict during the weeks they spent together immediately before their return to New York. Mead was, moreover, a very rapid worker. In a letter to A. R. Radcliffe-Brown from New York dated July 1, 1935, she wrote of turning out her Arapesh monograph "at a stint of 20,000 words a week."[2]

At the American Museum of Natural History, she had been given "a grand office" in the sixth-floor tower. Her first assignment as assistant curator was to rearrange the South Seas Hall, which she thought "dreadful," as half of the cases were filled with weapons. By October 29, she had already made a plan to do this. She was assisted first by Kenneth Emory of the Bishop Museum and then by H. D. Skinner of the Otago Museum, New Zealand, who was visiting the United States on a Carnegie Traveling Fellowship. She was fortunate, however, in being able to give much of her time during November and December 1926 to writing her report for the National Research Council. Before Boas sailed from New York for Bremen in the North German Lloyd liner *Columbus* on December 14, 1926, to spend Christmas with his sister in Berlin, there had been ample time for Mead to discuss her Samoan research with him and to gain his approval of the form that her report would take. Indeed, on December 13, the day before his departure for Germany, Boas wrote to the Committee for Fellowships on Child Development of the National Research Council about the "results" of Miss Mead's study of "adolescent girls in Samoa."[3]

On December 20, in a reply to a request from Gregory for a report on her activities as an associate in ethnology of the Bishop Museum, Mead informed him that during her time in Samoa she had been able to "collect material for an account of the ethnology of Manu'a, exclusive of the details of material culture, tattooing designs and mythology." She was proposing to begin work on the writing of this ethnology soon after January 1, 1927, and to have it completed before she sailed for Europe in June to study "the Polynesian collections in German museums." Although still sharing an apartment with Luther Cressman, Mead remained in active correspondence, "punctuated by the verses" that they wrote to one another, with Reo Fortune. By December 20, 1926, as her report to Gregory indicates, she was already planning to visit Germany, where, among other things, she could be with Reo once again. Since taking up her position at the American Museum of Natural History, she had, she told Gregory, devoted her time "to writing up a particular psychological problem—that of the adolescent girl in an alien culture," which, under the terms of her National Research Fellowship in the Biological Sciences, she had to "prepare for publication as soon a possible."[4]

The next day, in sending to Handy a copy of her report to Gregory, she noted that "what with getting settled in civilization" and starting work at the American Museum of Natural History, she had had no time at all since her return to New York to "touch" ethnology; but her work on the adolescent girl, so she told Handy, was flourishing. A fortnight later, in a memorandum of January 5, 1927, to the American Museum of Natural History, she formally recorded the completion of her report to the National Research Council. It was entitled "The Adolescent Girl in Samoa," was 56,000 words long, and had been written, while also performing her curatorial duties, in the astonishingly short time of ten weeks.[5]

In the first paragraph of the introduction to "The Adolescent Girl in Samoa," Mead stated that the question her report was intent on answering was this: "Are the attitudes, the conflicts, the perplexities, the ambitions of the adolescent girl correlates of a special period of physiological development or are they rather to be attributed to the civilization in which she lives?" As already noted, in her letter to Boas of January 5, 1926, Mead had asked: "If I simply write conclusions and use my cases as illustrative material will it be acceptable?" Boas was "very decidedly of the opinion" that "the characterization of a selected number of cases must necessarily be the material" with which she would "have to operate." Mead had eagerly accepted this advice. Her "generalizations," she noted in the introduction to her report to the National Research Council, would be "illustrated by case histories." The chief of these "generalizations" was the same as in her letter to Boas of March 14, 1926, written immediately after she had been hoaxed by Fa'apua'a and Fofoa: that in Samoa there is at puberty no curb on sexual activity. In chapter 1, "The Education of the Samoan Child," Mead says of the adolescent girl that "all of her interest" is "expended on clandestine sex adventures." In chapter 8, "The Experience and Individuality of the Average Girl," she states that one of the "uniform and satisfying ambitions" of the adolescent girl in Samoa is to live "with many lovers as long as possible."[6]

With the exception of the "deviants" discussed under the heading of "The Girl in Conflict," adolescence in Samoa, so Mead asserts, "represented no period of crisis or stress." And this being so, adolescent behavior, she concludes, was not a correlate of "a special period of physiological development" but rather something that is "relentlessly shaped and molded" by the "patterns" of the culture to which the adolescent belongs. To all appearances, she had triumphantly validated the central dogma of Boasian culturalism, the supposition that "the nature of man had to be derived from cultural materials."[7]

On January 13, 1927, Mead wrote to Edith Elliott, the secretary of the Board of National Research Fellowships in the Biological Sciences, stating that her report, "The Adolescent Girl in Samoa," was "in typewritten form awaiting Dr. Boas' inspection on his return from Europe" in the middle of February. After making "any changes" that Boas might suggest, she would be able, she said, to get a copy of her report to the board for its meeting in May 1927.[8]

Boas's "inspection" of Mead's report to the National Research Council on a research project of which he had been the instigator and of which he was the formally appointed supervisor was of great importance. It was Boas's personal responsibility as supervisor of Mead's research in Samoa to assure the Board of National Research Fellowships in the Biological Sciences that the account contained in her report was based on reliable data and that her general conclusion about adolescence was scientifically warranted.

A typewritten copy of "The Adolescent Girl in Samoa" was awaiting Boas on his return to New York from Germany in the second week of February 1927. On March 4, 1927, in a letter to her mother, Mead was able to announce: "Dr. Boas is completely satisfied with my book." That Boas should have been "completely satisfied" with Mead's "full report" on her "investigation of the adolescent girl" in Samoa as "a study in heredity and environment" is entirely understandable. Her "vastly important" conclusion, as Mead judged it to be, that adolescent behavior is "relentlessly shaped and molded" by cultural patterns was something in which Boas himself had long believed and, as Mead's class notes demonstrate, was part of the anthropological ideology that he had imparted to Mead at Barnard College in his lectures of 1922–1923. It is therefore fully understandable that Boas should have accepted Mead's account, as she reports in her autobiography, with no other criticism than that she had not "made clear the difference between passionate and romantic love."[9]

What this report also indicates is that, "completely satisfied" as he was with Mead's conclusion, Boas clearly failed to subject her evidence and arguments to an adequately thorough critical examination. By placing credence in the statements she had made to him after she had been hoaxed by Fa'apua'a and Fofoa, he had, like Mead herself, become cognitively deluded about Samoa. If only Boas, having been informed by Mead that premarital heterosexual promiscuity was the norm in Manu'a, had critically appraised her report, he could not but have noticed in table 1 of "The Adolescent Girl in Samoa," that of the twenty-five girls enumerated, all of them having reached puberty, no fewer than fourteen, or 56 percent, are listed as having had "no heterosexual experience," an outright contradiction of Mead's claim that in Samoa "sexual life begins with puberty in most cases."[10]

In table 1 of "The Adolescent Girl in Samoa," Mead lists eleven girls as having had heterosexual experience. On May 10, 1968, I wrote to Dr. Mead about this table, asking if a "yes" under the heading of "heterosexual experience" referred "in all cases to full sexual intercourse (i.e., with intromission)." In her reply of November 6, 1968, Dr. Mead stated: "When I used the term heterosexual I was referring to full intercourse, not to other practices." In her table 1 in "The Adolescent Girl in Samoa," Mead records that eight of the eleven girls listed (as having had heterosexual experience) were either three years (six cases) or four years (two cases) past their menarche. Thus, during three years and more, these eight girls had (on Mead's own evidence) been ovulating while also engaging (according to Mead) in "years of casual love-making," with full intromission and no kind of contraception. Yet none of them had become pregnant. Here we have an evident anomaly that would cause any perceptive reader to question the account of "free-lovemaking" on which Mead's general conclusion in "The Adolescent Girl in Samoa" was based. Nonetheless, Boas, whose mind, according to Lowie, was "in the highest degree critical," fully accepted her account, while Mead herself sought to justify her report with the bizarre rationalization that "in Samoa," premarital promiscuity seemed to ensure "against pregnancy."[11]

If Boas had only given due attention to table 1, he would also have noted that over one-third of the "girls past puberty" studied by Mead were resident in the house of the Christian pastor of their village, where they were "so severely watched that sexual activities were impossible," a state of affairs that Mead herself fully documents and which can only mean that her central generalization that in Manu'a the community made no attempt "to curb" sexual activity at puberty is in outright error. And if Boas had critically analyzed the chapter in "The Adolescent Girl in Samoa" entitled "The Girl in Conflict," he would have realized that the numerous cases of delinquency that Mead describes provide the clearest possible evidence of "storm and stress" among Samoan female adolescents, for these cases, as a moment's reflection shows, are as much the products of Samoan society as are the other adolescents in Mead's sample and constitute a delinquency rate as high as that to be found in other societies. Again, if only Boas had taken note of Mead's reference in her report of January

6, 1926, to the institution of ceremonial virginity and to the public testing of virginity at marriage even in the case of "girls of lesser rank," he would have been forced to consider why such institutions were present in a society that, so Mead claimed, made no attempt to curb sexual activity at puberty. And if he had consulted the readily available literature on Samoa, particularly the writings of Augustin Krämer, Otto Stuebel, and other German ethnographers of Samoa, he would have realized that Mead had seriously misdescribed the sexual mores of the Samoans. Yet Franz Boas did no such thing in 1927. Instead, despite the blunders, misconceptions, and fallacies Mead's report contained, he declared himself "completely satisfied" with it.[12]

It so happens that 1927 was the year when, during a visit to New York, Jacob Epstein sculpted a portrait of Franz Boas. Boas's face, according to Epstein, was "scarred and criss-crossed with mementos of many duels of his student days in Heidelberg, but what was still left whole in his face was as spirited as a fighting cock." While involved in the nature-nurture controversy, Boas had been fighting for well over a decade to establish his belief in "the complete molding" of human behavior "by social conditioning," and when Margaret Mead presented him with an apparent proof of this belief, he grasped it eagerly. As Liam Hudson and Bernadine Jacot have put it: "What Mead showed Boas was what he wanted to see and having seen what he wanted to see, considerations of science and scholarship went by the board." Convinced, as he was, of the "truth" of his ideas, all that mattered to him was that he had "won."[13]

On April 24, 1927, Mead dispatched to Dr. F. Lillie, chairman of the Board of National Research Fellowships in the Biological Sciences, the top copy of her "report upon the special problem" for which she had received her fellowship in 1925. The next day, two additional copies of "The Adolescent Girl in Samoa" were sent to the secretary of the board, with the assuring statement that her supervisor Dr. Boas had "read and approved the manuscript." Mead also told the board that in consultation with Dr. Boas, she had organized the manuscript in a form "sufficiently untechnical to appeal to a commercial publisher." As "The Adolescent Girl in Samoa" was "too clumsy a title for commercial publication," she was thinking, "with Dr. Boas' approval," of using the title "Coming of Age in Samoa" instead. She was anxious to have the manuscript approved by the board as soon as possible, so that she could submit it to a publisher before she sailed for Germany. Mead received this approval on May 10, 1927. The text of "The Adolescent

Girl in Samoa," as approved by Franz Boas and the Board of National Research Fellowships in the Biological Sciences of the National Research Council, could now be "sent questing for a publisher." On the advice of Dr. George Dorsey, who had suggested the title "Coming of Age in Samoa," the typescript was sent to Harper and Brothers, which had published Dorsey's immensely successful *Why We Behave Like Human Beings* in 1925, when Mead was in Samoa.[14]

In forwarding "The Adolescent Girl in Samoa" to Frank Lillie, Mead had described her "year of research" in Samoa as having laid "a firm foundation" for "the pursuit of psychological problems among primitive peoples." In his acknowledgment of April 27, 1927, Lillie expressed his "gratification" that Mead's fellowship had "resulted in such a very fine contribution." It gave him "much satisfaction," he said, to be able to congratulate her "personally" on her work. Yet in retrospect, it is highly ironic that Mead, while holding a fellowship "in the Biological Sciences," should have concluded that adolescent behavior is not in any way a correlate of "a special period of physiological development" but rather is "relentlessly shaped and molded" by cultural patterns and then have this one-sided and quite unscientific conclusion formally approved by the Board of National Research Fellowships in the Biological Sciences of the National Research Council. The irony was further compounded as several members of this board, including F. R. Lillie, T. H. Morgan, E. L. Thorndike, and R. S. Woodworth, had previously expressed an interactionist view similar to that of Edwin G. Conklin that "neither environment nor heredity is all-important, both are necessary to development." It can only be surmised that they did not seriously examine Mead's report but instead relied on the judgment of Professor Franz Boas, who in 1919 had been described by the Division of Anthropology and Psychology of the National Research Council as "the most eminent anthropologist in America," whom they had formally appointed as supervisor of Mead's Samoan research in May 1925. What can be said with certainty is that without Franz Boas, who was also the instigator of Mead's "investigation of the adolescent girl" in Samoa, the whole extraordinary affair would never have happened.[15]

In the spring of 1927, with word that Reo Fortune, in Cambridge, had been awarded a fellowship by the Australian National Research Council, Mead decided to proceed with her plan to meet him in Germany. Discontinuing work on her ethnology of Manu'a, she left New York early in June 1927 for a six-week tour of the museums of Bremen,

Hamburg, Berlin, Dresden, Cologne, Frankfurt, Stuttgart, Nuremberg, and Munich. From Bremen, which was so "clean" that "you could eat off the streets," she wrote to say that she felt "more at home" in Germany than anywhere else in Europe, including even England. By June 25, she was in Berlin, where after a "tempestuous" meeting, she agreed to obtain a divorce so that she could marry Reo Fortune on the completion of the fieldwork he was to do in Melanesia. Then, having notified her husband in New York of this denouement, she continued with her museum tour while Fortune headed for Australia. On August 19, 1927, soon after her return to New York, Luther Cressman agreed to move out of their "conjugal domicile" and thus initiate grounds for a divorce. It was finally granted in Mexico on July 31, 1928. On October 8, 1928, Margaret Mead and Reo Fortune were married in Auckland, New Zealand, en route to the Admiralty Islands of New Guinea to do fieldwork together at Manus. On August 31, 1928, in London, the prescient Luther Cressman had married Dorothy Loch, whom he had gotten to know there more than six months before Margaret Mead and Reo Fortune, in Sydney, Australia, became fellow passengers on the S.S. *Chitral*.[16]

For Mead, the year she spent in New York City after her return from Germany late in the summer of 1927 was unsettled and "troubled." With the breakup of her marriage to Luther Cressman, she went to live at 507 West 124th Street with several of her Barnard College friends, all of whom were struggling with "various forms of heartbreak." In December 1926, she had written to Stella Jones at the Bishop Museum about her firm intention to return to Samoa. On January 24, 1927, she also told its director, Herbert Gregory, of her eagerness to get back to Samoa. But a few months later, just before leaving to meet Reo Fortune in Berlin, when it became known that the New Zealand ethnologist Dr. Peter Buck, was to visit the Samoan islands, she wrote to H. D. Skinner: "So there's an end to my work in Samoa, I shall publish my book and look about for a new field and for another psychological problem." With her promise of June 1927 to marry Reo Fortune, the "new field" became Melanesia, and her "psychological problem" became the study of "the thought of the pre-school child," a topic that she had hammered out in discussion with her husband-to-be. In the fall of 1927, when Gregory wrote saying that he would welcome any further project Mead might have for Samoa, she replied that she had already "made other plans" for her "next fieldwork," which she expected to extend into 1929. After that, however, she would, she told Gregory, "like very much to do more work in Samoa." In fact, she never again did fieldwork anywhere in Samoa. Her next stay there, except for a four-hour stopover at Pago Pago in 1933, was not until 1971, when from November 10 to 15 she visited American Samoa as the guest of Governor and Mrs. John M. Haydon, to attend the dedication of a museum in Pago Pago and to open an electric power station at Faleasao on the island of Taʻū.[17]

During the summer of 1927 while Mead was in Germany, Ruth Benedict had been doing fieldwork among the Pima of Arizona. From her research base there, she wrote to Boas and described as "unbelievable" the contrast between the Pima and the Zuni, whom she had previously studied. It presented, she wrote later, "probably the most abrupt cultural break" in America. According to Mead, Benedict had recognized, with "a sense of revelation," the fundamental differences between "those American Indian cultures that emphasize ecstasy (for which she adopted Nietzsche's term Dionysian) and those that emphasize moderation and balance (for which she adopted Nietzsche's term Apollonian)." This brilliant insight, as Mead felt it to be, Benedict at once developed in her paper "Psychological Types in the Cultures of the Southwest." Nietzsche, in his studies of Greek tragedy, Benedict pointed out, had named and described two diametrically different ways of arriving at the values of existence, the Dionysian and the Apollonian. Comparable value systems, she claimed, were to be found in the Southwest of the United States, so that among the Zuni, as among other Indian tribes of the region, "a fundamental psychological set" had "created an intricate cultural pattern to express its own preferences."[18]

In the fall of 1927 then, Benedict and Mead became more convinced than ever that in all human societies, cultural patterns set the mold into which human nature flows. Mead, who was working on her ethnology of Manuʻa, eagerly grasped the opportunity of applying Benedict's newly conceived theory of culture as "personality writ large" to her Samoan materials. Together, she and Benedict "spent hours discussing how a given temperamental approach to living came so to dominate a culture that all who were born in it would become willing or unwilling heirs to that view of the world," taking as their example the Samoans about whom Mead was then writing. Thus, the first application of Benedict's revised theory of cultural pattern appeared in Mead's manuscript "Social Organization of Manuʻa," in her account of the "dominant cultural attitudes" of the Samoans, "every detail" of the "phrasing" of which was "thrashed out" by Benedict and Mead, as they "discussed at length the kind of personality that had been institutionalized in Samoan culture."[19]

In the monograph on Manu'a that Mead was writing with Benedict's active assistance at the end of 1927, there is an unequivocal avowal of the same extreme cultural determinist conclusion that she had reached in December 1926 in the final chapter of her report to the National Research Council, a conclusion that she repeated in February 1928, when, at the request of her publisher, William Morrow, she added two chapters to her book *Coming of Age in Samoa*. This avowal takes the form of an unconditional acceptance of what Mead, following Benedict, called "the phenomenon of social pressure and its absolute determination in shaping the individuals within its bounds." This assumption that cultural patterns determine human behavior in an "absolute" way, to the complete exclusion of biological variables, was thus the highly doctrinaire and unscientific mindset of both Benedict and Mead early in 1928, when the anthropological message of *Coming of Age in Samoa* was finally formulated.[20]

At the end of 1927, as Mead worked with Benedict on the "dominant cultural attitudes" of the Samoans, she had still found no publisher for her report to the National Research Council, which, under the title "Coming of Age in Samoa," had been rejected by Harper and Brothers. She was at a loss as to "what to do next." Then one day at a literary luncheon, George Dorsey happened to sit next to William Morrow, who had just started a new publishing house in New York City. When Dorsey told him about Mead's manuscript on the adolescent girls of Samoa, Morrow arranged to meet her, and having read her report, put to her the question: "What would you have to say if you wrote some more about what all this means to Americans?"[21]

On January 25, 1928, Mead sent to Morrow a brief "abstract" of a proposed "final discussion" she would be willing to incorporate into her book. It began with the statement that her research in Samoa had been "an experiment to find out whether the difficulties of our adolescent girls are due to the physiological changes which take place at puberty or to the civilization in which they grow up" and went on to assert that "there is nothing inherent in the period of adolescence which produces the difficulties which our children have." By February 11, 1928, within just over a fortnight of his having accepted her proposal, "two new concluding chapters," in which, according to Mead, she had pushed "speculation" to "the limit of permissibility," were on their way to William Morrow. Then on February 21, Morrow was sent "a new Introduction," of which Mead wrote: "I have tried to tie it up as much as possible with the kind of treatment which I developed in the conclusion."[22]

In this new introduction, claiming that she had "gathered many detailed facts" about the girls she had studied "through the nine months" she had been in Samoa, Mead went on to remark that "because one girl's life was so much like another's" in an "uncomplex, uniform culture like Samoa," she felt "justified in generalizing." In the opening paragraph of the first of her "two new concluding chapters," she advanced the same generalization as she had in her letter to Boas of March 14, 1926, after having been hoaxed by Fa'apua'a and Fofoa to the effect that "the lives of Samoan girls" include "as many years of casual love-making as possible." Then, in its third paragraph came the unqualified conclusion that adolescent behavior could be explained only in environmental terms.[23]

This extreme environmentalist conclusion, as is evident in the phrasing of statements in "Social Organization of Manu'a," which they had "thrashed out" together, was totally accepted by Mead's devoted confidante, Ruth Benedict. Even more important for the reception of *Coming of Age in Samoa* by the anthropologists of the day, it was also fully accepted by Franz Boas. Thus, on March 8, 1928, Mead informed Francis Phillips, a director of William Morrow and Company, that "with a few minor changes in phrasing," Professor Boas had "approved" all of the "new material" that she had added to the text of *Coming of Age in Samoa*. Boas, she noted, thought it would not be necessary to submit this "new material" to the National Research Council, and "at any rate it was unlikely," in Mead's view, that the Board of National Research Fellowships in the Biological Sciences would "make any suggestions" over Boas's "approval." It is thus evident that Margaret Mead's *Coming of Age in Samoa* of 1928, which had resulted from a research project of which he was both the instigator and the supervisor, was a text that Franz Boas fully accepted and approved right down to "minor changes in phrasing."[24]

Early in March 1928, Mead sent to William Morrow for possible inclusion in the text a brief sketch entitled "A Day in Samoa." It had been originally written as the "opening section" of the discussion in "Social Organization of Manu'a" of the "dominant cultural attitudes" of the Samoans on which Mead had worked with Ruth Benedict in the fall of 1927, only to be discarded as "too literary." It is a highly fanciful idyll in which Samoa is misleadingly depicted, as it had been by Fa'apua'a and Fofoa, as a paradise of free love, where at first light "lovers slip home from trysts beneath the palm trees" and where at the end of the day "there is only the mellow thunder of the reef and the whisper of lovers, as the village rests until dawn." Romantically setting the scene, as it beguilingly did, for the erroneous generalizations that followed, Mead's enchanting vignette, which William Morrow "very much" liked, was at once added to her report to the National Research Council to become the second chapter of *Coming of Age in Samoa*.[25]

With the manuscript complete and its publication scheduled for the fall of 1928, Mead was at last in a position to ask Boas for a foreword to her account of the investigation she had carried out, on his behalf, in Samoa. The standing of *Coming of Age in Samoa* within anthropology would, she well knew, very much depend on what Franz Boas would have to say about it.

The handwritten note that Margaret Mead sent to Boas from the American Museum of Natural History on May 22, 1928, immediately after she had received his highly approving foreword, is a poignant revelation of the depth of her infatuation with Franz Boas and his ideas.

> Dear Papa Franz,
> Thank you so very much for the foreword. I am more deeply appreciative than I can possibly tell you of your willingness to place the stamp of your approval—the highest medal of honor that we know—upon this work of mine. Through my whole trip my greatest worry was that I would have failed to do the work which I was to do well. So now my greatest joy is that it has in any way been found satisfactory to you.
> Affectionately,
> Margaret Mead[26]

The "work" that she had done for him in Samoa, it is evident, was wholly to his satisfaction, and in the foreword he wrote, at Mead's request, Boas noted that, like other anthropologists, he doubted that "childhood and adolescence" were "unavoidable periods of adjustment through which everyone had to pass." He was grateful to Miss Mead, whose "painstaking investigation" of "Samoan youth" had shown "that much of what we ascribe to human nature is no more than a reaction to the restraint put on us by our civilization." With this stamp of approval from Franz Boas, "the most influential anthropologist" of the day, the general acceptance of Margaret Mead's *Coming of Age in Samoa*, was, as she joyfully knew, assured.[27]

Earlier in May 1928, after having been awarded a research fellowship by the Social Science Research Council, Mead had applied to Dr. Clark Wissler for "leave of absence without salary" from the American Museum of Natural History "from September 1, 1928 to October 1, 1929," to do "ethnological research" in the Admiralty Islands to the north of New Guinea, where Professor Radcliffe-Brown had suggested that she and Reo Fortune should work. From June until she left New York late in August 1928 to travel via San Francisco and Honolulu to join Reo Fortune in New Zealand, Mead shared her apartment with Ruth Benedict. During this time, she attended to the proofs of her doctoral dissertation, which was finally being published by Columbia University Press, and continued writing "Social Organization of Manu'a," of which she sent a copy, except for an appendix of "about a hundred pages," to the Board of National Research Fellowships in the Biological Sciences on August 10, 1928, in completion, as she put it, of her "Fellowship work." This was with the approval of Franz Boas, who, in 1928, gratified at the outcome of Mead's Samoan "work," thus sanctioned the ethnological research that, in 1925, he had repeatedly instructed her not, under any circumstances, to undertake. Mead took another copy of the manuscript of "Social Organization of Manu'a" with her to Manus, whence, on March 18, 1929, it was finally sent to the Bishop Museum for publication after she had decided she would not be able, as she had hoped, to spend two months in Samoa before returning to New York. Instead, after leaving Manus, while Reo Fortune made a brief return visit to Dobu, she lived for six weeks on a plantation on the island of New Britain with Mrs. C. P. Parkinson, from whom she obtained a completely apocryphal account of the Samoan defloration ritual at marriage, calculated to support the account of the sexual mores of the Samoans she had given in *Coming of Age in Samoa* and which, when *Social Organization of Manu'a* was published by the Bishop Museum in 1930, was disingenuously incorporated in its text, as though this account had in fact come from Samoan informants in Manu'a.[28]

Early in August 1928, a number of advance copies of *Coming of Age in Samoa*, complete with its foreword by Franz Boas, were sent by its printers, Quinn and Boden of Rahway, New Jersey, to William Morrow and Company in New York City. At the suggestion of George Dorsey, one of these copies was sent off to the other leading anthropologist of the day, Bronislaw Malinowski, of the University of London, inviting his comments. On discovering this, Mead wrote to Malinowski on August 9 about the copy of *Coming of Age in Samoa* that her publisher had sent to him. She told Malinowski:

> I had wished to send this to you myself, feeling that no student who attempts to do psychological fieldwork should fail to acknowledge the debt that is owing to you in the field which you originated, ploughed, sowed and made fruitful for those who try to do the same kind of work, however indifferently they may succeed. This book is a work of apprenticeship, my first fieldwork, undertaken before much of your definition of the problem was published. I hope very much that I may have the benefit of your criticism.

When Malinowski's response reached New York, Mead was already on her way to the Admiralty Islands. It was so favorable that William Morrow "almost staged a celebration."[29]

After Mead had agreed to supplement her book in the way William Morrow had suggested, he assured her that he would do everything in his power to see that *Coming of Age in Samoa* would have "a real show with the general public." This was principally achieved by the expertly concocted illustration on the dust jacket of the first edition, which Mead, before leaving New York, had seen and approved. It shows, by the alluring light of a just-risen full moon, a bare-breasted Samoan girl, inflamed with passion, leading her half-naked lover to what Mead, in her fanciful text, called a tryst beneath the palm trees. On March 14, 1926, after her hoaxing by Fa'apua'a and Fofoa, Mead had quite mistakenly concluded that in Samoa there is at puberty no curb on sexual activity. By the fall of 1928, this fiction, as was flamboyantly depicted on its dust jacket, had become the leitmotiv of a book vouched for by Franz Boas as a "painstaking investigation."[30]

Mead's vexing problem in *Coming of Age in Samoa* was to reconcile the fiction that she had taken to be fact with all of the other information she had collected about Samoa and, at the same time, produce an account of a problem-free society that would warrant the desired generalization of universal applicability that "the difficulties of adolescent girls" cannot be explained other than in terms of the "social environment." This she attempted to do in the first of the two chapters added to *Coming of Age in Samoa* at William Morrow's request. She began with the fiction of the adolescent girl's "many years of casual love-making" and then proceeded to airy denial of anything that might detract from what she called "the general casualness of the whole society."[31]

In this chapter, as in her other writings on Samoa, Mead totally ignored facts well known to her that were inconsistent with the cultural pattern she was intent on establishing. The belief on the part of Mead and Benedict in patterns that lie beyond the empirical variability of the observable world is a latter-day version of an idealist notion that can be traced back to Plato. For Plato, the variable world of phenomena was "nothing but the reflection of a limited number of fixed and unchanging forms," *eide*, as he called them, or "essences as they were called by the Thomists." It is these that are believed to be real, with variation being attributed to the imperfect expression of an underlying essence. Thus, for fervent upholders of cultural patterning like Benedict and Mead, departures from a postulated cultural pattern are "viewed as merely accidental, and as having little theoretical significance," a stance that readily leads to denials and distortions of a quite flagrant order.[32]

Thus, although on New Year's Day, 1926, Mead lived through a hurricane that, as she described it at the time, "destroyed every house" in a nearby village and caused a severe famine, she nonetheless claimed, in seeking to establish a pattern of "general casualness," that "neither poverty or great disasters" threaten the people of Samoa. Although she knew that Sotoa, the high chief of Lumā, had in 1924 been dismissed from his position as district governor of Manu'a for opposition to U.S. government policy, she nonetheless described Samoa as a place where "no one suffers for his convictions." In her loose-leaf folder, she recorded two cases of forcible rape, one on Ta'ū and the other on Olosega. Yet in her paper "The Role of the Individual in Samoan Culture," which, with the approval of Franz Boas, was submitted to the National Research Council in November 1927 as part of her report, she states that "the idea of forceful rape or of any sexual act to which both participants do not give themselves freely is completely foreign to the Samoan mind." Her notes from her interview with To'aga of December 16, 1925, on virginity and ritual defloration contain this unambiguous information: "In the marriage of a taupou the tokens of virginity are taken by the boy's *tulāfale* (i.e., talking chief). In the marriage of an ordinary girl, the ceremony takes place in the house, only the family and the boy's friends are present and some elder man, chosen by the boy, performs the ceremony." Yet, as it was wholly inconsistent with the cultural pattern formulated by Mead after her hoaxing by Fa'apua'a and Fofoa that in Samoa there is at puberty no curb on sexual activity, To'aga's testimony is totally ignored in *Coming of Age in Samoa,* where Mead invents the supplementary fiction that the *taupou* alone was "excepted" from "free and easy experimentation" in "love affairs," while parents of lower rank "complacently ignore their daughters' experiments." Similarly, because chastity was required of unmarried church members, Mead, not to have her "pattern" in any way jeopardized, quite falsely asserts that no one joined the church until after marriage, even though her own field notes of February 1926 record that Lotu (number 9 in table 1 in *Coming of Age in Samoa*) had been a church member "for three years." In *Coming of Age in Samoa,* characterizing Samoa as it was at the time of her research, she claims that prohibitions against "personal violence" had "worked like a yeast" but made no mention of the fact that on October 1, 1925, when she attended the High Court of American Samoa, one of the cases she witnessed concerned two adolescent Samoan girls, aged about fifteen, one of whom had bitten off the other's ear in a fight. In one of her letters, she describes how "a Samoan boy," a nephew of County Chief Ufiti, of whose family in Vaitogi she was an adopted member, had shot and killed another youth who had "worsted him in love." Yet in defining the pattern of their culture, she claims of the Samoans that "they never hate enough to want to kill anyone," and that there is no jealousy among them. In each instance, an imagined "cultural pattern" completely supplants realities that, as the relevant historical sources show, were, in fact, well known to Mead.[33]

These and the numerous other flights from factual reality that are to be found in *Coming of Age in Samoa,* as elsewhere in Mead's Samoan writings, graphically demonstrate the way in which, by superlative rhetoric, she sought to convince others of the validity of a "cultural pattern" about which she had been hoaxed and on which she based her entirely unwarranted conclusion that "the difficulties of adolescent girls" cannot be explained other than "in terms of the social environment." In the words of Hudson and Jacot, for Margaret Mead, when she was writing *Coming of Age in Samoa,* "a story was true if it carried an unusually powerful persuasive charge; if it enabled her to execute a psychological manoeuvre she needed to execute; and if it placed a listening audience in the palm of her hand."[34]

In so behaving, Mead, who "did not doubt" that in Samoa she was "doing scientific work," was not acting duplicitously or in bad faith,

at least not in any deliberate kind of way. Rather, as a student of Franz
Boas and Ruth Benedict, she had been cognitively blinded to the complex nature of human behavior by the simplistic ideology that "the nature of man had to be derived from cultural materials." It was as a fervent devotee of this ideology that Margaret Mead went to Manu'a, and
in *Coming of Age in Samoa*, she constructed, with consummate literary skill, an apparent substantiation of Boasian culturalism that, from
the 1930s onward, came to be quite generally accepted in American
anthropology and throughout the Western world.[35]

# 15

# The Mythic Process

IN THE JOURNAL *Nature* IN 1983, a leading American anthropologist described how Margaret Mead's *Coming of Age in Samoa* became "an all-time best-seller," went through "numerous editions and translations," was "assigned to countless undergraduates," was "quoted and expanded upon by other social and behavioral scientists," and was still to be found "in nearly every American library and bookstore." In her memoir of 1979, Sey Chassler has recorded how, when it was published in 1928, *Coming of Age in Samoa* established Margaret Mead almost immediately as a major figure, not only in her own field but in the world at large as well. From the 1930s onward, the fame of *Coming of Age in Samoa* steadily grew, until it came to be generally regarded as "a seminal work in cultural anthropology," and in 1967, with Mead's approval, it was claimed that it was "the permanent glory of *Coming of Age in Samoa* that it helped to define and effect the transformation of anthropological emphasis in a manner that is peculiar to only the richest works of art." "Rightly recognized as a classic scientific study," *Coming of Age in Samoa* was, it was said, "one of the books that grace our century." At that time, some four decades after its first publication, having gone through numerous paperback editions, *Coming of Age in Samoa* was still selling about 100,000 copies a year. Then, in 1978, half a century after its publication, George Spindler of Stanford University instanced *Coming of Age in Samoa* as a book that was "the epitome of anthropology." How is all this to be accounted for? And how was it that a book with conclusions based on the untruths and hyperbole of Fa'apua'a and Fofoa could have come to be regarded as "a classic scientific study" and "the epitome of anthropology"?[1]

Although Mead, according to Ruth Benedict, was much interested in becoming famous, *Coming of Age in Samoa* was not written "as a popular book," and it became a best-seller "quite without" Mead's "expectation or intent." Yet with its publication by William Morrow and Company in the fall of 1928 at $3 a copy, sales were "maintained at a good rate from the very start." By December 31, 1928, 3,144 copies had been sold in the United States, "about 80 copies" in Canada, and there had already been a third printing. Moreover, not only did *Coming of Age in Samoa* at once become, and for decade after decade remain, a best-seller, but it was also unique, as David Thomas has pointed out, in being "both a scholarly and popular success." Nothing like it had ever previously been published: "An extraordinary accomplishment" in "the domain of erotics," in the words of Frederick O'Brien, the author of *Mystic Isles of the South Seas*, it was also vouched for as a "painstaking investigation" by "the most eminent anthropologist in America," Professor Boas of Columbia University. It was this avowal by Franz Boas that led to its immediate acceptance, as in the *New York Times Book Review* of November 1928, as a "careful scientific work."[2]

*Coming of Age in Samoa* was based, in Boas's words of December 1926, on Margaret Mead's study of "adolescent girls in Samoa for the purpose of determining in how far certain social attitudes of adolescence are due to physiological conditions and in how far they may be due to cultural conditions," a study that he himself had instigated and supervised. According to Mead, Boas thought that her study of adolescents in Samoa "would indicate that culture is very important," and when, in chapter 13 of *Coming of Age in Samoa*, she proclaimed "cultural conditions" to be all-important, Boas accepted this conclusion with alacrity. Thus, not only did Boas vouch for *Coming of Age in Samoa* as a "painstaking investigation," but in discussing Mead's Samoan research in his book *Anthropology and Modern Life* of 1928, he repeated, as though it were a fully substantiated anthropological fact, Dr. Margaret Mead's entirely false claim that in Samoa, where there was "freedom of sexual life," the "adolescent crisis disappears." That Boas behaved in this highly partisan way shows how eager he was to promote the idealist ideology of which for decades he had been a prominent advocate. Most certainly, Boas's active promotion of *Coming of Age in Samoa* as a "painstaking investigation" was crucial in securing its widespread acceptance by anthropologists and others as "careful scientific work."[3]

Boas, moreover, was not alone in his uncritical fervor. The dust jacket of the December 1928 printing of *Coming of Age in Samoa* displayed an even more forthright seal of approval from the other renowned anthropologist of the 1920s, Bronislaw Malinowski of the University of London. In 1926, Malinowski had had an enthusiastic discussion with Ruth Benedict when on a visit to New York. Indeed, Benedict, in a letter to Margaret Mead dated March 5, 1926, recounts that when she expounded Boas's ideas to Malinowski, whom she describes as "so excellent an ally," he commented, "If only I'd known, Boas was my spiritual father all the time."[4]

In Malinowski's estimation, Margaret Mead's *Coming of Age in Samoa* was "an absolutely first-rate piece of descriptive anthropology" as well as "an excellent sociological comparison of primitive and modern conditions in some of the most problematic phases of human culture such as sex, maturation and the development of the individual." "Miss Mead's fieldwork," Malinowski averred, seemed "beyond cavil and criticism." Her style was "fascinating as well as exact," and her book, which provided "excellent reading: convincing to the specialist and attractive to the layman," was "an outstanding achievement."

In November 1928, in the *American Mercury*, of which he was the editor, H. L. Mencken, a celebrated layman of the day, having informed his readers of "the sexual freedom which begins with adolescence" in Samoa, then went on to attest that Miss Mead had gone to "a great deal of trouble to establish her facts," wholly unaware, like Malinowski, Boas, and Mead herself, that she had been hoaxed. The people of the South Seas, Mencken declared, lived in Miss Mead's "precise, scientific pages" even more vividly than they lived in "the works of such romantic writers as Frederick O'Brien."[5]

In the *New York Times Book Review* of November 4, 1928, in an unsigned appraisal, *Coming of Age in Samoa* was given comparable approbation. Its author, having enthusiastically accepted her extreme environmentalist conclusion, then pronounced:

> As Miss Mead's careful scientific work deserves the most earnest tribute, so her method of presenting its results calls for the highest praise. Her book, broad in its canvas and keen in its detail, is sympathetic throughout, warmly human yet never sentimental, frank with the clean, clear frankness of the scientist, unbiased in its judgement, richly readable in its style. It is a remarkable contribution to our knowledge of humanity.

Never before had any book by an anthropologist been given such acclaim by specialist and layman alike. In forwarding a copy of this "splendid review" to Mead on January 11, 1929, William Morrow told

her there would be a redoubling of efforts to keep her "superbly written" *Coming of Age in Samoa* "before the public" and to see that it
continued "to sell for many years." In this, William Morrow and
Company were signally successful. By the time of Mead's death in
1978, fifty years after its first publication, *Coming of Age in Samoa*
had become "an all-time best-seller" and the most famous anthropological work ever written.[6]

The unqualified approval of Mead's Samoan research by Malinowski
and Boas, both of whom had no firsthand knowledge of Samoa, was
strongly reinforced by Ruth Benedict in two separate reviews. The
"concrete evidence" of the "excellent ethnological picture" in *Coming of Age in Samoa* was, Benedict declared in the *Journal of Philosophy*, "more convincing than any a priori argument" for the "plastic-
ity" of human nature. It was also, she emphasized in the *New
Republic* of November 28, 1928, a book in which "the student of sex
problems" would find "an example of consistent cultural behavior in a
society that develops no neuroses in its members," so identifying
*Coming of Age in Samoa* from the very start as depicting a sexual
utopia.[7]

It was this aspect of Mead's book that especially attracted Havelock
Ellis, the renowned author of the encyclopedic seven-volume *Studies
in the Psychology of Sex*. When in the fall of 1928 William Morrow received Ellis's gloss that *Coming of Age in Samoa* was "not only a fascinating book to read, but most instructive and valuable," these words
appeared on a bright red band around the already beguiling dust jacket.
This "stunt," according to Morrow, "helped the sales materially." The
next year, in *Sex and Civilization*, a volume edited by V. F. Calverton
and Samuel D. Schmalhausen and hailed in the *American Mercury* as
"the book of the epoch," Havelock Ellis, relying on the professional
assurances of Malinowski and Boas, gave lavish praise to *Coming of
Age in Samoa* as "a highly competent and judicious investigation"
and as "the outcome of a real acquaintance with the group studied."
Miss Mead, Ellis reported, had revealed the existence of a society of
"wholesome simplicity," in which "freedom of relationships" was
"practically unhampered before marriage." As a result, as Ellis recounted in his *Psychology of Sex: A Manual for Students*, "a whole
field of neurotic possibility" had been legislated "out of existence"
and Samoa had a society in which there was "no neurosis, no frigidity,
no impotence." Again, in advocating, on the basis of Margaret Mead's
"enlightening study," the adoption of sexual promiscuity by Ameri-

cans, Samuel D. Schmalhausen in his widely read book of 1929 entitled *Our Changing Human Nature*, cited "the innocent, strangely impersonal, naively mechanistic-behavioristic sexing of the light-hearted youths and maidens in far-off Samoa."[8]

In other words, what Mead had provided as a vehicle for her fervent belief in "the phenomenon of social pressure and its absolute determination in shaping the individuals within its bounds" was a captivating account of free love in "far-off Samoa." There could not have been a more mentally seductive concoction, and with Franz Boas and Bronislaw Malinowski vouching for its credibility, it was eagerly accepted by the anthropologists and intelligentsia of the day, as well as by the general public.

In reviewing Franz Boas's *Anthropology and Modern Life* in the *New Republic* of January 23, 1929, Sapir observed that Boas's thinking was "prevented by a certain fierce delicacy from ever declaring more than it manifestly must." Boas was quite ready, however, to endorse what Paul Rabinow has called the "unabashed crusading" of Margaret Mead. Again, when early in 1929 Ruth Benedict presented him with a copy of an article entitled "The Science of Custom," in which she repeated the extreme conclusion Mead had reached in *Coming of Age in Samoa* and used it as proof that "traditional patterns of behavior" set the mold into which human nature flows, Boas told her he thought it would "do more good" than his own recently published *Anthropology and Modern Life*.[9]

As this indicates, Boas, like his students Benedict and Mead, was deeply engaged in a campaign to gain acceptance for his impassioned belief in the sovereignty of culture. It was to this end, as Mead was very well aware, that Boas had sent her to Samoa. Thus, in a letter she wrote on October 18, 1928, Mead reported that in discussing her study of adolescence in Samoa with A. R. Radcliffe-Brown, a professor of anthropology at the University of Sydney, she had told him that it was a "problem" that had been assigned to her by Boas, adding "I simply did as I was told according to the training which I had received."[10]

In 1930, Mead's conclusion about adolescence in Samoa, vouched for as it was by Boas and Malinowski, was incorporated in the *Encyclopedia of the Social Sciences*, in a subsequent volume of which Franz Boas reiterated his conviction that the "genetic elements which may determine personality" are "altogether irrelevant as compared with the powerful influence of the cultural environment." In this way, using Margaret Mead as his highly proficient agent, Franz Boas was able by the fourth decade of the twentieth century to establish cultural determinism as the ruling dogma of American anthropology.[11]

All this happened at a time when human nature was being "newly conceived as flexible and malleable and plastic," especially in the writings of J. B. Watson, whose *The Ways of Behaviorism* was also published in 1928. In Watson's judgment, the years before and including 1928 were a period of "social renaissance," a preparation for a change in mores "that was likely to become much more of an epoch in history than the scientific renaissance which began with Bacon." The zeitgeist of Watson's generation was expressed in a massive volume entitled *The New Generation*, published in 1930. It had a soaring introduction by Bertrand Russell, in which he dwelled on the changing attitudes of the day and on how it had become clear that "the scientific psychologist, if allowed a free run with children," could "manipulate human nature" as freely as Californians manipulated the desert. Its editors, V. F. Calverton and Samuel D. Schmalhausen, who were passionately dedicated to the notion that human beings could attain "beauty and high utility" by "a courageous transformation of the social system," singled out for special mention among their many distinguished contributors the leader of behaviorism, J. B. Watson, and Margaret Mead, the gifted young anthropologist whose "enlightening study" of Samoa had furnished those who had "faith in the environment" with evidence of a singularly significant kind.[12]

That Margaret Mead should have so impressed the likes of H. L. Mencken and V. F. Calverton is a tribute to her extraordinary literary skills. According to Jane Howard, Gregory Bateson thought the "infinite facility of Mead's brain," as evinced in the game of *bouts-rimés* (set rhymes), to be "fantastic," as in the couplet:

*My pen leaps on, retracts, evades, until*
*My thoughts inchoate, tumble to a spill.*

This remarkable facility with words, by which, as W. H. Auden put it,

*A sentence uttered makes a world appear*
*Where all things happen as it says they do,*

was used by Mead, who, according to Luther Cressman, "never did anything by halves," to construct from the discrepant and delusive evidence she had brought back from Manu'a a brilliantly persuasive text. In 1929, in the *Spectator*, J. H. Driberg remarked on the "distinctive charm" of Mead's writing, and half a century later in the journal *Science*, Roger Reveille declared that "no one who has read the beautiful opening pages of *Coming of Age in Samoa* can fail to be caught" by Mead's "poetic spell." Thus, as well as being acknowledged as an "enlightening study" by the intelligentsia of the day, Mead's account of Samoa had immense popular appeal, and especially so in what T. S. Eliot, late in 1928, called "an unsettled age." In particular, *Coming of Age in Samoa* appealed to American readers because it was a romantic renewal of the American dream of an earthly paradise. It was as if the land "that flowered once for Dutch sailors' eyes—a fresh green breast of the new world," of which F. Scott Fitzgerald wrote in 1925 on the final page of *The Great Gatsby*, had flowered again in the remote islands of Samoa. In commending *Coming of Age in Samoa* to readers of the *Nation*, Freda Kirchway observed that "somewhere in each of us" is "a palm-fringed South Sea island" that promises "freedom and irresponsibility" and "love which is free, easy and satisfying." On January 3, 1929, in announcing to Miss Mead that he was "going to one of the South Sea islands" to get "local colour" for his "new novel," Henry Niel, of Battle Creek, Michigan, placed *Coming of Age in Samoa* "next to the Bible" as the "most interesting book" he had ever read.[13]

In this ambience, in the numerous reviews of *Coming of Age in Samoa* by the anthropologists and other academics of the day, there was no major questioning of Mead's conclusions. For Sapir, no longer enamored of the Ariel of his sonnet of December 1924, *Coming of Age in Samoa*, predictably, was "cheap and dull." In the fall of 1929, Dr. Paul Radin remarked to Laura Thompson, his graduate student in the Department of Anthropology at Berkeley: "I don't believe Margaret Mead can produce the records she claims to have collected from the girls in her sample." And, in his *The Method and Theory of Ethnology*, Radin's cavil against Mead was "the amazing assumption that any outsider can obtain the type of information she specifies except after an intensive study of a lifetime." Ellen Winston, using Mead's own data, questioned her generalization as to "the lack of neuroses among the Samoans." However, none of these criticisms was a serious challenge either to Mead's conclusion about adolescence or to her depiction of the sexual mores of the Samoans.[14]

Lowie, in the *American Anthropologist*, did point to various inconsistencies in Mead's account, which, if he had taken them further, would have quickly revealed just how unsound her account was; but on the basis of "a purely recreational visit" he had made to Tahiti in 1925 and without any independent knowledge of the Samoans, he mistakenly found "Miss Mead's graphic picture of Polynesian free-love" to be "convincing," as he believed it fell into line "with the reports of earlier travellers" and was, so he thought (lacking any appreciation of the major differences between Eastern and Western Polynesia), "supported by Dr. Handy's evidence from the Marquesas." A. L. Kroeber, having read *Coming of Age in Samoa*, wrote to Mead on October 11, 1929, saying: "Somehow I have confidence that your diagnoses are right even when your facts are few or not printed in full. I think you have given us all a mark to shoot at." Then in 1931, he included Mead's "The Role of the Individual in Samoan Culture" in the much-used *Source Book in Anthropology*, which he and T. T. Waterman coedited.[15]

With this, the acceptance of Mead's conclusions about Samoa by Boas and his principal followers was complete. In that same year, chapter 7 of *Coming of Age in Samoa*, "Formal Sex Relations," appeared between excerpts from the writings of Bronislaw Malinowski and Sigmund Freud in V. F. Calverton's "Golden Treasury of Anthropology," *The Making of Man*, and Mead's "extraordinary, illuminating book," as George Dorsey called it in the *Nation* of September 5, 1928, was republished by Doubleday as a Blue Ribbon paperback. Never before in the history of anthropology had there been such a meteoric rise to fame. Edna St. Vincent Millay's Second Fig, which Mead, when a student of Franz Boas and Ruth Benedict at Barnard College, took as her motto, ends with the euphoric words: "Come and see my shining palace built upon the sand."

By the early 1930s, *Coming of Age in Samoa*, her "investigation into the erotic freedom of Samoan girls," as Clifford Geertz has approvingly called it, had truly become Margaret Mead's "shining palace," and this it remained for as long as she lived, until eventually the sand upon which it was built came to be seen for what it really is.[16]

In 1934, in her own best-seller, *Patterns of Culture*, which also had an approving introduction by Franz Boas, Ruth Benedict again made use of Mead's writing, claiming wholly inaccurately that in Samoa, adolescence was "quite without turmoil." By the end of the 1930s, *Coming of Age in Samoa* was "standard reading" in the "behavioral" and "human sciences," and the myth Mead had created about Samoa had become generally accepted. Indeed, as Harriot Jardine has recorded, for those who went through college in the United States in the 1930s, *Coming of Age in Samoa* "was not only required reading but a revered classic of universal truths."[17]

So much was this the case that in 1939, when reviewing her anthropological career that had begun with her fieldwork in Samoa, Mead felt able to claim that "the battle which we once had to fight with the whole battery at our command, with the most fantastic and startling examples we could muster, is won." That same year, she received a National Achievement Award from a committee of which Eleanor Roosevelt was a member, and in 1940, she was awarded her first honorary doctorate. Margaret Mead was on her way to becoming an American icon.[18]

In 1949, *Coming of Age in Samoa* was published as a Mentor paperback in the New American Library of World Literature. With a colorfully inaccurate illustration on its front cover and priced at only 60 cents, it sold exceptionally well. By 1962, there had been fourteen reprintings. In her introduction of July 9, 1949, to this Mentor paperback, Mead made an emphatic claim for the scholarly standing of the research she had carried out on Boas's behalf: "To the extent that an anthropologist records the whole picture of any way of life, that record cannot fade." And in a similar vein, in another preface of December 1952, she wrote of the "extraordinary historical accident" by which the girls of whom she had written in *Coming of Age in Samoa* had been given "an enduring existence."[19]

By this time, *Coming of Age in Samoa* had become known throughout the English-speaking world, having been published in Great Britain in 1943 as a Pelican paperback. In January 1950, in a profile of Margaret Mead in the London *Observer*, it was said of *Coming of Age in Samoa* that "nothing quite like it had ever been done before." This is most certainly true. Dr. Mead had "proved," it was asserted without any discussion of the evidence, "that it was culture, not physiology, which determined the calmness or explosiveness of adolescence." By midcentury, then, Mead's categorical conclusion of 1928 had become for knowledgeable men and women something that, having been "proved," could be dependably believed in. Through the rhetoric of Boas, Benedict, and Mead, a major anthropological myth had been firmly established not only among the general public but throughout the discipline of anthropology as well. For example, in 1948, in his influential textbook, *Man and His Works: The Science of Cultural An-*

*thropology*, Melville Herskovits, a professor of anthropology at North-western University, asserted on the basis of Mead's Samoan research that the "emotional reactions" of adolescence are "culturally, not biologically, determined." And in 1951, E. E. Evans-Pritchard, a professor of social anthropology at the University of Oxford, singled out *Coming of Age in Samoa* as "a good example of the single-problem kind of study," written by "a highly intelligent woman" who had shown that in Samoa there was no crisis or stress during adolescence and that it was one of the ambitions of adolescent Samoan girls to live with "many lovers as long as possible."[20]

The uncritical acceptance of Mead's writings on Samoa in the anthropological texts of the 1930s (in publications by George Murdock, Raymond Firth, Irving Hallowell, and others) continued throughout the 1950s (as for example in all editions of Ralph Beals and Harry Hoijer's *An Introduction to Anthropology*, recognized by Walter Goldschmidt as having been one of "the most widely used of all anthropological textbooks"; in John Honigmann's *Culture and Personality* of 1954; and in Adamson Hoebel's *Man in the Primitive World* of 1958).[21]

In her presidential address of 1960 to the American Anthropological Association, Mead characterized anthropology as a "science" that involved "a willingness to suspend judgment." Nonetheless, she continued to view *Coming of Age in Samoa* in the context of what she called "the absoluteness of monographs on primitive societies." These monographs, of which *Coming of Age in Samoa* was one, were, she averred in April 1961, "like well-painted portraits of the famous dead" and "would stand forever for the edification and enjoyment of future generations, forever true because no truer picture could be made of what was gone." She was conscious, she added, "of the historical caprice which had selected a handful of young girls on a tiny island to stand forever like the lovers on Keats' Grecian urn."[22]

There was thus obviously no basis at all for reconsidering Mead's account of the sexual mores of the Samoans. In her *Male and Female* of 1948, she had described Samoa as one of the "best-studied examples" of "premarital freedom." Fifteen years later, in her introduction of April 15, 1961, to the Pelican edition of *Male and Female*, she noted that if she had been writing this book in the early 1960s rather than in the late 1940s, she would have laid "more emphasis on Man's specific biological inheritance from earlier human forms." This was largely due to the friendship she had formed in 1954 with the eminent ethologist Konrad Lorenz, whose photograph she had on the wall of her office in the American Museum of Natural History. However, this recognition by Mead in 1961 of "man's specific biological inheritance" did not lead to any reconsideration of her conclusion of 1928 that "we cannot make any explanations" of adolescent behavior in terms of the process of adolescence itself, this being the doctrine on which her anthropological reputation was based.[23]

Indeed, in June 1972, her retort to Samoan university students who, by this time, were vociferously insisting that her account was in outright error, was to assert that to revise *Coming of Age in Samoa* "would be impossible." "It must remain," she wrote, "as all anthropological works must remain, exactly as it was written, true to what I saw in Samoa and what I was able to convey of what I saw." Thus, from the time of its first publication in the fall of 1928 until Dr. Mead's death fifty years later, no part of the "scientific classic" on which her reputation as an anthropologist was primarily based was revised in any way whatsoever. Instead, even the typographical errors that had crept into the text of 1928 were repeated in edition after edition after edition, with no recognition at all being given to the mounting evidence that in *Coming of Age in Samoa*, the sexual mores of the Samoans had been fundamentally misreported.[24]

By this time Dr. Mead had become, in the eyes of her colleagues, "truly the most famous and influential anthropologist in the world." In 1969, *Time* magazine dubbed her "Mother to the World," declaring that *Coming of Age in Samoa*, with its "almost lyrical prose," was based on "solid proof." This continued without exception to be the assessment of *Coming of Age in Samoa* in countless textbooks and encyclopedias, including David Hunter and Phillip Whitten's *Encyclopedia of Anthropology* of 1976 and the *Encyclopedia Americana* of 1978.[25]

In 1975, Dr. Mead was elected to the National Academy of Sciences "with one of the highest votes ever recorded in an Academy election." In 1976, she became president of the American Association for the Advancement of Science, as had Boas before her. In the words of her biographer, Jane Howard, she had become "indisputably the most publicly celebrated scientist in America." At the time of her death on November 15, 1978, her fictitious sexual utopia *Coming of Age in Samoa*, with its approving foreword by Franz Boas, was still by far the most celebrated and influential of her many books. In 1982, Melvin Konner, for whom Mead was "one of the greatest of all social scientists," gave it as his view that "if she had become the first such scientist to win the Nobel Prize in Medicine and Physiology," this would have "done credit to the Swedish Academy." A huge impact crater on the planet Venus, measuring 175 miles across, has been named after her.[26]

In *The Republic*, Plato wondered if it might be possible to contrive a convenient story or magnificent myth that would carry conviction with the whole community. It was just such a myth that Margaret Mead created in *Coming of Age in Samoa*, and although it was based on entirely false information derived directly from her hoaxing on the island of Ofu on March 13, 1926, this myth, after *Coming of Age in Samoa* had been vouched for by Franz Boas, Bronislaw Malinowski, Ruth Benedict, and other cognoscenti, came to carry conviction with a whole community of anthropological and other cognitively deluded believers, in America as elsewhere in the world. Such magnificent myths, once a sufficient number of individuals have come fervently to believe in them, achieve an aura of invincible propriety and are defended, when challenged, with the utmost vehemence. This was the case when Mead's demonstrably erroneous conclusions about Samoa were seriously questioned for the first time early in 1983. Indeed, before the year was out, the scientific standing of Margaret Mead's Samoan research had become the ruling cause célèbre of twentieth-century anthropology.[27]

# Afterword

IN 1939, WHEN MARGARET MEAD was writing in New York of
how the ideological "battle" she had fought since beginning her
fieldwork in Samoa in 1925 had been "won," I was a twenty-two-
year-old university student in Wellington, New Zealand, already a
keen admirer of her accomplishments and determined, if at all possible, to travel to the islands of Samoa to extend there, through inquiries
of my own, her research of some fourteen years earlier.[1]

At Victoria University College, I became a student of Dr. Ernest
Beaglehole, who had come to the college in 1937 after studying anthropology with Sapir at Yale, and had done fieldwork as a Bishop Museum Fellow on Pukapuka, an isolated atoll in the Cook Islands of
Central Polynesia. Beaglehole's approach to anthropology, as Thomas
Gladwin has noted, was "in many ways similar to that of Margaret
Mead," with his attention being focused, as was Mead's, on "the shaping of personality by the totality of expectations and pressures exerted
on and communicated to a person by other persons sharing the same
culture." In the late 1930s, Ernest Beaglehole imparted this approach
to me at Victoria University College while extolling the virtues of Dr.
Margaret Mead's *Coming of Age in Samoa.* I soon became an enthusiastic proponent of cultural determinism, and in my "Anatomy of
Mind" of September 1938, I echoed Franz Boas and Margaret Mead, declaring that "the aims and desires that determine behavior" are all derived from "the social environment."[2]

In his "Polynesian Anthropology Today," published in the *American Anthropologist* in 1937, Ernest Beaglehole noted that although
Margaret Mead's studies had "adequately covered" Manu'a in Eastern
Samoa, there remained "other islands of the Samoan group" and that
"in order to study pattern and pattern variation in one of the largest
and most interesting groups in Western Polynesia," there was a "vital
need for studies at least from Upolu and Savai'i." From 1920 onward,

the islands of Upolu and Savai'i had been under New Zealand administration in the Mandated Territory of Western Samoa, and so in 1939,
encouraged by Ernest Beaglehole, I applied to become a schoolteacher
in Upolu in the hope of being able to confirm and extend Dr. Mead's
findings of 1925–1926 by fieldwork of my own in Western Samoa.
When I sailed from Wellington for Apia on April 9, 1940, I was embarking, though I had no notion of it at the time, on an involvement
with the Samoan writings of Margaret Mead that was to become, in
the words of the song of Guiderius in Shakespeare's *Cymbeline*, my
"worldly task."[3]

So complete was my acceptance of Dr. Mead's Samoan writings on
my arrival in Upolu that in my early inquiries, I dismissed or ignored
all evidence that ran counter to her findings. Indeed, it was not until
after I had become fluent in the Samoan language, had been adopted
into a Samoan family, and, having been given a *mānaia* title, had begun attending chiefly courts, or *fono mānu*, that I became fully aware
of the extent of the discordance between Mead's account and the realities that I was regularly witnessing. When I left Samoa in November
1943, after a stay of over three and one-half years, it had become apparent to me, after prolonged inquiry, that Mead's depiction of Samoa
was gravely defective in numerous ways and that her account of the
sexual mores of the Samoans was in outright error.

Back in New Zealand, while waiting to sail for England as a member
of the Royal New Zealand Naval Volunteer Reserve, I informed Ernest
Beaglehole, as well as my other anthropological mentor, H. D. Skinner, director of the Otago Museum, of my misgivings about Dr. Mead's
account of Samoa. Neither of them took me seriously. That so famous
an anthropologist as Margaret Mead could have been so mistaken was
beyond belief, besides which, she was, in each instance, a valued personal friend. This was also my experience when, as a student in the
Department of Anthropology at the London School of Economics during the years 1946–1948, I reported my misgivings about Mead's account of Samoa to Professor Raymond Firth and others. By this time,
Dr. Mead's reputation was securely established, and Raymond Firth,
as he told Mead in 1950, had "a very real respect and admiration" for
her work.[4]

During 1946 and 1947, when I was in London, I made a thorough
study of the Samoan archives of the London Missionary Society. These
archives, which contain extensive information on Manu'a from 1830
onward, fully confirmed my view of Mead's research of 1925–1926;

however, in 1949 instead of returning to Samoa as I had planned, I began several years of fieldwork among the Iban of Borneo. With this diversion, which later took me to Cambridge University to complete my doctoral studies and then led me in new anthropological directions, I did not return to Samoa until 1965, after a crucially important meeting with Dr. Mead in November 1964.

In 1961, I had corresponded briefly with Dr. Mead about a student of hers who had come to work at the Australian National University under my supervision. Then, on August 27, 1964, I had delivered to me in Sydney Harbor, on the S.S. *Fairstar*, in which I had just returned to Australia after a year in England, a cable that read: "Passing through Australia November. Discussion of Samoa possible then. Regards Margaret Mead." In my reply, I informed Dr. Mead of my intention to resume fieldwork in Samoa in 1965 and added, "I would greatly appreciate being able to discuss with you certain of the conclusions you reached following your researches in Manu'a in 1925–26." Dr. Mead and I did have this discussion during a meeting of two hours and forty minutes in my study in the Research School of Pacific Studies at the Australian National University on the afternoon of Tuesday, November 10, 1964.[5]

Throughout our wide-ranging discussion, it was evident that Dr. Mead, since leaving Manu'a in April 1926, had had a set of absolutely assured beliefs about the sexual mores of the Samoans that she had elaborated in *Coming of Age in Samoa* and other of her writings. Yet, while continuing confidently to avow these beliefs, she was, at the same time, obviously taken aback by the detailed ethnographic and historical evidence with which I presented her, all of which indicated that the conclusions she had reached in *Coming of Age in Samoa* were in error. Indeed, as Lola Romanucci-Ross has recorded, a few days later, when she was alone with Mead in Rabaul, Mead admitted that this evidence "had proven her wrong." I told Dr. Mead in a letter written on the day after our discussion:

> It is plain to me that our conclusions about the realities of adolescent and sexual behavior in Samoa are fundamentally at variance. For my part I propose (as in the past) to proceed with my research with as meticulous an objectivity as I can muster. This, I would suppose, is going to lead to the publication of conclusions different from those reached by you, but I would very much hope that, however we may disagree, there should be no bad feeling between us. You have my assurance that I shall strive towards this end.[6]

The concluding sentence in Dr. Mead's reply of December 2, 1964, was the exemplary statement: "Anyway, what is important is the work." I was able to return to this work at the end of 1965. From January 1966 to January 1968, from my research base in Sa'anapu on the south coast of Upolu, where I had also worked in the 1940s, I was able to investigate further all of the issues I had discussed with Dr. Mead in November 1964. Then in September 1967, I made a twelve-day visit to Manu'a. Fa'apua'a had already gone to live in Hawaii, but I was able to discuss life as it was in Manu'a in 1926 with numerous individuals who were adults at the time of Mead's visit and who had clear memories of that period. From their detailed testimony about the sexual mores of Manu'a in the 1920s, there could be no doubt that Dr. Mead's account of these sexual mores in *Coming of Age in Samoa* was comprehensively in error, but I remained totally mystified about how an error of such magnitude could possibly have been made. At no stage did I conceal from Dr. Mead the results of my inquiries into the ethnographic issues we had discussed in 1964. Thus, on March 20, 1969, in informing her of the data I had assembled from court records on the incidence of rape in Samoa, I wrote:

> There is ample evidence that rape behavior occurred in the 1920s, just as it occurs today. For this, and a range of comparable reasons, I am not in agreement with your depiction of sexual behavior in Samoa as "a light and pleasant dance" and as one of the "smoothest" adjustments "in the world." Indeed, I am greatly puzzled as to what evidence could have led you to this erroneous conclusion.

At this time there had been no suggestion, from any quarter, that Margaret Mead, during her fieldwork of 1925–1926 in Manu'a, might have been hoaxed.[7]

Dr. Mead made no reply to my letter of March 20, 1969. Then in 1972, despite having admitted in November 1964 that she had been "proven wrong," she totally rejected any prospect of revision by declaring that *Coming of Age in Samoa* "must remain exactly as it was written." With this declaration, there was every justification for writing a refutation of the demonstrably erroneous conclusion Dr. Mead had reached in *Coming of Age in Samoa*. However, because of other anthropological interests and academic responsibilities, it was not until March 1978 that I was able to turn to this task.[8]

In August 1978, after having made some headway, I wrote to Dr. Mead asking if she would like to see the draft of my discussion of the sexual mores of the Samoans, while warning her that it was "acutely critical" of the accounts she herself had given. In reply, I received a letter from New York dated September 14, 1978, in which I was informed by an assistant that Dr. Mead had "been ill" and that I would be notified if she had "an opportunity to read and comment on my manuscript." I heard no more from Dr. Mead's office until after her death in November 1978. With this, I turned for a time to other work, and the first draft of my refutation was not completed until August 1981.[9]

In her addendum of 1969 to the second edition of *Social Organization of Manu'a*, while admitting the "serious problem" of reconciling the "contradictions" between her reports and those of other observers, Dr. Mead proposed that it was just possible that Manu'a at the time of her fieldwork in 1925–1926 "might have represented a special variation of the Samoan pattern, a temporary felicitous relaxation" of the behaviors others had recorded. This was a possibility I still had to investigate. In September 1981, I returned to Western Samoa to submit my refutation to the critical scrutiny of Samoan scholars. I then undertook detailed research in the archives of the High Court of American Samoa and the manuscript holdings of the Bishop Museum in Honolulu on Manu'a and Tutuila in the 1920s. This research showed that no "special variation of the Samoan pattern" had existed at the time of Dr. Mead's fieldwork in Manu'a. By the end of October 1981, my research was complete, and on December 14, I accepted an offer from the syndics of Harvard University Press to publish what an external reader described as a book making a case "unique in anthropology."[10]

Just how widely known my refutation was destined to become became apparent when, on January 31, 1983, an article entitled "New Samoa Book Challenges Margaret Mead's Conclusions," appeared on the front page of the *New York Times* and was republished in newspapers throughout the world. Within a few months, the refutation contained in my book *Margaret Mead and Samoa: The Making and Unmaking of an Anthropological Myth* had given rise to what Dr. Paul Shankman, in opening the national conference "Margaret Mead: Legend and Controversy" in Boulder, Colorado, on October 15, 1983, described as "the greatest controversy in the history of anthropology." This was something I had not anticipated. My refutation of Mead's conclusions about Samoa had been written in the naive expectation that other anthropologists would acknowledge the needfulness of my attending to what Karl Popper called "the critical method of error elimination" in the case of Samoa. I could not have been more mistaken. In the preface to my refutation, I emphasized that my concern was *"not* with Margaret Mead personally, nor with any aspect of her ideas or activities that lie beyond the ambit of her writings on Samoa." Yet during the impassioned controversy that followed its publication, the scientific purpose of my refutation was, for the most part, quite ignored.[11]

What I had not realized was the extent to which Margaret Mead had become, in the words of a professor of anthropology of the University of California, "the Mother-Goddess of American Anthropology." Thus, my refutation, instead of being viewed as a scientifically warranted correction of Dr. Mead's conclusions about Samoa, came to be thought of by many American anthropologists as a personal attack on this "Mother-Goddess." This attitude was directly linked to the way in which Mead's conclusions of 1928 had come to be believed in as proven truths by a great many American anthropologists. In the face of contrary evidence, there is, as John Ziman has put it, "a natural psychological tendency for each individual to go along with the crowd, and to cling to a previously successful paradigm." For over fifty years, or two generations, Mead's conclusions, which had never been seriously challenged in print, had been central to the belief system of American cultural anthropology, being viewed as one of its glories and a solid proof of Boasian culturalism. Then, early in 1983, without warning and for all to witness, an entire edifice of belief was revealed as being without empirical foundation. For many American anthropologists, it was, as Theodore Schwartz has termed it, "a seismic event," and as they surveyed the fallen masonry, the embarrassment of those whose beliefs had been so rudely shaken soon turned to fury, and in no time at all, as Harriot Jardine has recorded, there were many who "seemed willing to tear Freeman from limb to limb." Thus, from February 1983 onward, I was subjected to a highly emotional and, at times, flagrantly ad hominem campaign that reached its apogee in Chicago during the Eighty-Second Annual Meeting of the American Anthropological Association, when, on November 18, there was a special session (to which I was not invited) devoted to the evaluation of my refutation.[12]

The session, which was crowded, began conventionally enough with a series of formal presentations, but when the general discussion began, it degenerated into a delirium of vilification. One eyewitness described it as "a sort of grotesque feeding frenzy." Another wrote to me saying, "I felt I was in a room with 200 people ready to lynch you." And at the Annual Business Meeting of the American Anthropological Association on the evening of November 18, 1983, a formal motion denouncing my refutation as "poorly written, unscientific, irresponsible and misleading" was moved, put to the vote, and passed.[13]

That the members of a professional association could seek to dispose of a major scientific and scholarly issue in this undisguisedly political way, attempting to dismiss, by a show of hands, a refutation based on a cogent array of factual evidence, is a striking demonstration of the extraordinary way in which belief can come to dominate the thinking of scholars and scientists and of how a hallowed doctrine can blind its devotees to empirical reality. Indeed, with the authentication of how Margaret Mead came to her erroneous conclusions about Samoa after being hoaxed by Fa'apua'a and Fofoa on the island of Ofu in March 1926, the principal significance of the impassioned controversy over my now fully vindicated refutation of 1983 is the light it sheds on the way in which a set of beliefs, once implanted, impels even highly educated individuals to cling fervently to doctrines that have been shown to have no scholarly or scientific basis.

In both science and scholarship, as Charles S. Peirce once put it, "any inquirer must be ready at all times to dump his whole cartload of beliefs the moment experience is set against them." Yet it is precisely against this ideal of enlightened action that belief militates. As Edmund Burke long ago observed, "when men have suffered their imaginations to be long affected with any idea, it so wholly engrosses them as to shut out by degrees almost every other and to break down every partition of the mind which would confine it." And added to this, there is a marked reluctance to admit to having entertained error, for humans, in the words of Leo Tolstoy, "can seldom discern even the simplest and most obvious truth if it be such as obliges them to admit the falsity of conclusions they have formed, perhaps with much difficulty—conclusions of which they are proud, which they have taught to others and on which they have built their lives." It is in these terms, then, that the excesses that occurred at the Eighty-Second Annual Meeting of the American Anthropological Association are to be understood.[14]

There is certainly abundant evidence that from the 1920s onward, American cultural anthropology has had many of the characteristics of a belief system, with Margaret Mead's *Coming of Age in Samoa* standing in the checkered history of cultural anthropology as a deeply instructive instance of the way in which human understanding can be misled by uncritical adherence to a cherished dogma rather than to the demanding discipline of impartially objective scholarly inquiry. As Garret Hardin has observed, dogmas become "silently built into the psyche so firmly that questioning them becomes, quite literally, unthinkable."[15]

In 1956, Leon Festinger and his colleagues, in *When Prophecy Fails*, drew attention to a key characteristic of the behavior of the devotees of belief systems. Their classic study showed that when a belief is held with "deep conviction," the presence of "undeniable disconfirmatory evidence" can lead to the belief in question being "maintained with new fervor." This reaction, most interestingly, was evinced by many American anthropologists from 1983 onward. At the national conference "Margaret Mead: Legend and Controversy" held in Boulder in 1983, it was affirmed that Dr. Mead's methods and influences had, as a result of my refutation, "emerged stronger than ever." In 1986, the late Professor Roy A. Rappaport of the University of Michigan, then president-elect of the American Anthropological Association, asserted in the *American Scholar* that *Coming of Age in Samoa* remained a "humane and liberating text"; that same year, president-elect of the Wenner-Gren Foundation for Anthropological Research, Professor Sydel Silverman of the City University of New York, declared in the *New York Times Book Review* that Margaret Mead's "message" in *Coming of Age in Samoa* was "as timely as ever." Only time will tell whether such credulous, not to say idolizing, attitudes will persist now that the exact details are known about how Margaret Mead, when just twenty-four years of age, was hoaxed on the island of Ofu on March 13, 1926. On past indications, I shall not be altogether surprised if they do. As Max Planck once noted, new realizations do not triumph by convincing their opponents but because these opponents eventually pass away and a new generation takes their place.[16]

Since 1983, Margaret Mead's Samoan research has become an anthropological cause célèbre. No fewer than eight books dealing either in whole or in part with Mead's Samoan research have been published. One of these is *The Samoan Reader* of 1990. Edited by Hiram Caton, it contains an account of the Samoan controversy to the year 1989. It appeared too soon, however, for the evidence of Fa'apua'a Fa'amū to be fully considered and before any study of Mead's papers in the Manuscript Division of the Library of Congress had been completed. Other books, such as those by Lowell Holmes, James Côté, and Adam Kuper, written in the absence of adequate historical research, are radically misleading. They all reach seriously misinformed conclusions about Mead's Samoan research by totally ignoring the indispensably important primary sources on which any scholarly account of this research must be based.[17]

Two studies based on manuscript sources have so far been published. They are by George Stocking and Martin Orans. In Stocking's insightful essay of 1989, there is a valuable if brief discussion of Mead's Samoan research, in which use is made of the papers of Mead and Boas. Stocking's purview, however, is narrow. For example, there is no mention of Mead's crucially important meeting with Dr. Edward Craighill Handy on her way to Samoa or of the extensive ethnological research for the Bishop Museum that Mead carried out in Manu'a. All that we are told of her stay in Honolulu—where, during her visit to the Bishop Museum, she was inexpertly briefed about Samoa by Dr. Handy—is that Honolulu was a place "where 'wandering mists' hid 'all signs of industrial civilization.'" Again, Stocking was not able to take into account the testimony of Fa'apua'a Fa'amū.[18]

Martin Orans has produced, from primary sources, a detailed account of one aspect of Mead's fieldwork in Manu'a. In his analysis of Mead's field notes, Orans has been able to demonstrate that various of the statements she made in her letters to Boas and in *Coming of Age in Samoa* are "totally contrary to her field data." Indeed, Orans has concluded that Mead's "profoundly unscientific" and "seriously flawed" work on Samoa is "filled with internal contradictions and grandiose claims to knowledge that she could not possibly have had." If this is so (and Orans presents detailed evidence to show that it is), then the conclusions that Mead reached in her official report of April 1927 to the National Research Council cannot possibly have been correct. This, however, is an issue that Orans has avoided. Instead, he has come to the idiosyncratic conclusion that Mead's writings on Samoa are "so mistaken" that "she is not even wrong"![19]

About the unscientific nature of Mead's Samoan research, Orans and I, from our independent examinations of the relevant documents, are in substantial agreement. But Orans has gone on to assert that in making her claims about "the acceptability of premarital sex for unmarried adolescent females," Mead "knew better" and that "rather than being misled she is misleading." In other words, it is Oran's view that Mead's conclusions about adolescent sexual behavior in *Coming of Age in Samoa* and elsewhere involved deliberate falsification. This charge may appear warranted when one limits one's attention, as does Orans, to Mead's field notes and published texts. It cannot be sustained when her Samoan research is analyzed in its full historical context.[20]

Orans has told us that he is only concerned with the "appraisal" of Mead's Samoan fieldwork and not with any "appraisal" of Mead herself. This, however, is altogether too confined a frame of reference: *There can be no adequate understanding of the one without the other.* Nor can the course of Mead's Samoan fieldwork be understood without detailed consideration of her commitment to the ideology with which she operated in Samoa, that human behavior is wholly determined by cultural patterns. Equally, there must also be full consideration of her misleading briefing by Edward Craighill Handy about adolescent sexual behavior in Polynesia and her inordinate involvement, as far as her investigation of adolescent behavior was concerned, in ethnological research on behalf of the Bishop Museum. These important historical issues are completely ignored by Orans. He has not had access to all of the information contained in the testimony of Fa'apua'a Fa'amū. He has never visited Manu'a.

When all of the pertinent historical circumstances are taken into account, the notion that Margaret Mead engaged in deliberate falsification in the way suggested by Orans is seen to be baseless. Rather, after she had been hoaxed, she at once sought, on the basis of the false information she had been given by Fofoa and Fa'apua'a, to solve the problem Boas had assigned to her by resorting, in accordance with her training at Columbia University, to the theory that human behavior is determined by "cultural patterns." There can be no doubt that this way of proceeding involved such psychological mechanisms as denial and rationalization, but this does not amount to deliberate falsification. If Margaret Mead had indeed been involved in deliberate falsification, she would never have made her papers available for public scrutiny in the Library of Congress. A Boasian ideologue she may have been; a deliberate cheat about major anthropological issues she was not. Rather, Margaret Mead's Samoan research will go down in the history of the behavioral sciences as an example of the way in which a highly intelligent investigator can be blinded to empirical reality by an uncritical commitment to a scientifically unsound assumption.[21]

It was in 1888, at the very outset of his anthropological career, that Franz Boas declared that "not only our ability and knowledge but also the manner and ways of our feeling and thinking [are] the result of our upbringing as individuals and our history as a people." After she had been to Samoa, this unevolutionary notion, which is basic to Boasian culturalism, was repeated by Margaret Mead in her claim that "human nature" is "the rawest, most undifferentiated of raw material." Then, in 1965, at the University of Chicago, Clifford Geertz outdid both Boas and Mead in his claim that "our ideas, our values, our acts, even our emotions are, like our nervous system itself, cultural products"—this being the most egregiously absurd formulation of the tabula rasa assumption of Boasian culturalism to be found anywhere in the literature of anthropology. Moreover, some eight years after the publication in New York of Wilder Penfield and Theodore Rasmussen's *The Cerebral Cortex of Man: A Clinical Study of Localization of Function*, it was an unthinking claim that entirely ignored the fundamental advances that, by that time, had been made in the neurosciences, genetics, and other of the life sciences.[22]

As Geertz has recorded in his 1995 work, *After the Fact*: "The first index entry nowadays in books surveying the field is often: Anthropology, crisis of." How could this possibly have happened within living memory of the year in which Margaret Mead, having posed the question "What is human nature?" had claimed to have decisively won the battle for Boasian culturalism?[23]

The answer is that Boasian culturalism has been rendered ineffectual and obsolete by fundamentally significant advances, since the 1930s, in all of the life sciences. Many of these findings are integral to the understanding of human behavior, yet cultural anthropologists have conspicuously failed to take them into account. Thus, in *After the Fact* (the index of which contains twenty entries for "Anthropology, crisis of"), there is no mention whatsoever of evolutionary theory, of primatology, of human ethology, of the cognitive neurosciences, or of any of the other life sciences, the findings of which during recent decades have been crucially relevant to any genuine discipline of anthropology.

It was as late as 1934 that Franz Boas asserted that "the genetic elements which may determine personality" were "altogether irrelevant as compared with the powerful influence of the cultural environment," and in 1939, three years before his death in 1942, he gave it as his opinion that there was "little doubt" that as time went on "the study of genetics" would wear down. He was massively mistaken. By 1942, Oswald Avery and his colleagues were already actively exploring the characteristics of DNA, and, since the determination of its three-dimensional configuration by Francis Crick and James Watson in 1953, an event ranked by John Maynard Smith as "the most important discovery in biology since Darwin," the biological sciences have effloresced in the most prodigious way. "We have witnessed," as Ernst Mayr has recorded, "unprecedented breakthroughs in genetics, cellular biology and neuroscience." Never before have there been such fundamental advances in our understanding of the mechanisms of life.[24]

Further, during these same decades, there have been fundamental advances in evolutionary biology. Central to these is what John Tooby and Leda Cosmides have called "the modern technical theory of evolution," consisting of "the logically derivable set of causal principles that necessarily govern the dynamics of reproducing systems." This phase of development began with the publication in 1964 of W. D. Hamilton's now-classic paper, "The Genetical Evolution of Social Behaviour" and, in 1966, of George C. Williams's *Adaptation and Natural Selection*. In 1989, Irenäus Eibl-Eibesfeldt published his monumental 848-page *Human Ethology*, which Robert Provine has rightly described as a "handbook of human nature." This was followed in 1992 by *The Adapted Mind: Evolutionary Psychology and the Generation of Culture*, with contributions by various members of the Human Behavior and Evolution Society and, in 1995, by *The Cognitive Neurosciences* (1466 pages), in which Cosmides and Tooby present evidence to show that the human brain (which is the organ of behavior) is "an information-processing device which was designed by the evolutionary process."[25]

On July 17, 1990, the president of the United States proclaimed the 1990s to be the Decade of the Brain. The decade was ushered in by the publication of Paul MacLean's book *The Triune Brain in Evolution*, in which it is shown that the human brain contains three phylogenetically given formations—the reptilian, the paleomammalian, and the neomammalian—which both anatomically and biochemically reflect an ancestral relationship to reptiles, early mammals, and late mammals.[26]

The principal feature of the paleomammalian brain is the limbic system, which is primarily concerned with visceral processes and the emotions. It is in this phylogenetically ancient part of our brain, which is virtually identical with the limbic systems of our primate cousins, the chimpanzees, and which evolved long before the emergence of cultural adaptations, that much of our human nature is physiologically programmed.

Thus, Joseph LeDoux and his colleagues have recently shown that the amygdala (which is part of what MacLean calls the limbic system) has to do, in all species that have an amygdala, with fear responses. According to LeDoux, "The remarkable fact is that at the level of behavior, defense against danger is achieved in many different ways in different species, yet the amygdala's role is constant," and has been "maintained through diverse branches of evolutionary development." The amygdala, then, is one of the "emotion systems" of the human brain, "each of which," as LeDoux has put it, "evolved for a different functional purpose and each of which gives rise to different kinds of emotions." Further, "these systems operate outside of consciousness" and "constitute the emotional unconscious." The amygdala in Homo sapiens is thus in no sense the "product" of recent social or cultural conditioning. These findings make arcane nonsense of Geertz's notion, following Boas and Mead, that "our emotions, like our nervous system itself" are "cultural products." Rather, as Roger Shepard noted in his contribution to *Characterizing Human Psychological Adaptations* (1997), certain elements of human cognition and behavior are phylogenetically given. As W. D. Hamilton has precisely put it, "The *tabula* of human nature was never *rasa* and it is now being read."[27]

Even more important are the frontal lobes of our brains, often described as "the neocortex of the limbic system," the seat of consciousness and of the human capacity to make choices. This capacity, as the research of J. Z. Young, John Tyler Bonner, Antonio Damasio, and others has demonstrated, is *biologically given*. As Richard Passingham, one of the foremost researchers in the field has put it: "Human beings are capable of voluntary action in the most restrictive sense; that is, voluntary action involving the conscious comparison of alternative courses of action."[28]

The human capacity to make choices, from which human cultures spring, is, then, biologically given. And further, in the light of recent research, it is evident that the two main mechanisms that have operated in the course of human evolution and history are the related mechanisms of natural selection and choice, for it was natural selection that produced the brain in the frontal lobes, where the capacity to make choices is located.

What evolutionary biology also tells us is that all humans, belonging as they do to the same species, have the same phylogenetically given human nature, with their differing cultures having come into being during quite recent times, through the varying exercise of choice. Our biologically given capacity for choice is then of enormous human significance. Further, as R. J. Rose has noted, "We inherit dispositions, not destinies. Life outcomes are consequences of lifetimes of behavior choices. The choices are guided by our dispositional tendencies, and the tendencies find expression within environmental opportunities that we actively create." Thus, as Matt McGue and Thomas Bouchard have remarked, "the heritability of psychological function does not imply the genetic determinism of human behavior."[29]

Toward the end of Clifford Geertz's *After the Fact*, there occurs the despairingly relativistic cri de coeur: "There are, indeed, no master plots." Like Boas and Mead before him, Geertz is mistaken. As Daniel Dennett has recently put it: "The fundamental core of contemporary Darwinism, the theory of DNA-based reproduction and evolution, is now beyond dispute among scientists"; and in the words of George C. Williams, "There is no aspect of human life for which an understanding of evolution is not a vital necessity." It is entirely understandable, then, that Boasian culturalism, with its antievolutionary ideology, has run aground in the 1990s and that Nancy Scheper-Hughes has written of Geertz's book: "From this retrospective by one of the master anthropologists of our time, it may be deduced that the end of modern 'realist' anthropology has arrived, and that something new is waiting in the wings."[30]

What is clearly waiting in the wings is an anthropology that takes note of the tested findings of evolutionary biology and of evolutionary psychology, and, on this basis, studies the social and cultural adaptations of the human species.[31]

As Jerome Barkow, Leda Cosmides, and John Tooby note in *The Adapted Mind*:

> Culture is not causeless and disembodied. It is generated in rich and intricate ways by information-processing mechanisms situated in human minds. These mechanisms are, in turn, the elaborately sculpted product of the evolutionary process. Therefore, to understand the relationship between biology and culture one must first understand the architecture of our evolved psychology.

Further, in the light of the research of the past half century or so, there is now no mystery regarding the primordial origin of human culture. Through prehistoric archaeology and paleoanthropology, we can trace its development beyond the horizon of recorded history to a time when our ancestors were wandering the savannah with a culture little more elaborate than that of existing chimpanzee groups. Yet we can be sure, in evolutionary terms, that these hominids from whom we are descended possessed a phylogenetically given nature, just as do chimpanzees. It follows from this that all human cultures, past and present, are the historical creations of human populations, all of whose members possessed, as they still possess, a phylogenetically given primate nature and, further, that this primate nature, which is principally programmed in the limbic systems of their paleomammalian brains, is *ever present*, in all human groups, *coexisting with their cultural institutions.*[32]

In 1965, Clifford Geertz defiantly declared: "There is no such thing as human nature independent of culture." This is most certainly true. What can be said at the end of the twentieth century is that it is equally true that "there is no such thing as culture independent of human nature."[33]

It was Margaret Mead's view that anthropology would evolve into "an increasingly exact science." It is now evident that the way in which this is likely to be achieved is by the emergence of *a new anthropological paradigm in which full recognition is given to both biological and cultural variables and to their complex interaction.*[34]

In 1987, in an editorial in *Science*, Daniel E. Koshland Jr. declared: "the debate on nature and nurture in regard to behavior is basically over. Both are involved, and we are going to have to live with that complexity." This is unquestionably the case, and at the end of the twentieth century, it is crystal clear that anthropology, of necessity, must operate within an interactionist paradigm. And this, ineluctably, involves the abandonment of Boasian culturalism, which is now a completely superseded belief system. In adolescent behavior, as in *all* human behavior, *both* "physiological conditions" *and* "cultural conditions" (to use Boas's terms) are *always involved*, in varying degree: It is *never* "nature *or* nurture" but always "nature *and* nurture."[35]

The time is thus conspicuously at hand for an anthropological paradigm that gives full recognition to the radical importance of *both* cultural and biological variables, and of their past and ongoing interaction.

*To enact this is the principal task of the anthropology of the twenty-first century.*

# Appendix:
# From the Correspondence of
# Franz Boas and
# Margaret Mead, 1925–1926

This appendix contains ten letters, four of them by Franz Boas and six of them by Margaret Mead. These letters document the course of Mead's research in Manu'a. They are listed in chronological order and, in each instance, the full text is given. (Mead's misspelling of Samoan words has been corrected.)

(1) Franz Boas's letter to Margaret Mead of July 14, 1925, written in New York on the eve of her departure for Samoa. In this letter, Boas, who had already instructed Mead not to engage in ethnological research in Samoa, mentions again the "practical danger" that "regular ethnological questions" might become "so attractive" to her that she might be tempted to slight her principal task, which was the study of heredity and environment in relation to adolescence.

July 14, 1925

My dear Margaret,

I suppose the time is drawing near when you want to leave. Let me impress on you once more first of all that you should not forget your health. I am sure you will be careful in the tropics and try to adjust yourself to conditions and not work when it is too hot and moist in the day time. If you find that you cannot stand the climate do not be ashamed to come back. There are plenty of other places where you could solve the same problem on which you propose to work.

I am sure you have thought over the question carefully, but there are one or two points which I have in mind and to which I would like to call your attention, even if you have thought of them before.

One question that interests me very much is how the young girls react to the restraints of custom. We find very often among ourselves during the period of adolescence a strong rebellious spirit that may be expressed in sullenness or in sudden outbursts. In other individuals there is a weak submission which, however, is accompanied by repressed rebellion that may make itself felt in peculiar ways, perhaps in a desire for solitude which is really an expression of desire for freedom, or otherwise in forced participation in social affairs in order to drown the mental troubles. I am not at all clear in my mind in how far similar conditions may occur in primitive society and in how far the desire for independence may be simply due to our modern conditions and to a more strongly developed individualism.

Another point in which I am interested is the excessive bashfulness of girls in primitive society. I do not know whether you will find it there. It is characteristic of Indian girls in most tribes, and often not only in their relations with outsiders, but frequently within the narrow circle of the family. They are often afraid to talk and are very retiring before older people.

Another interesting question is that of crushes among girls. For the older ones you might give special attention to the occurrence of romantic love, which is not by any means absent so far as I have been able to observe, and which, of course, appears most strongly where the parents or society impose marriages which the girls may not want.

I presume your work will be of such a character that a great deal of what you are particularly interested in can be obtained only indirectly, and will leave a lot of time for other things. Here there is a practical danger that when this happens some of the regular ethnological questions may become so attractive to you that you may be tempted to slight the principal object of your trip. I wish you would always bear in mind that whatever you decide to do in addition to the principal object of your journey, the most important contribution that we hope you will make will be the psychological attitude of the individual under the pressure of the general pattern of culture. It is, of course, impossible to tell from here what the most promising lines of attack may be. I am, however, clear in my mind that anything that pertains to this subject will be of greatest importance for the methodological development of ethnological research. Such studies like that of the behavior of the individual artist to his or her work, his preferences, the character of his inventiveness, his dependence or independence of prevailing patterns, such as Ruth Bunzel in the puebloes and Haeberlin on the Northwest coast tried to solve, are the kind of thing I mean. The same problem of course will appear in the attitude towards members of the family, in religious affairs and so on. I believe you have read Malinowsky's paper in *Psyche* on the behavior of individuals in the family in New Guinea. I think he was too much influenced by Freudianism, but the problem which he had in mind is one of those which I have in mind.

Good luck. I hope you will let us know soon how you are getting on. I trust that your trip will be successful in every way. Don't forget your health.

With kindest regards,

Yours very sincerely,

[Franz Boas]

(2) Margaret Mead's letter to Boas of October 11, 1925, informing him that she is proposing to work on the island of Ta'ū, Manu'a, while living in the "white household" of the U.S. Naval Dispensary; she asks Boas to write to her at once if he feels that she should not do this and that it is "not right" for her to "neglect any opportunity" to increase her "knowledge of the language and intimacy with the people."[1]

Pago Pago, Tutuila, Samoa,
October 11, 1925

Dear Dr. Boas,

It is not possible for me to tell you in this letter of my immediate plans because they are dependent upon the arrival of the Australia boat a day after this letter goes to you. But I want to tell you in some detail of my decisions for the next six months' work so that if you have any suggestions to give I may receive them before I actually put my plans into effect.

I have now visited almost every village on this island. They are divided into two types; those which are along the bus line, and those which are practically inaccessible except by difficult mountain trails or by water. The villages along the bus line have been very much influenced by American goods and American visitors and do not present a typical picture of the original culture. The villages off the bus line present two disadvantages; they are very difficult to reach and very small. No one of them boasts more than four or five adolescents, and so the difficulty of getting from one to the other makes them impossible places to work. To find enough adolescents I would have to spend all my time climbing mountains or tossing about in the surf in an open boat, both extremely arduous and time consuming activities. There are only two villages which are really large enough for my purposes: Pago Pago and Leone, and both of these are overrun with missionaries, stores and various intrusive influences.

Because of these disadvantages I have decided to go to Ta'ū, one of the three small islands in the Manu'a group about 100 miles from here. The Manu'a islands are included in the American Concession and a government steamer goes back and forth every three weeks. They are much more primitive and unspoiled than any part of Samoa, being equalled in this respect only by part of western Savai'i. There are no white people on the island except the Navy man (and his wife) in charge of the Dispensary and two corps men. There is a large village, or rather a cluster of four villages there within a few minutes walk of each other. The chief, Tufele, who is also District Governor of Manu'a, was educated in Honolulu and speaks excellent English, and is probably the most co-operative chief in American Samoa.

---

[1]All letters from Mead to Boas courtesy of the Institute for Intercultural Studies, Inc., New York.

Furthermore this is the only place where I can live in a white household and still be right in the midst of these villages all the time. This is the point about which I am particularly anxious to have your advice. If I lived in a Samoan house with a Samoan family, I might conceivably get into a little more intimate touch with that particular family. But I feel that such advantage as would be reaped would be more than offset by the loss in efficiency due to the food and the nerve-wracking conditions of living with half a dozen people in the same room, in a house without walls, always sitting on the floor and sleeping in constant expectation of having a pig or a chicken thrust itself upon one's notice. This is not an easy climate to work in; I find my efficiency diminished about one half as it is, and I believe it would be cut in two again if I had to live for weeks on end in a Samoan house. It is not possible to get a house of my own, which would of course be optimum. Of course if I lived in a Samoan household I would have to speak Samoan every minute and my progress in the language would be considerably accelerated. You may feel that it is not right for me to neglect any opportunity to increase my knowledge of the language and intimacy with the people. If you do will you please write me at once, as I have arranged to live with the Holts on Ta'ū and I would have to make several alterations in my plans and equipment.

By the time I go to Ta'ū I will have a fairly comprehensive survey of the life of Samoan girls, ceremonies and observances surrounding birth and marriage, her theoretical functioning in the communities and the code of conduct which governs her activity. In the course of gathering this material I have, of course, collected a good deal of information of value ethnologically but not bearing with particular force upon my problem. However, this other material will be valuable and worth publishing, and I am in some doubt as to how much time I should give to checking it. Most of the observances which I am recording are still going on; my informants are of the chiefly class and well informed. How much checking would you consider it necessary and legitimate for me to do?

My knowledge of the language is progressing more slowly than at first. I take texts several hours a day, and have one definite lesson, and then prospect about for chances of conversation. For the next five or six weeks I hope to divide my time between a Samoan girls boarding school where no English is spoken and a half caste family in Leone where I can hear Samoan most of the time. These two places are only three miles apart. But I can't be sure about going to the school until the teacher returns from Australia next week.

I am quite well and standing the climate with commendable fortitude.

My very best wishes,

Sincerely yours,

Margaret Mead

(3) Margaret Mead's letter of November 1, 1925, written in Pago Pago, American Samoa, to Dr. Edward Craighill Handy, senior ethnologist of the

Bernice P. Bishop Museum, Honolulu, on the eve of her departure for Manu'a. In this letter, Margaret Mead agrees to work on an "ethnology of Manu'a" that would, she had been assured in Honolulu, be published as a bulletin of the Bernice P. Bishop Museum.[2]

November 1, 1925

My dear Dr. Handy,

This next week will complete my formal study of the language, and the following week I go to Manu'a. All the villages on this island which are large enough for my problem are too greatly under foreign influence, so I have decided to go to Ta'ū. This is the island where Tufele the governor who was educated in Honolulu lives, and I expect to get a good deal of help from him. I am going to live in the Naval Dispensary there, as living in a Samoan family for seven months seems hardly practical, in the wet season. And there is the additional difficulty that for my problem I must not have too definite rank. I have been living in Vaitogi with the County Chief, who adopted me and gave me the ceremonial *taupou* name for the village of Vaitogi. Working thus under the shadow of the throne was excellent as long as I wanted only practice in the language and straight ethnological information, because I had the enthusiastic help and co-operation of all the chiefs and *tulāfales* in the village. But my status was such that I could never cross the village alone, nor enter the house of a commoner. So for my adolescent girl study, I've got to devise ways and means of not being so thoroughly absorbed into the aristocratic structure. It's too confining. I have enjoyed living *fa'aSamoa* very much and found it very comfortable except in wet weather. Then the fact that all the beasties tramp merrily in and out of the house, is a decided drawback.

I remember your wondering somewhat discouragingly if I could contrive a stunt to intrigue my Samoan hosts or guests, in as much as I could neither dance or sing. But, there is one thing which the Samoans like even better, that is talking. And learning to use the three-fold courtesy language is my "stunt," and a frightfully nerve-wracking one at that, as half a dozen ancients listen for misapplied pronouns, or the use of a *tulāfale*'s word to a chief.

I shall be able to cover the subjects of birth, childhood and its training, games, the simpler domestic arts practised by the girls, marriage, relationship system, its tabus and obligations; rank in its relation to the organization of the household, and to the ceremonies of birth, marriage and death, and the routine of festival and daily life. This leaves untouched mythology (and I haven't taken many folk tales in text because conversation is so sparse in them and that was what I needed), tattooing designs, cinet designs, weaving (which would be a study of two or three months at least), dancing and music and any additional work you might want done on the actual construction of houses and canoes. For religion I can't make any promises until I reach Ta'ū. All my questions leave me with my original impression that it was very sparsely developed here. Most of the functions previously exercised by the ghosts have been shifted to the Christian God with remarkably little effort. Before God came, the ghosts are reputed to have punished the infringement of tabus and so forth. The now extinct Tui Manu'a seems to have had many of the same prerogatives as the Tui Tonga and from all I hear of Manu'a custom, I think this will be a fruitful field.

I have been talking with some Upolu chiefs and apparently usage in the matter of government and rank differed greatly on Tutuila from the usage of Western Samoa. Do you suppose you'd have time to see whether Churchill's material covers Tutuila and Manu'a also? If it doesn't I shall attempt to pick up whatever seems in danger of passing out of knowledge.

There are a large number of cinet lashing patterns at use at the present day here in Tutuila, and I have obtained the names of the virtuosos in the art. Many of these are very complex and take hours to record from a distance of several feet below. Would the Museum be interested in paying one of these *tufuga* [craftsman] to make a series for its collection? They would be much easier to study in this form and to use for comparative work.

The dictionary continues to be a godsend.

With best wishes to Mrs. Handy and the members of the Museum staff.

I am, very sincerely yours,

Margaret Mead

(4) Boas's letter to Mead of November 7, 1925, in which he tells her to use her own judgment "in regard to the question of how best to keep in close contact with Samoan girls" and at the same time be in a position where she could "work advantageously," adding that he knew "from personal experience" how hard it was "to find time for serious work in a native house where there are constant interruptions of all sorts." (This letter did not reach Mead in Manu'a until early in January 1926.)

Columbia University in the City of New York,
Department of Anthropology
Nov. 7, 1925

Miss Margaret Mead,
Pago Pago,
Tutuila,
Samoa

My dear Margaret,
I have just returned from Europe and find your two letters of September 17th. and October 11th. It is very difficult for me to give advice in regard to the

question of your locating with the Holts in Ta'ū, or go to some other place. I am quite sure that you will use your own judgement in regard to the question of how best to keep in close contact with the Samoan girls and at the same time be in a position where you can work advantageously. I know from personal experience how hard it is to find time for serious work in a native house where there are constant interruptions of all sorts and I presume that if you are located with the Holts you will nevertheless be able to spend many hours in succession during the day or evening with the people. The only danger in such an arrangement is if the behavior of the whites interferes with close and friendly contact with the people on account of their own attitude, but I hardly think that is the case in that family. I have not yet had time to read your reports to Ruth Benedict because I'm just wading through all the accumulated material that has come in this summer.

I am fully aware that the subject that you have selected is a very difficult one and is the first serious attempt to enter into the mental attitude of a group in a primitive society. Great, of course, will be the satisfaction if you succeed in getting even part of what you would like to find and I believe that your success would mark a beginning of a new era of methodological investigation of native tribes. At the same time I trust you will not feel discouraged if the results are coming slowly and not to the extent that you would like to get. Conditions are such that even if you do not get all you want in your principal subject, there are plenty of other aspects in regard to which material will be accumulated all the time and that will be of value and many of which will have a bearing on the matter that you really want to investigate.

I am not writing any more today because I want to reply at once to your question. I shall write, however, again more fully very soon.

With kindest regards,

Yours as ever,

Franz Boas

(5) Mead's airmail letter to Boas of January 5, 1926, written after she had been in Manu'a for almost two months, asking him: "If I simply write conclusions and use my cases as illustrative material will it be acceptable?"

Ta'ū, Manu'a, American Samoa,
January 5, 1926

Dr. Franz Boas,
Columbia University,
New York City
Dear Dr. Boas,
This will acknowledge your letter of November 7th. Thank you for all your generous haste in answering it, it reached me after I had been settled in

Manu'a for six weeks. Which very neatly demonstrates the hopelessness of trying to correspond about anything down here.

I am enclosing my report to the Research Council which is required by the first of March. I have sent them two copies under separate cover and registered. If by any chance they should fail to reach the Council and they should advise you of that fact would you see that they get a copy, please. I have to take endless precautions because there is no regular mail service here and we have to entrust our mail to the good nature of a series of irresponsible individuals. I realize how irregular it is for you not to have had an opportunity to criticise and approve this report. But if I had sent it earlier I should have had two weeks instead of five to report on and furthermore there would have been no time for your criticisms to have reached me. It therefore seemed advisable to send my report directly to the Council with a definite statement that you had neither seen nor approved it in any way. I hope that I said nothing in the report of which you would actively disapprove.

As to the content of the report, I have, as you see, made it exceedingly brief and tentative. While making absolutely no showing in conclusions at all, I could hardly enlarge further than I have done. Every conclusion I draw is subject to almost certain modifications within the next ten days and is therefore pretty valueless. If the report satisfies the Council that I am working with passable efficiency, it will have accomplished as much as it could under the circumstances.

And now, what I need most is advice as to method of presentation of results when I finally get them. Ideally, no reader should have to trust my word for anything, except, of course, in as much as he trusted my honesty and averagely intelligent observation. I ought to be able to marshall an array of facts from which another would be able to draw independent conclusions. And I don't see how in the world I can do that. Only two possibilities occur to me and both seem inadequate. First, I could present my material in a semi-statistical fashion. It would be fairly misleading at that because I can't see how any sort of statistical technique would be of value. But I could say "Fifty adolescents between such and such ages were observed. Of these ten had step-mothers, and five of the ten didn't love their step-mothers, two were indifferent and three were devoted. Fifteen had had some sex experience, five of the fifteen before puberty, etc." All of which would be quite valueless, because whether fifty is a fair sample or not could be determined only on the basis of my personal judgment. And saying you don't love your step-mother, or that you rebel against your grandfather but mind your older sister, or any of the thousand little details on the observation of which will depend my final conclusions as to submission and rebellion within the family circle, are all meaningless when they are treated as isolated facts. And yet I doubt whether the Ogburns of science will take any other sort of result as valid.

Then I could use case histories, like this: "Anovale, L7-3 is a girl of 12 or 13. (Ages always have to be doubted as that). She is just on the verge of puberty. Her father is a young man with no title and a general reputation for shiftlessness. Her mother is likewise young and irresponsible, given to going off visiting and leaving Anovale with the care of her five younger brothers and sisters. Anovale is nevertheless excessively devoted to her mother, showing an unusual amount of demonstrative affection for her. The girl is decidedly overworked and is always carrying a baby. They are quite poor and she never has any even passably respectable clothes. Her mother is a relative of the high chief of Lumā, Sotoa, and as poor relations a great (deal) of unpleasant work falls to the share of Anovale and her sister of 9. Her younger sister is much prettier and more attractive and is the mother's favorite. (The father is negligible). Anovale is tall, angular, loud voiced and awkward, domineering towards all her younger relatives, obstinate, sulky, quick to take offence. She regards her playmates as so many obstacles to be beaten over the head. She has no interest in boys whatsoever, except as extra antagonists. All her devotions seem to be reserved for her mother and the pretty little sister, etc." I can probably write two or three times as much about each of them before I leave. But to fill such case histories with all the minutiae which make them significant to me when they are passing before my eyes is next to impossible. And the smaller the details become, the more dangerous they become if they are to be taken just as so many separate facts which can be added up to prove a point. For instance, how many other little girls carry babies all the time, and how many other mothers go visiting. Facts which possess significance in one case but which are mere bagatelles of externality in another would have to be included in each case history or they would not be comparable.

As I indicated in my report, I am making a thorough personnel study of the whole community. These provided me with a tremendous back ground of detail. I will quote here the information contained on one household card to give you an idea of just what this means.

L30 (Lumā, 30th. house). Rank, high chief. (Title) Richest family in village, seven houses. 1. Sotoa, aged about 60, has tb. 2. Toaga, his wife, belongs to the family of the Tui Manu'a (kings of Manu'a). Her father was a half caste, son of an Englishman who married into the Tui Manu'a family. She is the widow of a Pharmacist's Mate in the U.S. Navy and has $10,000 insurance. Continuing to live and work *fa'aSamoa* she has great influence and prestige. She works all the girls in her household to death, and one of them, Vaito'ilau, L30-5 has just run away. The girls in her household are not allowed to go out walking in couples with boys. She has one child, illegitimate, a boy of 5, son of another Pharmacist's Mate.

The other members of the household are: 3. Aviata, an unmarried boy of 25, the illegitimate son of Sotoa, his mother is dead. 4. Moeva, boy of 24, son of

the sister of Sotoa, Sasa, a widow of 60 who lives in household no 7. 5. Numela, brother of 4. Moeva, boy of 21, has just left to work in Tutuila. 6. Ifo,
boy of 18, son of the dead brother of Sotoa, and his sister Vaito'ilau, girl of 17
who formerly lived in the pastor's household, ran away from there and has
now run away to Si'ufaga. 8. Logono, boy of 16, son of Sotoa by his first marriage; his mother is living and remarried in Upolu. 9. Iloa, the married daughter of Sasa, and her husband Suivale, also her child, illegitimate Sualosa, a boy
of 6, and three children (names and ages) by her husband Suivale; Tupu, a girl
of 14, daughter of the daughter of the brother of Sotoa's father, orphan; Sane,
Toaga's half caste illegitimate child, etc. There are several more. As rank does
not depend on primogeniture nor necessarily upon being the son of a chief
rather than a relation, one must know in addition who are the favorites, and
why, etc. But you see what type of information this gives me, and the numerous questions I can answer on the basis of it. I had to have it anyhow in order
to thread my way through the mass of gossip and village happenings.

But how to use it? If I simply write conclusions and use my cases as illustrative material will it be acceptable? Would it be more acceptable if I could
devise some method of testing the similarity of attitudes among the girls, in a
quantitative way. For instance, no Samoan who knows I'm married ever fails
to say "Have you any children?" No. *Talofa e.* Poor you. This is the universal
response from men and women, except in the case of the boarding school girls.
Now it would be more convincing if I could present an array of such responses
indicating attitudes with actual numbers and questions—as "Of the fifty girls
questioned, 47 said they hoped to marry soon and 45 wanted at least five children." I wouldn't feel any wiser after collecting information in that style but
maybe the results would be strengthened. It will, of course, be fairly easy to
demonstrate a fairly dead level of background and information.

I am sorry to bother you with so much detail, but this is a point on which I
am very much at sea. I think I should be able to get an answer in time to get
some help. On second thought, I'll not enclose my report in this letter (the reports contains nothing which I haven't written to you), but send it air mail. If
you could dash me off an air mail answer I might get it some time in March.
You will see that is quite late, and will perhaps forgive my importunity.

The hurricane has messed everything up nicely, but as Tutuila and Western
Samoa were equally wrecked, I shan't make any change in my plans. It will
considerably lessen my chances of getting ethnological information by observation, as nothing important can occur without a feast and there will be a
famine here for months where every morsal of food will have to be hoarded.
My health continues to withstand the onslaughts of the tropics.

With very best wishes,
Sincerely yours,
Margaret Mead

(6) Boas's letter to Mead of February 15, 1926, in which he states, "I am very decidedly of the opinion that a statistical treatment of such a intricate behavior as the one you are studying, will not have very much meaning and that the characteristics of a selected number of cases must necessarily be the material with which you have to operate."

(Boas's letter of February 15, 1926, did not reach Mead until March 18, 1926, four days after she had, on the island of Ofu, written her letter to Boas of March 14, 1926.)

I was very glad to receive today three letters from you: a little personal note, a letter with the enclosure to Dr. Lillie also containing the report and your letter in which you asked me a few questions.

I have written to Washington and told them that you expect to be here in New York next year and that you will have an opportunity to work up your material here and that it would be unwise to have you interrupt your work now in order to write a report. Considering this I do not think that you need worry just at present about the question of the final formulation of your results.

However, I am anxious to answer your questions as well as I can, although I am quite aware that I think in the progress of your work you will find yourself the best way of presentation and that some of the difficulties that upset you in the beginning will have disappeared.

I am very decidedly of the opinion that a statistical treatment of such an intricate behavior as the one you are studying, will not have very much meaning and that the characteristics of a selected number of cases must necessarily be the material with which you will have to operate. Statistical work will require the tearing out of its natural setting, some particular aspect of behavior which, without that setting, may have no meaning whatever. A complete elimination of the subjective use of the investigator is of course quite impossible in a matter of this kind but undoubtedly you will try to overcome this so far as that is at all possible. I rather imagine that you might like to give a somewhat summarised description of the behavior of the whole group or rather of the conditions under which the behavior develops as you have indicated in your letter to the Research Council and then set off the individual against the background.

If you should give a purely statistical treatment I fear that the description would resemble the results of a questionaire which I personally consider of doubtful value.

I am under the impression that you have to follow somewhat the method that is used by medical men in their analysis of individual cases on which is built up the general picture of the pathological courses that they want to describe. There would be no difficulty in guarding yourself by referring to the variety of personal behavior that you will find.

APPENDIX

I hope that the hurricane has not disturbed your work too much. Perhaps it is quite interesting to see how the people behave under stress.

I wonder whether you will not find, when this letter arrives, that you have answered your own question better than I can do from here. However, I want to help you as much as I can.

With kindest regards,
Yours very sincerely,
[Franz Boas]

(7) Mead's letter to Boas of March 14, 1926, written the day after she had been hoaxed by Fa'apua'a and Fofoa. (When she wrote this letter on the island of Ofu, Mead had not received Boas's letter to her of February 15, 1926.)

Ofu, Manu'a, Samoa,
March 14, 1926

Dear Dr. Boas,

I am over on one of the other islands of the Manu'a group for a week doing a little comparative ethnology. School has just started in Ta'ū and all the children are much too excited to manage. And I've concluded that I will be able to write an *Ethnology of Manu'a* (excluding such aspects of the culture as have no direct bearing on my problem and would take a long time to collect i.e. tapa designs, knots used in weaving fish nets; types of adzes, tattooing designs, etc.), and so I want to spend time on the other two islands of the group to round out this study. There was an assurance that the station ship could be here within ten days so that I needn't spend longer than that here, so I came over in a row boat and I'll go back on the *Tanager* on Wednesday.

It's a vacation of sorts too, to escape from that tiny island and the society of the tiny white colony on it. Over here I am living native entirely, which I thoroughly enjoy but which, I am still convinced, would have been impossible in the village where I did my problem.

My problem is practically completed. I await your answer to my airmail letter with the greatest interest as it will partly determine how I will use the next six weeks. If you want statistics I'll have to spend some time counting them out, likewise if you want case studies for all my children. I've made out informative tests to test the community of response of various age groups and to measure the degree to which various age groups participate in the culture of the adult community. I also have achievement scales of proficiency in the arts and crafts. There is so little variability in these aspects that unless you have written me that many statistics are valuable, I'll not test the other 20 girls. What I have already tested [is] one in the 46. Because I feel absolutely safe in generalizing from the material I have. Aside from such matters, checking up my family cards, and getting a little more on individuals sex experiences, I'm practically thru. My results summarized briefly read like this:

1. From the standpoint of submission to the group, and rebellion either against family or community authority, the period of adolescence does not present a focus point. Children reach the height of rebellious behavior at the age of 8 or 9, and thereafter are gradually submerged, not asserting themselves again until (20–25) or marriage—these are usually synonymous. Of course, I have endless illus. and details of this to make it thoroughly realistic.
2. From the standpoint of religious and philosophical development, both church and community shift all religious responsibilities from the adolescent to the adult, and the adolescent acquiesces cheerfully in this arrangement.
3. Sexual life begins with puberty in most cases. Fairly promiscuous intercourse obtains until marriage and there is a good deal after marriage. It is the family and not the community (except in the case of the *taupou*) which attempts to preserve a girl's virginity—and this attempt is usually secretly frustrated rather than openly combatted by the adolescent. The development of sex interest, of coquetry, etc. is quite sudden and coincident with puberty. The neuroses accompanying sex in American civilization are practically absent, such as frigidity, impotence and pronounced perversions. (Then, I have detailed information on sexual interests and beliefs and standards and preferences.)

So, the sum total of it all is adolescence is a period of sudden development, of stress, only in relation to sex, and where the community recognizes this and does not attempt to curb it, there is no conflict at all between the adolescent and the community, except such as arises from the conflict of personalities within a household (and this is immediately remedied, as I have shown, by the change to another relationship group); and the occasional delinquent—of any age from 8 to 50, who arouses the ire of the community. I think I have ample data to illustrate all these points. As far as I understand, it is this that is the sort of thing that you wanted. I plan to write up my material on the boat going to Europe which would give me time to send in a report to the Research Council by the first of August, provided it was not first submitted to you. I could say that it was subject to endless revision and send it in. Will you write me please to the steamer as to whether you think it advisable for me to send in a preliminary report of this sort—or to postpone sending in any until you can look over the material. If you wish that, I'll simply write up my material roughly, and finish up the *Ethnology of Manu'a* for the Bishop Museum. I'll have 5 weeks of uninterrupted time and a typewriter on ship board.

I hope you'll be pleased.

Sincerely,

Margaret Mead

(8) Mead's letter to Boas of March 19, 1926, written after she had received
Boas's letter of February 15, 1926, informing him that she had decided to "finish up" her research on the island of Ta'ū "in the next month."

Ta'ū,
March 19, 1926

Dear Dr. Boas,
After receipt of your letter on presentation of results, and because of the increasing difficulty of living in Manu'a with so many people quartered at the
Dispensary for me to stay there and a famine in native foods, I've decided to
finish up my work here in the next month and to leave Samoa on the *Sonoma*,
sailing April 27 from San Francisco and May 10 from Pago Pago. I will get my
results pretty thoroughly written up for the Council on my 6 week voyage.

Thank you so much for your letter and the help and encouragement it contained.

Very sincerely,
Margaret Mead

(9) Boas's letter to Mead of April 20, 1926, written in New York on the day
on which he received her letter of March 14, 1926, telling her he was "glad"
she had been "able to do so well" with her "difficult problem" as to be able to
state her results "so succinctly."

Columbia University in the City of New York,
Department of Anthropology
April 20, 1926

My dear Flower of Heaven,
I have to hurry now, if I want to send you the letter that I have intended to
write to you for many weeks. It is so difficult to do what we want to do! Your
summary which reached me this morning sounds very interesting and I am
glad you were able to do so well with your difficult problem that you feel able
to state your results so succinctly. I am very curious to see the material on
which you base your conclusions. In regard to your report, I believe you do not
need to take the requirement of a final report this year too strictly. The Research Council will be satisfied if they hear of your general results or the completion of your fieldwork. On the other hand you must remember that your
new position will take a lot of time and that your thesis will have to be completed. I presume you will simply plod away at your observations on the boat
and copy down with [illegible]. I should not spend too much time on a formal
report which will only be pigeonholed. I think it would not be amiss to write a
short report for publication in the *Anthropologist*. I am sorry I cannot meet
you in Rome, but it will be impossible. You know that Ruth Benedict, Gladys
and Oetteking will be there so we are well represented. I wish I could say

something; but, although Samoa "belongs" to us (by what right?), it is not known in a scientific sense. Before we know it you will be here. I hope you will have a splendid time in Europe after all the hardships of this year.

Yours very sincerely,

Franz Boas

(10) Mead's letter to Boas of July 13, 1926, in which she tells him, quite untruthfully, that she "was seasick the whole trip and utterly incapable of doing any consecutive work on ship board."

> c/o Bankers Trust Co.,
> 3–5 Place Vendome.
> Paris,
> France.
> July 13, 1926

Dear Dr. Boas,

Your long letter reached me on sailing day and how much I did appreciate it and the fact that you had taken some of your precious time to write it in long hand.

I am enclosing my letter to the Council. It was a case of following your suggestions entirely and to the letter. I was seasick the whole trip and utterly incapable of doing any consecutive work on ship board. I find now that I am very tired and I'm just beginning to realize how strenuous this year has been, coming as it did on top of my work at Columbia. I fear that if I am to adequately discharge my duties next year and write up my fieldwork also, I shall have to give these two months in Europe to rather thorough relaxation. Having gotten all my field note books safely over the reef, my anxiety in that respect is somewhat allayed. Luther will take them home next week and put them in a safe.

I am so disappointed that you will not be at the Congress. I had supposed all along that you would be. With very best wishes to Mrs. Boas and the members of the Department.

Very sincerely,

Margaret Mead

Mead's letter to Handy of November 1, 1925, is in the collections of the Manuscript Division of the Library of Congress. All of the other letters are in the archives of the American Philosophical Society.

# Notes

## Abbreviations

ANRC: Archives, National Research Council, National Academy of Sciences, Washington, D.C.

PFB: Papers of Franz Boas, American Philosophical Society, Philadelphia.

PMM: Papers of Margaret Mead, Manuscript Division, Library of Congress, Washington, D.C.

## Introduction

1. In a letter dated March 3, 1967, to S. E. Blazer, editor of the 1968 Dell paperback edition of *Coming of Age in Samoa*, Mead wrote that it was "rightly recognized as a classic scientific study," PMM. This phrase was then used by S. E. Blazer; E. D. Hirsch Jr., J. F. Kett, and J. Trefil, *The Dictionary of Cultural Literacy* (Boston, 1988), 395; D. Freeman, *Margaret Mead and Samoa: The Making and Unmaking of an Anthropological Myth* (Cambridge, Mass., 1983).

2. F. Heimans, letter to Meloma Afuola, from Sydney, August 4, 1987; Galea'i Poumele died in Pago Pago, American Samoa, on July 27, 1992.

3. D. Freeman, "Fa'apua'a Fa'amū and Margaret Mead," *American Anthropologist* 91 (1989), 1017–1022. As I noted in this publication (p. 1021), I have translated the term *pepelo*, which was used by Fa'apua'a on November 13, 1987, to describe her response to Mead's questioning about sexual matters, as "fibbing" to indicate that she and Fofoa were only joking, as Fa'apua'a makes plain in the rest of her testimony. In Pratt's *Grammar and Dictionary of the Samoan Language* (1911), p. 248, the connotation of *pepelo* is: "v. to lie, to deceive." *Pepelo*, however, is applied both to culpable lying, as in the phrase *molimau pepelo*, meaning perjury, and to lighthearted deception and fibbing, as in joking behavior.

4. M. Mead, *Letters from the Field, 1925–1975* (New York, 1977), 55; M. Mead, *Coming of Age in Samoa* (New York, 1928), viii.

5. In the original Samoan, the lines cited from Fa'apua'a's letter of April 17, 1926, read as follows: "*E le galo 'oe ia te a'u, e manatua pea i lo'u mafaufau lo 'oe agalelei ia te a'u. E manatua pea lou alofa ia te a'u i aso e tele sa taua feoa'i solo ai. O lea, aua nei galo masaniga lelei e manatua pea lava e a'u.*"

6. A. Lewis, *They Call Them Savages* (London, 1938), 178, 184.

7. Leulu F. Va'a, in *The Samoa Times*, January 6, 1989, 1ff.

8. T. O'Meara, personal communication, 1995; R. Bolt, *A Man for All Seasons* (New York, 1960), xiii.

9. On January 1, 1994, the Research School of Pacific Studies of the Institute of Advanced Studies of the Australian National University became the Research School of Pacific and Asian Studies.

10. R.F.G. Spier, *Encyclopedia Americana* (New York, 1987), vol. 4, 118; F. Boas, letter to chairman, Board of National Research Fellowships in the Biological Sciences, January 4, 1926, ANRC; Douglas Cole, with whom I was in correspondence about Franz Boas from 1990 onward, died in Vancouver on September 18, 1997.

11. F. Boas, letter to M. Mead, July 14, 1925, PFB.

12. F. Boas, letters of M. Mead, November 7, 1925, January 4 and February 15, 1926, PFB; M. Mead, letters to F. Boas, January 4 and March 19, 1926.

13. Secretary, Board of National Research Fellowships in the Biological Sciences, letter to M. Mead, February 15, 1930, ANRC.

14. H. Gregory, letter to M. Mead, June 6, 1925; M. Mead, letter to H. Gregory, June 16, 1925; M. Mead, letter to E.S.C. Handy, November 1, 1925, PMM.

15. M. Mead, *Blackberry Winter: My Earlier Years* (New York, 1972), 45.

16. G. W. Stocking Jr., "The Ethnographic Sensibility of the 1920s and the Dualism of the Anthropological Tradition," in G. W. Stocking Jr., ed. *Romantic Motives: Essays on Anthropological Sensibility* (Madison, Wis., 1989), 242; M. Mead, letter to F. Boas, January 5, 1926, PFB.

17. M. Mead, bulletin 14, March 24, 1926, PMM.

18. In Samoan: *E fili e le tai aga a le va'a.*

# Chapter One

1. A. Kroeber, "Franz Boas: The Man," *American Anthropological Association Memoir* 61 (1943), 23.

2. R. H. Lowie, review of *Race, Language, and Culture* by Franz Boas, *Science* 91 (1940), 599; A. Goldenweiser, "Recent Traits in American Anthropology," *American Anthropologist* 43 (1941), 153.

3. G. W. Stocking Jr., "Ideas and Institutions in American Anthropology: Thoughts Towards a History of the Interwar Years," in *Selected Papers from the American Anthropologist, 1921–1945* (1976), ed. G. W. Stocking Jr., 3;

G. W. Stocking Jr., "Franz Boas," *Dictionary of American Biography*, supp. 3 (1973), 86.

4. In a letter to his sister, Toni, dated December 10, 1886, Boas called himself *"ein unverbesserlichere Idealisten"* (D. Cole, personal communication, 1997). Boas was primarily referring to what (in 1938) he called "the ideals of the revolution of 1848," which he had derived from his mother. But also, as noted in Chapter 1, when only twenty-three years old, he became converted to a form of neo-Kantian idealism. For a discussion of the political and related values of Franz Boas, with which I am not here concerned, compare chap. 5, "The Scientist as Citizen," in M. J. Herskovits, *Franz Boas* (New York, 1953).

5. F. Boas, "An Anthropologist's Credo," *Nation* 147 (1938), 201; D. Cole, *"A Certain Work Lies Before Me": The Early Years of Franz Boas, 1858–1906* (unpublished manuscript, 1995), 20ff.; G. W. Stocking Jr., ed., *The Shaping of American Anthropology, 1883–1911* (New York, 1974), 43; Boas, "An Anthropologist's Credo," 201; F. Boas, curriculum vitae, 20, PFB; Cole, *A Certain Work*, 48.

6. Stocking, *Shaping of American Anthropology*, 43.

7. F. Gregory, *Scientific Materialism in Nineteenth-Century Germany* (Dordrecht, 1977), 9, 13.

8. W. M. Montgomery, "Germany," in T. F. Glick, ed., *The Comparative Reception of Darwinism* (Austin, 1972), 82; A. Kelly, *The Descent of Darwinism* (Chapel Hill, N.C., 1981), 21, 29; "Darwin und Darwinismus," *Illustrierte Zeitung* 50 (1868), 323–326.

9. L. W. Beck, foreword to K. C. Kohnke, *The Rise of Neo-Kantianism* (Cambridge, 1991), xii; B. Russell, introduction to F. A. Lange, *The History of Materialism* (London, 1925), vi; D. D. Runes, *Dictionary of Philosophy* (New York, 1983), 224; Kohnke, *Rise of Neo-Kantianism*, 205, 279.

10. D. Blackbourne, *The Marpingen Visions: Rationalism, Religion, and the Rise of Modern Germany* (London, 1995), 106; E. Acherknecht, *Rudolf Virchow: Doctor, Statesman, Anthropologist* (Madison, Wis., 1953), 239.

11. *Nature* 16 (October 4, 1877), 491; E. Haeckel, "The Present Position of the Evolution Theory," *Nature* 16 (October 4, 1877), 492, 494; R. Virchow, "The Liberty of Science in the Modern State," *Nature* 17 (November 22 and 29 and December 6, 1877), 74, 113; E. Haeckel, "Charles Darwin as an Anthropologist," in A. C. Seward, ed., *Darwin and Modern Science* (Cambridge, 1909), 145; see also J. Diamond, *The Rise and Fall of the Third Chimpanzee* (London, 1991), 17, in reference to the current evidence on the genetic relationship of Homo sapiens to other primates.

12. Virchow, "Liberty of Science," 74; Kelly, *Descent of Darwinism*, 60; E. Haeckel, *Freedom in Science and Teaching* (London, 1879), 7; F. Darwin, *The Life and Letters of Charles Darwin* (London, 1888), vol. 3, 236; Prince Von Bulow, *Memoirs, 1849–1897* (London, 1932), 439; Kohnke, *Rise of Neo-Kantianism*, 281.

13. Ibid., 247, 210.

14. Cole, *A Certain Work*, 115; M. Stockhammer, *Kant Dictionary* (New York, 1972), 6.

15. C. Kluckhohn and O. Prufer, "Influences During the Formative Years," in W. Goldschmidt, ed., *The Anthropology of Franz Boas* (Washington, D.C., 1959), 9; E. Haeckel, "Darwin, Goethe, and Lamarck," *Nature* 26 (September 28, 1882), 534; F. Boas, "Rudolf Virchow's Anthropological Work," *Science* 16 (1902), 441; P. Radin, "The Mind of Primitive Man," *New Republic* 98 (1939), 303; J. J. Williams, "Boas and American Ethnologists," *Thought* 11 (1936), 194; Acherknecht, *Rudolf Virchow*, 236; Acherknecht maintained that Boas's arguments "against social evolutionism" were to a large extent transcriptions of Virchow's polemics against Haeckel on the question of biological monism.

16. Cole, *A Certain Work*, 157ff.

17. F. Boas, "The Study of Geography," *Science* 9 (February 11, 1887), 139; G. W. Stocking Jr., *Race, Culture, and Evolution* (New York, 1968), 143; according to Stocking (1968, 154), Boas's "The Study of Geography" was "apparently in process as early as January 1885"; review of *The Philosophy of Kant* by John Watson, *Science* 12 (August 17, 1888), 18; Virchow, "Liberty of Science," 112; in 1887, in the *Contemporary Review* (p. 768), it was noted that "the principle of evolution" had been "accepted as the guiding idea in the investigation of Nature."

18. R. Benedict, "Franz Boas as an Ethnologist," *American Anthropologist* 45 (1943), 31; Boas's 1940 translation into English fails to translate the words *"unser Konnen"* ("our ability") from the German version (published in New York in 1889). Thus, Boas's assertion in German of March 8, 1888, is even more strongly idealist than the words cited by Benedict in 1943; F. Boas, *Die Ziel der Ethnologie* (New York, 1889), 23. The phrase "the biology of behavior" is from Konrad Lorenz's preface in the University of Chicago Press edition of 1965 of Charles Darwin's *The Expression of the Emotions in Man and Animals* of 1872, a work that Boas studiously ignored throughout his anthropological career.

19. F. Boas, "Human Faculty as Determined by Race," *Proceedings of the American Association for the Advancement of Science* 43 (1894), 318.

20. T. Waitz, *Introduction to Anthropology* (London, 1863); F. A. Lange, *The History of Materialism* (London, 1925), vol. 3, 106; for further information on Theodor Waitz, see D. Freeman, *Margaret Mead and Samoa* (Cambridge, Mass., 1983), 26–29.

21. F. Boas, "Psychological Problems in Anthropology," in Stocking, *Shaping of American Anthropology*, 244; F. Boas, "The Question of Racial Puberty," *American Mercury* 3 (1924), 163; F. Boas, "Race," *Encyclopaedia of the Social Sciences* 13 (1934), 34.

22. F. Boas, "The Mind of Primitive Man," *Journal of American Folk-Lore* 14 (1901), 11; F. Boas, "The History of Anthropology," *Science* 20 (October 21, 1904), 523; Stocking, *Race, Culture, and Evolution*, 264.

23. A. L. Kroeber, "Eighteen Professions," *American Anthropologist* 17 (1915), 285; Stocking, introduction to *Shaping of American Anthropology*, 17; A. L. Kroeber, "The Superorganic," *American Anthropologist* 19 (1917), 208, 213; see also, in reference to Kroeber's "abyss," C. Stringer and R. McKie, *African Exodus* (London, 1996), 12: "[T]he biological abyss that was once supposed to divide human beings from the animals has been revealed to be the narrowest of genetic crevices"; C. Geertz, *Works and Lives: The Anthropologist as Author* (Stanford, 1988), 20.

24. R. H. Lowie, *Culture and Ethnology* (1917; New York, 1929), 66.

25. F. Boas, "Eugenics," *Scientific Monthly* 3 (1916), 476; L. Spier, "Some Central Elements in the Legacy," in *The Anthropology of Franz Boas*, ed. W. Goldschmidt, *American Anthropological Association Memoir* 89 (1959), 146; because of their historical significance, Spier's words have been put in italics.

26. K. McAleer, *Dueling: The Cult of Honor in Fin-de-Siècle Germany* (Princeton, 1994); Cole, *A Certain Work*, 71.

27. F. Boas, "The Question of Racial Purity," *American Mercury* 3 (1924), 163; F. Boas, "What Is a Race?" *Nation* 120 (1925), 89.

# Chapter Two

1. M. Mead, *Anthropologists and What They Do* (New York, 1965), 156.

2. M. Mead, *Blackberry Winter: My Earlier Years* (New York, 1972), 100, 109; official transcript of the record of Miss Margaret Mead, Barnard College, Columbia University, March 2, 1925, ANRC; J. Meyers, *Scott Fitzgerald* (New York, 1994), 66: "*The Smart Set: A Magazine of Cleverness* (H. L. Mencken and George Jean Nathan, eds.) was satiric and avant-garde, snobbish and stylish, witty and iconoclastic. It published Somerset Maugham's *Rain*, fiction by Willa Cather, James Branch Cabell, and Sinclair Lewis, more experimental work by D. H. Lawrence, James Joyce, and Ezra Pound and stories by Scott Fitzgerald."

3. R. Metraux, ed., *Margaret Mead: Some Personal Views* (London, 1979), 253; *Bucks County Daily News*, September 6, 1921; "The Buckingham Child's Quest," 1921.

4. Mead, *Blackberry Winter*, 19.

5. J. Houston, *A Mythic Life* (San Francisco, 1996), 243; compare *Sir Patrick Spens*, in J. MacQueen and T. Scott, *The Oxford Book of Scottish Verse* (Oxford, 1966), 280, where the image commented on by Jean Houston (who regards herself as having been "Margaret Mead's second daughter") has a very different meaning:

> Late late yestreen I saw the new moone,
> Wi the auld moone in her arme,

*And I feir, I feir, my dear master,*
*Tha we will cum to harme.*

For a discussion of Dr. Mead's religious and associated beliefs, see M. Gardner, *The New Age: Notes of a Fringe Watcher* (New York, 1988), 19–24.

6. J. Howard, *Margaret Mead: A Life* (New York, 1984), 14, 31, 286, 377; Mead, *Blackberry Winter*, 1; C. P. Snow, *Variety of Men* (London, 1966), 107; C. P. Snow, *George Passant* (London, 1940), 47; M. Mead, *Male and Female* (1950; London, 1962), 382; Metraux, *Margaret Mead*, 261.

7. H. E. Crampton, "Studies in the Variation, Distribution, and Evolution of the Genus *Partula*. The Species Inhabiting Tahiti," *Carnegie Institution of Washington Publications* 228 (1917), 1–311.

8. M. Mead, *An Anthropologist at Work* (New York, 1959), 9ff.

9. R. Benedict, Diary, 1923, in Mead, *Anthropologist at Work*, 57.

10. G. W. Stocking Jr., "Ruth Fulton Benedict," *Dictionary of American Biography*, supp. 4 (New York, 1974), 70ff.; J. Modell, *Ruth Benedict* (London, 1984), 87.

11. R. Benedict, Journal, 1912–1916, in Mead, *Anthropologist at Work*, 132; M. M. Caffrey, *Ruth Benedict: A Stranger in the Land* (Austin, Tex., 1989), 95.

12. J. Friedlander, "Elsie Clews Parsons," in *Women Anthropologists: A Biographical Dictionary* (New York, 1988), 286; A. L. Kroeber, "Elsie Clews Parsons," *American Anthropologist* 45 (1943), 253; R. M. Zumwalt, *Wealth and Rebellion: Elsie Clews Parsons, Anthropologist and Folklorist* (Urbana, Ill., 1992), 171.

13. A. A. Goldenweiser, *Early Civilization* (1922; New York, 1935), vii; Mead, *Anthropologist at Work*, 8.

14. Caffrey, *Ruth Benedict*, 363; Mead, *Anthropologist at Work*, 14.

15. M. Mead, *Ruth Benedict* (New York, 1974), 20; Caffrey, *Ruth Benedict*, 103, 104.

16. Mead, *Anthropologist at Work*, 4, 5.

17. F. Boas, lectures on anthropology, Barnard College, New York, October 1922–May 1923, recorded by M. Mead, PMM.

18. M. Mead, *Social Organization of Manu'a* (Honolulu, 1930), 83; F. Boas, lectures on anthropology, recorded by M. Mead; L. Spier, "Some Central Elements in the Legacy," in *The Anthropology of Franz Boas*, ed. W. Goldschmidt, *American Anthropological Association Memoir* 89 (1959), 146.

19. R. Benedict, "The Vision in Plains Culture," *American Anthropologist* 24 (1922), 1; E. Sapir, letter to Mrs. Benedict, Ottawa, June 25, 1922, in Mead, *Anthropologist at Work*, 49.

20. R. Benedict, "Towards a Social Psychology," *Nation* 119 (1924), 54; R. Benedict, "The Science of Custom," in V. Calverton, ed., *The Making of Man* (New York, 1931), 815, originally published in *Century Magazine* (April 1929); G. W. Stocking Jr., "Ruth Fulton Benedict," 73.

21. Mead, *Anthropologist at Work*, 5.

22. Ibid., 8; Mead, *Blackberry Winter*, 113, 114; Benedict, Diary, 1923, in Mead, *Anthropologist at Work*, 58, 60, 61.

23. R. Benedict, note of February 8, 1923, PMM; Benedict, Diary, 1923, in Mead, *Anthropologist at Work*, 58, 61, 66.

24. Mead, *Blackberry Winter*, 45; M. Mead, letter to Martha Mead, from Barnard College, March 11, 1923, PMM.

25. Benedict, Diary, 1923, in Mead, *Anthropologist at Work*, 68, 69; Mead, *Blackberry Winter*, 111, 127.

26. Official transcript of Margaret Mead, Barnard College, March 2, 1925, ANRC; letter, July 15, 1923, PMM.

27. Mead, *Blackberry Winter*, 107, 115, 119; Caffrey, *Ruth Benedict*, 191 and throughout.

# Chapter Three

1. L. Cressman, *A Golden Journey: Memoirs of an Archaeologist* (Salt Lake City, 1988), 91.

2. Ibid., 93; R. West, "Impressions of America," *New Republic*, December 10, 1924, 65; Ann Douglas, *Terrible Honesty: Mongrel Manhattan in the 1920s* (New York, 1995), 22; M. Mead, letter to Martha Mead, November 4, 1923, PMM.

3. M. Mead, *Blackberry Winter: My Earlier Years* (New York, 1972), 122; M. Mead, abstract of master's essay, Columbia University, 1924, ANRC.

4. M. Mead, transcript of record, Columbia University, March 6, 1925, ANRC; Mead, *Blackberry Winter*, 122.

5. W. F. Ogburn, *Social Change with Respect to Culture and Original Nature* (1922; New York, 1950), 337; M. Mead, *An Anthropologist at Work* (New York, 1959), 16; M. Mead, "Retrospects and Prospects," in A. Gladwin and W. C. Sturtevant, eds., *Anthropology and Human Behavior* (Washington, D.C., 1962), 121.

6. M. Mead, *An Inquiry into the Question of Cultural Stability in Polynesia* (New York, 1928); Mead, *Blackberry Winter*, 127.

7. Cressman, *Golden Journey*, 111; Mead, *An Inquiry*; M. Mead, letter to Martha Mead, February 19, 1924, PMM.

8. M. Mead, letter to Martha Mead, March 31, 1924, PMM.

9. E. Sapir, "Anthropology at the Toronto Meeting of the British Association for the Advancement of Science, 1924," *American Anthropologist* 26 (1924), 563; R. H. Lowie, review of *Language: An Introduction to the Study of Speech* by Edward Sapir, *American Anthropologist* 25 (1923), 93; M. Mead, "Rank in Polynesia," *Report of the Ninety-Second Meeting, British Association for the Advancement of Science, Toronto, August 6–13, 1924*.

10. Sapir, "Anthropology at the Toronto Meeting," 565; R. Darnell, *Edward Sapir: Linguist, Anthropologist, Humanist* (Berkeley, 1990), 181; Mead, *Blackberry Winter*, 124; Cressman, *Golden Journey*, 112; M. Mead, letter to R. Benedict, September 8, 1924, in Mead, *Anthropologist at Work*, 286.

11. M. Mead, letter of circa September 1924, container 2, PMM.

12. Ibid.; Mead, *An Inquiry*; Reverend Père Hervé Audran, "Traditions of and Notes on the Paumotu or Tuamotu Islands," *Journal of the Polynesian Society* 28 (1919), 31ff.; Paiore, "The Paumotu Conception of the Heavens and of Creation," *Journal of the Polynesian Society* 28 (1919), 210.

13. Mead, *Blackberry Winter*, 124, 125; Mead, *An Inquiry*, 12; see also C. Winick, *Dictionary of Anthropology* (New York, 1956), 193: "Ethnology. The study of culture on a comparative basis and the theory of culture; it is often called cultural anthropology. Ethnology is distinguished from ethnography as being more inclined toward theory and the comparative study of institutions."

14. F. Boas, "Eugenics," *Scientific Monthly* 3 (1916), 475; R. Benedict, "Nature and Nurture," *Nation* 118 (1924), 118.

15. Mead, *Blackberry Winter*, 128.

16. R. C. Cochrane, *The National Academy of Sciences: The First Hundred Years, 1863–1963* (Washington, D.C., 1978), 213; *Scientific American* 115 (1916), 256; *American Anthropologist* 25 (1923), 130; circular, National Research Council, from Washington, D.C., July 1, 1924.

17. A. P. Merriam, "Melville Jean Herskovits, 1895–1963," *American Anthropologist* 66 (1964), 84; G. W. Stocking Jr., *Race, Culture, and Evolution: Essays in the History of Anthropology* (New York, 1968), 300; Cressman, *Golden Journey*, 131; M. Mead, interview, November 1971, KVZK-TV, Pago Pago, American Samoa.

18. Mead, *Blackberry Winter*, 36, 128; Mead, *Anthropologist at Work*, 9, 305.

19. M. Mead, *Letters from the Field, 1925–1975* (New York, 1977), 19; Mead, *Blackberry Winter*, 129.

20. H. E. Gregory, *Report of the Director for 1925* (Bishop Museum, Honolulu), 5.

21. M. Mead, letter to Herbert E. Gregory, May 5, 1925, PMM.

22. M. Mead, application, February 27, 1925, ANRC.

23. Mead, *Blackberry Winter*, 39, 130.

24. V. C. Gildersleeve, letter, February 17, 1925; H. L. Hollingworth, letter, February 13, 1925, ANRC.

25. W. F. Ogburn, letter, February 27, 1925, ANRC.

26. F. Boas, letters, February 24 and April 23, 1925, ANRC.

27. *American Anthropologist* 22 (1920), 98.

28. A. L. Kroeber, "Pliny Earle Goddard," *American Anthropologist* 31 (1929), 4; P. E. Goddard, letter to F. Boas, PMM.

29. P. E. Goddard, letter to F. R. Lillie, March 3, 1925, ANRC.

30. Minutes of meeting of the Board of National Research Fellowships in the Biological Sciences held in Washington, D.C., April 30, 1925, ANRC.

31. Mead, *Blackberry Winter*, 106, 132; E. Wilson, ed., *The Crack-Up. F. Scott Fitzgerald* (New York, 1945); J. Gray, *Edna St. Vincent Millay* (New York, 1967), 8; Edna St. Vincent Millay, *Collected Poems* (New York, 1956), 127.

32. F. R. Lillie, letter to M. Mead, May 2, 1925, ANRC.

33. E. G. Conklin, *Heredity and Environment* (1915; Princeton, 1922), 220; T. H. Morgan, "Are Acquired Characters Inherited?" *Yale Review* 13 (1924), 726; F. R. Lillie, "The Gene and the Ontogenetic Process," *Science* 66 (1927), 363; R. S. Woodworth, *Psychology* (1921; London, 1922), 89.

34. Secretary, Board of National Research Fellowships in the Biological Sciences, letter to M. Mead, December 3, 1925; F. R. Lillie, letter to M. Mead, May 2, 1925; F. Boas, letter to F. R. Lillie, May 12, 1925, ANRC.

# Chapter Four

1. Secretary, Board of National Research Fellowships in the Biological Sciences, letters to M. Mead, May 26 and June 24, 1925, ANRC; M. Mead, letter to H. E. Gregory, May 5, 1925; H. E. Gregory, letters to M. Mead, May 20, May 25, and June 2, 1925, PMM.

2. M. Mead, *Blackberry Winter: My Earlier Years* (New York, 1972), 138; F. R. Lillie, letter to M. Mead, May 2, 1925.

3. H. E. Gregory, letter to M. Mead, June 16, 1925, PMM.

4. M. Mead, letter to E.S.C. Handy, November 1, 1925, PMM; M. Mead, report of January 6, 1926, to the National Research Council, 6, ANRC.

5. F. Boas, letter to M. Mead, July 14, 1925, PFB.

6. R. Darnell, *Edward Sapir* (Berkeley, 1990), 186; F. Boas, letter to R. Benedict, July 16, 1925, and R. Benedict, letter to F. Boas, July 18, 1925, in M. Mead, *An Anthropologist at Work* (New York, 1959), 288, 290.

7. J. Howard, *Margaret Mead: A Life* (New York, 1984), 65; Mead, *Anthropologist at Work*, 88, 286.

8. L. Cressman, *A Golden Journey: Memoirs of an Archaeologist* (Salt Lake City, 1988), 197; Mead, *Blackberry Winter*, 11.

9. Mead, *Anthropologist at Work*, 14, 171; M. C. Bateson, *With a Daughter's Eye* (New York, 1984), 125; M. Mead, letter to Martha Mead, August 3, 1925, PMM; Howard, *Margaret Mead*, 87.

10. M. Mead, letters to F. Boas, July 17, 19, and 24, 1925; F. Boas, letter to M. Mead, July 17, 1925, PFB.

11. M. Mead, letter to F. Boas, July 24, 1925, PFB; minutes, special meeting of December 23, 1925, of trustees; Archives, American Museum of Natural History.

12. Cressman, *Golden Journey*, 130; Mead, *Blackberry Winter*, 14.

13. Mead, *Anthropologist at Work*, 16, 291, 345; Mead, *Blackberry Winter*, 29, 128, 137, 138, 209; Cressman, *Golden Journey*, 129; M. Mead, "Apprenticeship Under Boas," in W. Goldschmidt, ed., *American Anthropological Association Memoir* 89 (1959), 31; "Margaret Mead," in G. Lindzey, ed., *A History of Psychology in Autobiography*, vol. 6 (Englewood Cliffs, N.J., 1974), 310; F. Boas, letter to F. R. Lillie, May 12, 1925, ANRC; M. Mead, *Letters from the Field, 1925–1975* (New York, 1977), 9; M. Mead, "On the Anthropological Age," *Psychology Today* 4 (1970), 59; M. Mead, letter to F. Boas, January 16, 1926, PFB.

14. Mead, *Anthropologist at Work*, 14, 16, 202; A. Lowell, *Selected Poems* (New York, 1928), 124; R. Benedict, "The Science of Custom," in V. F. Calverton, ed., *The Making of Man* (New York, 1931), 815, originally published in *Century Magazine*, April 1929.

15. Mead, *Anthropologist at Work*, 16, 202; R. Benedict, *Patterns of Culture* (New York, 1934), 2, 258.

16. Mead, *Anthropologist at Work*, 291, 292, 552; Howard, *Margaret Mead*, 100; M. Mead, letter to Martha Mead, August 3, 1925, PMM; J. Modell, *Ruth Benedict* (London, 1984), 292; Cressman, *Golden Journey*, 132; Mead, *Letters from the Field*, 21.

17. M. Mead, letter to Martha Mead, August 3, 1925, PMM; Mead, *Blackberry Winter*, 145; Cressman, *Golden Journey*, 132; Mead, *Letters from the Field*, 21.

# Chapter Five

1. W. Somerset Maugham, "Honolulu," in *The Trembling of a Leaf* (London, 1921), 207; M. Mead, bulletin, August 11, 1925, PMM; M. Mead, *Letters from the Field, 1925–1975* (New York, 1977), 26; M. Mead, *Blackberry Winter: My Earlier Years* (New York, 1972), 146.

2. W. C. McKern, review of *The Material Culture of the Marquesas Islands* by Ralph Linton, *American Anthropologist* 26 (1924), 543; "Anthropology in the Pan-Pacific Scientific Congress, Honolulu, August 2 to 20, 1920," *American Anthropologist* 22 (1920), 392; P. H. Buck, *An Introduction to Polynesian Anthropology* (Honolulu, 1945), 44; E. Beaglehole, "Polynesian Anthropology Today," *American Anthropologist* 39 (1937), 213.

3. *American Anthropologist* 22 (1920), 201; Buck, *Polynesian Anthropology*, 45; C. Fadiman, ed., *The American Treasury, 1455–1955* (New York, 1955), 567.

4. H. E. Gregory, *Report of the Director for 1920* (Bishop Museum, Honolulu, 1921), 4; E.S.C. Handy, *The Native Culture of the Marquesas* (Honolulu, 1923), 1; E.S.C. Handy, "Ethnology—The Marquesas," in Gregory, *Report of the Director for 1921*, 205; H. D. Skinner, review of *The Native*

*Culture of the Marquesas* by E.S.C. Handy, *Journal of the Polynesian Society* 33 (1924), 218; E. W. Gifford, review of *The Native Culture of the Marquesas* by E.S.C. Handy, *American Anthropologist* 26 (1924), 549.

5. E.S.C. Handy, *History and Culture in the Society Islands* (Honolulu, 1930), 5; Buck, *Polynesian Anthropology*, 49; E.S.C. Handy, *Polynesian Religion* (Honolulu, 1927); H. D. Skinner, review of *Polynesian Religion* by E.S.C. Handy, *American Anthropologist* 31 (1929), 800.

6. M. Mead, bulletin, August 14, 1925, PMM.

7. *Pratt's Grammar and Dictionary of the Samoan Language*, 4th ed., revised and enlarged by Reverend J. E. Newell (Malua, Western Samoa, 1922).

8. M. Mead, letter to H. E. Gregory, May 5, 1925, PMM.

9. M. Mead and R. Metraux, *A Way of Seeing* (New York, 1970), 34; M. Mead, "The Arts in Bali," *Yale Review* 30 (1940), 336.

10. H. Melville, *Narrative of a Four Months' Residence Among the Natives of a Valley of the Marquesas Islands* (London, 1846), 3, 226; D. Porter, *Journal of a Cruise Made to the Pacific Ocean . . . in the Years 1812, 13, and 14* (Philadelphia, 1815), 113.

11. Handy, *Native Culture of the Marquesas*, 139.

12. L. Thompson, *Beyond the Dream: A Search for Meaning* (Guam, 1991), 36; Handy, *Society Islands*, 6; Handy, *Polynesian Religion*, 232; M. Mead, *An Inquiry into the Question of Cultural Stability in Polynesia* (New York, 1928), 10; E. G. Burrows, "Western Polynesia: A Study in Cultural Differentiation," *Etnologiska Studier* 7 (1938); R. Linton, *The Tree of Life* (New York, 1962), 153.

13. M. Mead, *Social Organization of Manu'a*, 2d ed. (Honolulu, 1969), xvi.

14. M. Mead, letter to F. Boas, August 29, 1925, PFB.

15. M. Mead, letter to Martha Mead, August 24, 1925, PMM.

## Chapter Six

1. R. L. Stevenson, *In the South Seas* (London, 1922), 14; M. Mead, *Blackberry Winter: My Earlier Years* (New York, 1972), 142; M. Mead, *Letters from the Field, 1925–1975* (New York, 1977), 23.

2. H. F. Bryan, *American Samoa: A General Report by the Governor* (Washington, D.C., 1927), x.

3. Ibid.

4. Mead, *Letters from the Field*, 23; M. Mead, bulletin, August 31, 1925, PMM.

5. M. Mead, bulletin, September 2, 1925; M. Mead, letter to Dr. E. R. Stitt, September 17, 1927, PMM.

6. L. Cressman, *A Golden Journey: Memoirs of an Archaeologist* (Salt Lake City, 1988), 114.

7. M. Mead, letter to Dr. E. R. Stitt, September 17, 1927, PMM.

8. M. Mead, "Field Work in the Pacific Islands, 1925–1967," in P. Golde, ed., *Women in the Field* (Chicago, 1970), 318; M. Mead, bulletin, September 4, 1925; M. Mead, "Travel Hints for Samoa," PMM; M. Mead, letter to Freda Kirchway, January 20, 1928; M. Mead, letter to Dr. E. R. Stitt, September 17, 1927, PMM.

9. Mead, *Letters from the Field*, 24.

10. W. Somerset Maugham, "Rain," in *The Trembling of a Leaf* (London, 1921), 21; M. Mead, *An Anthropologist at Work* (New York, 1959), 57; M. Mead, bulletin, September 2, 1925, PMM.

11. Mead, *Letters from the Field*, 25; M. Mead, bulletin, September 14, 1925; M. Mead, letter to Martha Mead, September 9, 1925, PMM.

12. J.A.C. Gray, *Amerika Samoa* (Annapolis, Md., 1960), 172; M. Mead, bulletin, September 4, 1925, PMM; M. Mead, letter to F. Boas, September 17, 1925, PFB; Mead, *Blackberry Winter*, 148.

13. M. Mead, letter to Martha Mead, September 14, 1925; M. Mead, bulletin, September 14, 1925, PMM.

14. M. Mead, *Letters from the Field*, 26.

15. Ibid., 37; M. Mead, bulletins, September 14 and 27, 1925, PMM; Mead, *Blackberry Winter*, 148.

16. M. Mead, bulletin, September 27 to October 7, 1925, PMM.

17. M. Mead, bulletin, October 7, 1925, PMM.

18. M. Mead, letter to F. Boas, October 11, 1925, PFB; M. Mead, bulletin, October 13, 1925, PMM.

19. M. Mead, letter to F. Boas, October 11, 1925; F. Boas, letter to M. Mead, November 7, 1925, PFB.

# Chapter Seven

1. M. Mead, letter to F. Boas, October 11, 1925, PFB; M. Mead, bulletin, October 3, 1925, PMM.

2. M. Mead, typewritten field notes of September 30 and October 3, PMM; E.S.C. Handy, "Some Conclusions and Suggestions Regarding the Polynesian Problem," *American Anthropologist* 22 (1920), 227.

3. M. Mead, notes on informants; bulletin of October 11, 1925, PMM.

4. M. Mead, notes from Leone, October 10, 1925, on the *taupou*; informant, Helen Ripley Wilson, PMM; for an account of the *taupou* system of Samoa, see D. Freeman, *Margaret Mead and Samoa* (Cambridge, Mass., 1983), 228ff.

5. M. Mead, letter to F. Boas, October 11, 1925, PFB; H. F. Bryan, *American Samoa: A General Report by the Governor* (Washington, D.C., 1927), 63; M. Mead, bulletin, October 31, 1925, PMM.

6. J.A.C. Gray, *Amerika Samoa* (Annapolis, Md., 1960), 207ff.; A. F. Judd, "Expanded Notes, Ethnology, Etc., American Samoa, February 15–April 2,

1926," Archives, Bishop Museum, Honolulu; M. Mead, bulletin, October 31, 1925, PMM.

7. M. Mead, bulletin, October 31, 1925, PMM.

8. M. Mead, *Blackberry Winter: My Earlier Years* (New York, 1972), 148; M. Mead, bulletin, October 31, 1925, PMM.

9. M. Mead, bulletin, October 31, 1925, PMM; M. Mead, *Coming of Age in Samoa* (New York, 1928), vii; M. Mead, notes on fishing; informant, Tinitali of Vaitogi, October 1925, PMM. See M. Mead, *Letters from the Field, 1925–1975* (New York, 1977), 34, for a photo of Lolo, the talking chief from Western Samoa, who in Vaitogi, Tutuila, American Samoa, in October 1925, taught Margaret Mead "the rudiments of the graceful pattern of social relations which is so characteristic of the Samoans."

10. M. Mead, bulletin, October 31, 1925, PMM.

11. M. Mead, letter to E. Elliott, November 3, 1925; letter to E.S.C. Handy, November 1, 1925, PMM.

12. M. Mead, letter to H. E. Gregory, June 16, 1925; M. Mead, letter to E.S.C. Handy, November 1, 1925, PMM.

# Chapter Eight

1. M. Mead, *Blackberry Winter: My Earlier Years* (New York, 1972), 150; M. Mead, bulletin, November 14, 1925, PMM.

2. M. Mead, bulletin, November 14, 1925, PMM; M. Mead, letter to F. Boas, November 15, 1925, PFB; M. Mead, letters to Martha Mead, November 14 and 26, 1925, PMM; S. and B. Epstein, *She Never Looked Back: Margaret Mead in Samoa* (New York, 1980), 37.

3. M. Mead, letter to F. Boas, November 11, 1925, PFB.

4. M. Mead, letter to F. Boas, November 29, 1925, PFB; M. Mead, interview of December 16, 1925, on marriage and rank, PMM; M. Mead, report to the National Research Council, January 6, 1926, PFB.

5. M. Mead, letter to L. Cressman, December 6, 1925, PMM.

6. Mead, *Blackberry Winter*, 130; M. Mead, bulletin, December 20, 1925, PMM.

7. Minutes, December 1925, Board of Trustees, Archives, American Museum of Natural History; M. Mead, *Anthropologists and What They Do* (New York, 1965), 116; E. Elliott, letter to M. Mead, December 3, 1925; M. Mead, letter to F. R. Lillie, January 6, 1926, PMM.

8. M. Mead, bulletins, November 14, 1925, and January 26, 1926, PMM; M. Mead, letter to F. Boas, November 29, 1925, PFB; W. E. Calnon, *Seeing the South Sea Islands* (New York, 1926), 126; A. Lewis, *They Call Them Savages* (London, 1928), 170; M. Mead, letter to F. Boas, January 5, 1926, PFB.

9. E.S.C. Handy, letter to M. Mead, December 7, 1925, PMM.

10. M. Mead, bulletin, January 12, 1926; M. Mead, letter to E.S.C. Handy, January 6, 1926, PMM; M. Mead, *An Anthropologist at Work* (New York, 1959), 73; M. Mead, cable to F. Boas, January 10, 1926, PFB.

11. M. Mead, report, January 6, 1926, PFB; for an outline account of Samoan society, see D. Freeman, *Margaret Mead and Samoa* (Cambridge, Mass., 1983), chap. 8.

12. M. Mead, report, January 6, 1926.

13. F. Boas, letters to chairman, Board of National Research Fellowships in the Biological Sciences, and to M. Mead, January 4, 1926, PFB.

## Chapter Nine

1. M. Mead, letter to F. Boas, January 5, 1926, PFB.

2. M. Mead, *Letters from the Field, 1925–1975* (New York, 1977), 30, 45.

3. Ibid., 45, 47; M. Mead, letter to F. Boas, January 16, 1926, PFB.

4. M. Mead, bulletin, January 23, 1926, PMM.

5. M. Mead, letter to F. Boas, August 29, 1925, PFB; M. Mead, *Social Organization of Manu'a* (Honolulu, 1930), 197; A. Lewis, *They Call Them Savages* (London, 1938), 172, 184.

6. Fa'apua'a Fa'amū, letter to M. Mead, January 6, 1926, PMM; Mead, *Letters from the Field*, 50; Fa'apua'a Fa'amū, personal communication, May 2, 1988.

7. Mead, *Letters from the Field*, 47, 49.

8. M. Mead, bulletins, January 26 and February 14, 1926, PMM. See Mead, *Letters from the Field*, 48, for a photo of "Tufele's mother, Talala, a visiting high chief from Western Samoa, with her two female talking chiefs."

9. Mead, *Letters from the Field*, 50.

10. Ibid., 51; M. Mead, letter to F. Boas, February 15, 1926, PMM.

11. M. Mead, letter to F. Boas, February 15, 1926, PFB.

12. Ibid.

13. Ibid.

14. H. E. Gregory, *Report of the Director for 1926* (Bishop Museum, Honolulu), 14.

15. M. Mead, *Social Organization of Manu'a* (Honolulu, 1930), 196.

## Chapter Ten

1. M. Mead, *Letters from the Field, 1925–1975* (New York, 1977), 54.

2. Ibid., 51.

3. Ibid., 52.

4. M. Mead, bulletin, March 7, 1926, PMM.

5. N. A. Tuiteleleapaga, *Samoa: Yesterday, Today, and Tomorrow* (New York, 1980), vi, x.

6. M. Mead, Fieldwork Notebook no. 4, PMM; M. Mead, *Coming of Age in Samoa* (New York, 1928), 151, 157, 228.

7. Tuiteleleapaga, *Samoa* (New York, 1980), 43, 63.

8. M. Mead, Fieldwork Notebook no. 4, PMM; M. Mead, "Anthropology," in V. Robinson, ed., *Encyclopaedia Sexualis* (New York, 1936), 23; M. Mead, "On the Anthropological Age," *Psychology Today* 4 (1970), 64; M. Mead, "The Samoans," in M. Mead, *Co-operation and Competition Among Primitive Peoples* (New York, 1937), 310.

9. M. Mead, bulletin, March 7, 1926, PMM; M. Mead, letter to F. Boas, April 7, 1926, PFB.

10. M. Mead, letter to E. S. Mead, March 3, 1926; M. Mead, letter to Martha Mead, March 5, 1926, PMM.

11. M. Mead, *Letters from the Field*, 55.

12. Ibid.

# Chapter Eleven

1. M. Mead, letter to F. Boas, March 14, 1926, PFB; M. Mead, letter to R. Linton, May 18, 1931, PMM; M. Mead, *Social Organization of Manu'a*, 2d ed. (Honolulu, 1969), xiii, xviii; M. Mead, *Letters from the Field, 1925–1975* (New York, 1977), 57.

2. M. Mead, letters to F. Boas, March 14 and April 7, 1926, PFB; M. Mead, *Letters from the Field*, 55ff.

3. M. Mead, bulletin, March 24, 1926, PMM.

4. M. Mead, "Life as a Samoan Girl," in *All True! The Record of Actual Adventures That Have Happened to Ten Women of Today* (New York, 1931), 118; M. Mead, *Blackberry Winter: My Earlier Years* (New York, 1972), 153.

5. M. Mead, *Letters from the Field*, 56.

6. Ibid., 57.

7. M. Mead, report of January 6, 1926, to the National Research Council; M. Mead, letter to F. Boas, February 2, 1926, PFB; Mead had previously questioned another female informant in this same way. On September 16, 1967, in Si'ufaga, I interviewed Laula, whom Mead lists as one of her informants on p. viii of the first edition of *Coming of Age in Samoa*. According to Laula, Mead put it to her that in Manu'a if a boy stood outside the house of a girl, the girl would come out and the couple would make off into the bush (*sosola la'ua i le vao*). Laula stated that she had strongly denied this, telling Mead that this was definitely not the case (*ona ou fai atu lea i ai leai se mea fa'apena*).

8. A. Wendt, "Three Faces of Samoa: Mead's, Freeman's, and Wendt's," *Pacific Islands Monthly*, April 1983, 14; T. O'Meara, transcript of interview with Frank Heimans, Washington, D.C., October 30, 1987.

9. C. D. MacDougall, *Hoaxes* (New York, 1958); *Shorter Oxford English Dictionary* (Oxford, 1959), 908; E. Partridge, *Origins* (London, 1958), 323; G. B. Milner, *Samoan Dictionary* (London, 1966), 107, 205, 297; G. Pratt, *Grammar and Dictionary of the Samoan Language* (Malua, 1911), 66, 112, 304. In his ignorance of Samoan culture, Adam Kuper, in his book *The Chosen Primate* (Cambridge, Mass., 1994), 202, completely fails to realize that *taufa'ase'e* behavior is not outright lying but a "culturally ordained form of joking behavior." Then, having failed to cross this pons asinorum, he proceeds to pontificate about the "paradox of Epimenides the Cretan," a paradox that has no bearing at all on the highly conventional and culturally sanctioned hoaxing of Margaret Mead by Fa'apua'a and Fofoa.

10. Fa'apua'a Fa'amū, translated transcript of interview with Galea'i Poumele, Fitiuta, November 13, 1987.

11. G. Stein, *Encyclopedia of Hoaxes* (Detroit, 1993), xv.

12. Mead, report to the National Research Council; M. Mead, letter to F. Boas, March 14, 1926, PFB.

13. R. Benedict, in M. Mead, *An Anthropologist at Work* (New York, 1959), 204; M. Mead, "Apprenticeship Under Boas," *American Anthropologist* 61 (1959), 31; M. Mead, "Conclusions," in typescript of *The Adolescent Girl in Samoa*, 1927, 4, PMM; see also Jean Houston, who, in *A Mythic Life* (San Francisco, 1996), 240, reports Margaret Mead having said to her: "You're like me; you think in patterns."

14. Mead, report to the National Research Council, PFB; M. Mead, *The Adolescent Girl in Samoa*, 1927, table 1, PMM; M. Mead, *Coming of Age in Samoa* (New York, 1928), 285.

15. M. Mead, letter to F. Boas, March 14, 1926, PFB; Mead, *Coming of Age in Samoa*, 108; A. M. Noble and W. Evans, *Codification of the Regulations and Orders for the Government of American Samoa* (San Francisco, 1921), 25.

16. M. Mead, *Letters from the Field*, 57.

17. F. Boas, letter to M. Mead, February 15, 1926, PFB.

18. M. Mead, letter to F. Boas, April 7, 1926, PFB.

19. M. Mead, letter to F. Boas, March 19, 1926, PFB.

20. M. Mead, plan of research, February 1925, ANRC; Mead, report to the National Research Council, PFB; M. Mead, letter to Martha Mead, April 7, 1926, PMM; F. Scott Fitzgerald, *The Great Gatsby* (1926; New York, 1990), liii; M. Mead, bulletin, March 24, 1926, PMM.

21. L. Cressman, *A Golden Journey: Memoirs of an Archaeologist* (Salt Lake City, 1988), 194; Mead, *Anthropologist at Work*, 334; see also Mead's "very convenient hunch" about Samoa, which she describes in her letter of February 19, 1924, to Martha Mead, PMM.

22. M. Mead, letter to F. Boas, April 7, 1926, PFB.

23. M. Mead, letter to Martha Mead, April 7, 1926, PMM.

# Chapter Twelve

1. F. Boas, letter to M. Mead, April 20, 1926; M. Mead, letter to Emily Mead, March 4, 1927, PMM; Papers of Elsie Clews Parsons, Archives, American Philosophical Society, cited in R. L. Zumwalt, *Wealth and Rebellion: Elsie Clews Parsons, Anthropologist and Folklorist* (Urbana, 1992), 162.

2. F. Boas, letter to M. Mead, February 24, 1926, PFB.

3. M. Mead, *Blackberry Winter: My Earlier Years* (New York, 1972), 151; M. Mead, letter to F. Boas, April 7, 1926, PFB; M. Mead, letter to H. E. Gregory, May 5, 1926, PMM.

4. M. Mead, letter to E.S.C. Handy, November 1, 1925, PMM; M. Mead, *Letters from the Field, 1925–1975* (New York, 1977), 45.

5. Mead, *Blackberry Winter*, 156; M. Mead, letter to Martha Mead, December 5, 1925, PMM. Although the correspondence of R. Benedict and M. Mead for the years 1925–1926 is held in the Library of Congress, it is not available for public inspection. Until this correspondence has been critically assessed, the history of Mead's Samoan research will not be definitively known.

6. M. Mead, spiral notebook entry, PMM; the errors in Mead's spelling of Samoan words have been corrected and translations added.

7. L. Cressman, *A Golden Journey: Memoirs of an Archaeologist* (Salt Lake City, 1988), 112; M. Mead, interview, November 1971, KVZK-TV, Pago Pago.

8. H. Gregory, letter to M. Mead, May 25 and June 2, 1925; M. Mead, letter to H. Gregory, June 16, 1925, PMM.

9. In her report of January 6, 1926, to "the Board of Fellowships of the National Science Council," Mead noted (without indicating the extent) that "some aspects of Samoan culture" were "being studied in co-operation with the B. P. Bishop Museum." Boas was sent a copy of this report, but it was not until Mead wrote to Boas on March 14, 1926, that she made any mention of the "Ethnology of Manu'a" on which she had been working for the Bishop Museum. By the time this letter reached Boas in New York, Mead had already left Manu'a.

10. M. Mead, bulletin, November 14, 1925, PMM; M. Mead, letter to F. Boas, January 16, 1962, PFB.

11. M. Mead, letter to F. Boas, April 7, 1926, PMM.

12. E.S.C. Handy, letter to M. Mead, April 30, 1926; M. Mead, letter to E.S.C. Handy, December 21, 1926, PMM.

13. M. Mead, letter to F. Boas, February 15, 1926, PFB; M. Mead, *An Anthropologist at Work* (New York, 1958), 212; M. Mead, *Coming of Age in Samoa* (New York, 1928), 195.

14. Mead, *Coming of Age in Samoa*, tables 1, 2.

15. Mead, *Blackberry Winter*, 151; M. Mead, letter to F. Boas, April 7, 1926, PFB; M. Mead, letter to Martha Mead, April 7, 1926, PMM; M. Mead, letter to F. Boas, January 5, 1926, PFB; M. Mead, letter to F. Boas, January 16, 1926, PFB; Cressman, *Golden Journey*, 129; M. Mead, *New York Times*, August 9, 1964,

cited in *Simpson's Contemporary Quotations* (New York, 1988), 234; W. F. Ogburn, letter, February 27, 1925, ANRC.

16. H. Russell Bernard, *Research Methods in Cultural Anthropology* (Newbury Park, 1988), 178; H. Russell Bernard et al., "The Problem of Informant Accuracy," *Annual Review of Anthropology* 13 (1984), 503; Ronald P. Rohner, *The Ethnography of Franz Boas* (Chicago, 1969), 61; G. Stein, *Encyclopedia of Hoaxes* (Detroit, 1993), xv; William Bligh, *A Voyage to the South Sea* (London, 1792), 90; Jacques De Labillardière, *Voyage in Search of La Perouse* (London, 1792), vol. 2, 57.

17. C. Tudge, *The Day Before Yesterday* (London, 1996), 15.

18. Compare the judgment of Professor G. B. Milner—who, when compiling his *Samoan Dictionary* (1966), did field research in all parts of the Samoan archipelago—that "Mead's Samoan fieldwork was a disaster and its data unreliable in the extreme" (*School of Oriental and African Studies Bulletin*, vol. 47 [1984], 595); F. Boas, foreword, in Mead, *Coming of Age in Samoa*, xv.

19. J. Milton, *L'Allegro*, vol. 1 (1631), 25.

# Chapter Thirteen

1. M. Mead, bulletin, November 14, 1925, PMM; M. Mead, letters to F. Boas, March 14, March 19, and April 7, 1926, PFB; M. Mead, letter to Martha Mead, April 15, 1926, PMM.

2. Fa'apua'a Fa'amū, letters to M. Mead, March 25, 28, and 31 and April 1, 2, 10, 12, 16, and 17, 1926, PMM.

3. Fa'apua'a Fa'amū, letters to M. Mead, March 25 and April 17, 1926, PMM.

4. Fa'amotu Ufiti, letter to M. Mead, April 17, 1926; M. Mead, letter to B. F. Kneubuhl, March 24, 1926; M. Mead, letter to Martha Mead, April 15, 1926, PMM.

5. M. Mead, *Blackberry Winter: My Earlier Years* (New York, 1972), 155; Fa'amotu Ufiti, letter to M. Mead, May 26, 1931, PMM.

6. Mead, *Blackberry Winter*, 156.

7. M. Mead, letter to F. Boas, April 7, 1926, PFB; Mead, *Blackberry Winter*, 155; M. Mead, *Social Organization of Manu'a*, 2d ed. (Honolulu, 1969), xi, 3.

8. Mead, *Blackberry Winter*, 156, 157; M. Mead, letter to Martha Mead, May 19, 1926, PMM.

9. Mead, *Blackberry Winter*, 157, 158.

10. Ibid., 158, 159, 161; M. Mead, *Letters from the Field, 1925–1975* (New York, 1977), 20.

11. M. Mead, letter to Martha Mead, June 18, 1926, PMM; Mead, *Blackberry Winter*, 161; J. Howard, *Margaret Mead: A Life* (New York, 1984), 96.

12. L. Cressman, *A Golden Journey: Memoirs of an Archaeologist* (Salt Lake City, 1988), 132, 176, 177.

13. Ibid., 178; M. Mead, letter to Martha Mead, April 7, 1926, PMM.

14. L. Cressman, *Golden Journey*, 178, 181; M. Mead, letter to F. Boas, July 13, 1926, PFB.

15. M. Mead, letters to F. Boas, April 7 and July 13, 1926, PFB; F. Boas, letter to M. Mead, April 20, 1926, PMM.

16. Mead, *Blackberry Winter*, 163; M. Mead, *An Anthropologist at Work* (New York, 1959), 85, 153.

17. M. Mead, letter to Martha Mead, August 26, 1926, PMM.

18. M. Mead, letter to R. R. Tinkam, March 24, 1928; M. Mead, letter to H. E. Gregory, May 5, 1925, PMM; Cressman, *Golden Journey*, 181.

# Chapter Fourteen

1. M. Mead, letters to S. Jones, December 12 and October 29, 1926, PMM.

2. M. Smith, "G. A. Reichard," *American Anthropologist* 58 (1956), 914; M. M. Caffrey, *Ruth Benedict: A Stranger in the Land* (Austin, 1989), 122; L. Cressman, *A Golden Journey: Memoirs of an Archaeologist* (Salt Lake City, 1988), 184; M. Mead, letter to A. R. Radcliffe-Brown, July 1, 1935, PMM.

3. M. Mead, letter to R. R. Tinkam, March 24, 1928, PMM; F. Boas, letter to the National Research Council, December 13, 1926, PFB.

4. M. Mead, letter to H. E. Gregory, December 20, 1926, PMM; M. Mead, *Blackberry Winter: My Earlier Years* (New York, 1972), 164.

5. M. Mead, letter to E.S.C. Handy, December 21, 1926; M. Mead, memorandum to American Museum of Natural History, January 5, 1927, PMM.

6. M. Mead, typescript of "The Adolescent Girl in Samoa," PMM; M. Mead, letter to F. Boas, January 5, 1926; F. Boas, letter to M. Mead, February 12, 1926, PFB.

7. M. Mead, typescript of "Adolescent Girl," PMM; M. Mead, *An Anthropologist at Work* (New York, 1959), 16.

8. M. Mead, letter to E. Elliott, January 13, 1927, PMM.

9. M. Mead, letter to Emily Mead, March 4, 1927, PMM; Mead, *Blackberry Winter*, 121.

10. Mead, typescript of "Adolescent Girl," PMM; M. Mead, letter to F. Boas, March 14, 1926, PFB.

11. Mead, typescript of "Adolescent Girl," PMM; D. Freeman, letter to M. Mead, May 10, 1968; M. Mead, letter to D. Freeman, November 6, 1968; R. Lowie, "Franz Boas, Anthropologist," *Scientific Monthly* 56 (1943), 184.

12. Mead, typescript of "Adolescent Girl," PMM; M. Mead, letter to F. Boas, March 14, 1926, PFB; M. Mead, "Adolescence in Primitive and Modern Society," in V. F. Calverton and S. D. Schmalhausen, eds., *The New Generation* (London, 1930), 174; J. R. Swanton, "The President Elect," *Science* 73 (1931), 148.

13. J. Epstein, in R. Buckle, *Jacob Epstein, Sculptor* (London, 1963), 160; L. Hudson and B. Jacot, *Intimate Relations: The Natural History of Desire* (New Haven, 1995), 40. Thus, it can be said that Boas's "particular fault" was wanting to win at any cost; compare the lines in *Hamlet*, act 1, scene 4, beginning, "So, it chances in particular men."

14. M. Mead, letter to F. R. Lillie, April 24, 1927; M. Mead, letter to E. Elliott, April 25, 1927; E. Elliott, letter to M. Mead, May 10, 1927, PMM; M. Mead, *Anthropologists and What They Do* (New York, 1965), 121.

15. M. Mead, letter to F. R. Lillie, April 24, 1927; F. R. Lillie, letter to M. Mead, April 27, 1927, PMM; E. G. Conklin, *Heredity and Environment* (Princeton, 1915), 220.

16. Mead, *Blackberry Winter*, 165, 168; M. Mead, report to American Museum of Natural History for June-October, 1927; M. Mead, letter to Martha Mead, June 12, 1927, PMM; Cressman, *Golden Journey*, 191, 229, 491. Reo Fortune, according to J. Howard in *Margaret Mead: A Life* (New York, 1984), 431, "fell down a flight of stairs in the library of Wolfson College at Cambridge University" in December 1979 and died of injuries a few days later." Luther Cressman died in Eugene, Oregon, on April 4, 1994. Margaret Mead died in New York on November 15, 1978.

17. Howard, *Margaret Mead*, 104; Mead, *Blackberry Winter*, 165, 166; M. Mead, letter to S. Jones, December 21, 1926; M. Mead, letter to H. E. Gregory, January 24, 1927; M. Mead, letter to H. D. Skinner, May 24, 1927; M. Mead, letters to H. E. Gregory, October 22, November 11, and December 4, 1927; M. Mead, letter to Mrs. J. Haydon, September 20, 1971, PMM; Mead, *Anthropologist at Work*, 207; M. Mead, "Return to Samoa," *Redbook Magazine* 139 (1972), 29ff.

18. Mead, *Anthropologist at Work*, 206; Mead, *Blackberry Winter*, 195; R. Benedict, "Psychological Types in the Cultures of the Southwest," *Proceedings of the Twenty-Third International Congress of Americanists, September 1928* (New York, 1930), 572.

19. Mead, *Anthropologist at Work*, 206, 207.

20. M. Mead, *Social Organization of Manu'a* (Honolulu, 1930), 83.

21. M. Mead, *Anthropologists and What They Do*, 121.

22. M. Mead, letter to W. Morrow, January 25, 1928; M. Mead, abstract of proposed concluding chapter of *Coming of Age in Samoa*; M. Mead, letters to W. Morrow, February 11 and 21, 1928, PMM.

23. M. Mead, *Coming of Age in Samoa* (New York, 1928).

24. M. Mead, letter to H. D. Skinner, November 11, 1927; M. Mead, letter to F. Phillips, March 8, 1928, PMM.

25. Mead, *Anthropologist at Work*, 547; Mead, *Coming of Age in Samoa*, 14, 19.

26. M. Mead, letter to Franz Boas, May 22, 1928, PFB.

27. F. Boas, foreword to Mead, *Coming of Age in Samoa*, xv; A. Lesser, "Franz Boas," *International Encyclopedia of the Social Sciences*, vol. 2 (1968), 99.

28. M. Mead, letter to C. Wissler, May 8, 1928; M. Mead, letter to F. R. Lillie, August 10, 1928; M. Mead, letter to H. E. Gregory, March 18, 1929, PMM; M. Mead, *Social Organization of Manu'a* (Honolulu, 1930), 96. Mead repeated the apocryphal and quite false account she had been given by Mrs. C. P. Parkinson in M. Mead, "Cultural Determinants of Sexual Behavior," in W. C. Young, ed., *Sex and Internal Secretions* (Baltimore, 1961), 1436; also compare D. Freeman, *Margaret Mead and Samoa* (Cambridge, Mass., 1983), 250–253, and D. Freeman, "All Made of Fantasy," *American Anthropologist* 100 (1998), no. 4. Because the field research on which it was based was so hurried, Mead's *Social Organization of Manu'a* contains numerous errors; compare D. Freeman, "*Social Organization of Manu'a* (1930 and 1969) by Margaret Mead: Some Errata," *Journal of the Polynesian Society* 81 (1972), 70–78.

29. M. Mead, letter to B. Malinowski, August 10, 1928; W. Morrow, letter to M. Mead, January 11, 1929, PMM.

30. W. Morrow, letter to M. Mead, February 20, 1928, PMM.

31. Mead, *Coming of Age in Samoa*, 195, 198.

32. E. Mayr, *The Growth of Biological Thought* (Cambridge, Mass., 1982), 38; E. R. Sober, "Darwin's Nature," in J. Torrance, ed., *The Concept of Nature* (Oxford, 1992), 111.

33. M. Mead, letter to E.S.C. Handy, January 6, 1926, PMM; Mead, *Coming of Age in Samoa*, 98, 100, 198, 275; D. Freeman, "Inductivism and the Test of Truth," *Canberra Anthropology* 6 (1983), 105; M. Mead, memorandum on Mr. Taylor's letter, c. 1927, PMM; M. Mead, "Life as a Samoan Girl," in *All True! The Record of Actual Adventures That Have Happened to Ten Women of Today* (New York, 1931), 99; M. Mead, "The Role of the Individual in Samoan Culture," *Journal of the Royal Anthropological Institute* 58 (1928), 487; M. Mead, bulletin, September 27, 1925; M. Mead, typewritten field notes of December 16, 1925, PMM; M. Mead, "Americanization in Samoa," *American Mercury* 16 (1929), 269.

34. Hudson and Jacot, *Intimate Relations*, 43.

35. M. Mead, "Apprenticeship Under Boas," *American Anthropologist* 61 (1959), 31; Mead, *Anthropologist at Work*, 16.

## Chapter Fifteen

1. P. B. Glick, "Brouhaha Among the Breadfruit," *Nature* 302 (1983), 758; S. Chassler, "Afterword: Margaret Mead, 1901–1978," in R. Metraux, ed., *Margaret Mead: Some Personal Views* (London, 1979), 279; R. Ferrell, ed., *The Twentieth Century: An Almanac* (London, 1986), 158; M. Mead, letter to S. E. Blazer, editor, Laurel Editions, Dell Publishing Co., March 3, 1967, PMM;

*Reader's Digest*, August (1970), 120; G. Spindler, *The Making of Psychological Anthropology* (Berkeley, 1987), 87.

2. J. Howard, *Margaret Mead: A Life* (New York, 1984), 111; M. Mead, preface to 1973 edition of *Coming of Age in Samoa*; M. Mead, *Britannica Yearbook of Science and the Future* (New York, 1972), 108; W. Morrow, letter to M. Mead, January 11, 1929, PMM; D. H. Thomas, "Margaret Mead as a Museum Anthropologist," *American Anthropologist* 82 (1980), 358.

3. F. Boas, letter to Committee on Fellowships on Child Development of the National Research Council, December 13, 1926, PFB; M. Mead, *Coming of Age in Samoa* (New York, 1928), 158ff., 197; F. Boas, *Anthropology and Modern Life* (New York, 1928), 187.

4. R. Benedict, letter to M. Mead, March 5, 1926, in M. Mead, *An Anthropologist at Work* (London, 1959), 305.

5. H. L. Mencken, "Adolescence," *American Mercury* 59 (1928), 379.

6. W. Morrow, letter to M. Mead, January 11, 1929, PMM.

7. R. Benedict, review of *Coming of Age in Samoa*, *Journal of Philosophy* 26 (1929), 110; R. Benedict, review of *Coming of Age in Samoa*, *The New Republic* 57 (1928), 50.

8. W. Morrow, letter to M. Mead, January 11, 1929, PMM; H. Ellis, introduction to V. F. Calverton and S. D. Schmalhausen, eds., *Sex in Civilization* (London, 1929), 25; H. Ellis, *Psychology of Sex: A Manual for Students* (London, 1933), 89; S. D. Schmalhausen, *Our Changing Human Nature* (New York, 1929), 8.

9. E. Sapir, "Franz Boas," *New Republic*, January 23, 1929; P. Rabinow, "Humanism as Nihilism," in N. Haan et al., eds., *Social Science as Moral Inquiry* (New York, 1983), 73; R. Benedict, "The Science of Custom," *Century Magazine*, April 1929; R. Benedict, letter to M. Mead, January 16, 1929, in Mead, *Anthropologist at Work*, 311.

10. M. Mead, letter to F. Boas, October 18, 1928, PFB.

11. M. Van Waters, "Adolescence," *Encyclopaedia of the Social Sciences*, vol. 1 (1930), 438; F. Boas, *Encyclopaedia of the Social Sciences*, vol. 13 (1934), 34.

12. Schmalhausen, *Our Changing Human Nature*, 481; J. B. and R. Watson, *Psychological Care of Infant and Child* (London, 1928), 18; V. F. Calverton and S. D. Schmalhausen, eds., *The New Generation* (London, 1930), 13, 18.

13. Howard, *Margaret Mead*, 159; W. H. Auden, *Collected Poems* (London, 1976), 473; L. Cressman, *A Golden Journey: Memoirs of an Archaeologist* (Salt Lake City, 1988), 192; J. H. Driberg, review of *Coming of Age in Samoa*, *Spectator* 142 (1929), 787; R. Revelle, "Margaret Mead: An American Phenomenon, 1901–1978," *Science* 203 (1979), 39; T. S. Eliot, "The Idealism of Julian Benda," *New Republic* 57 (1928), 105; F. Scott Fitzgerald, *The Great Gatsby* (New York, 1926); Freda Kirchway, "Sex in the South Seas," *Nation* 127 (1928), 427; H. Neil, letter to M. Mead, January 3, 1929, PMM.

14. Sapir, "Franz Boas"; L. Thompson, *Beyond the Dream: A Search for Meaning* (Guam, 1991), 38; P. Radin, *The Method and Theory of Ethnology* (1933; New York, 1966), 178; E. Winston, "The Alleged Lack of Mental Diseases Among Primitive Groups," *American Anthropologist* 36 (1934), 234; Mead, *Coming of Age in Samoa*, 206.

15. R. H. Lowie, review of *Coming of Age in Samoa*, *American Anthropologist* 31 (1929), 532; R. H. Lowie, *Robert H. Lowie, Ethnologist: A Personal Record* (Berkeley, 1959), 110; A. L. Kroeber, letter to M. Mead, October 11, 1929, Archives, Bancroft Library, University of California, Berkeley.

16. V. F. Calverton, ed., *The Making of Man: An Outline of Anthropology* (New York, 1931), 586; F. Phillips, letter to R. Benedict, November 28, 1931, PMM; C. Geertz, "Margaret Mead, December 16, 1901–November 15, 1978," *Biographic Memoirs* 58 (1989), 339.

17. R. Benedict, *Patterns of Culture* (Boston and New York, 1934), 30; M. Mead, preface to 1961 edition of *Coming of Age in Samoa* (New York, 1961); H. Jardine, "Freeman's Book Fuels Controversy over Margaret Mead's Samoan Research," *Bear Pause* 12 (1983), 9.

18. M. Mead, *From the South Seas* (New York, 1939), x.

19. M. Mead, preface to 1949 edition of *Coming of Age in Samoa* (New York, 1949), x; M. Mead, preface to Modern Library edition of *Coming of Age in Samoa* (New York, 1953).

20. *Observer*, London, January 29, 1950; M. J. Herskovits, *Man and His Works: The Science of Cultural Anthropology* (New York, 1948), 44; E. E. Evans-Pritchard, *Social Anthropology* (London, 1951), 98.

21. G. P. Murdock, *Our Primitive Contemporaries* (New York, 1934), 72; R. Firth, *We, the Tikopia* (London, 1936), 199; A. I. Hallowell, "The Child, the Savage, and Human Experience" (1939), in *Culture and Experience* (Philadelphia, 1955), 29; R. L. Beals and H. Hoijer, *An Introduction to Anthropology* (New York, 1953), 586; W. Goldschmidt, "R. L. Beals, 1901–1985," *American Anthropologist* 88 (1986), 947; J. J. Honigman, *Culture and Personality* (New York, 1954), 294; E. A. Hoebel, *Man in the Primitive World* (New York, 1958), 285.

22. M. Mead, "Anthropology Among the Sciences," in *Anthropology, A Human Science: Selected Papers, 1939–1960* (Princeton, 1964), 5; M. Mead, preface to 1961 edition of *Coming of Age in Samoa*.

23. M. Mead, *Male and Female* (Harmondsworth, England, 1962), 17, 192; K. Lorenz, letter to M. Mead, December 22, 1954, PMM.

24. M. Mead, preface to 1973 edition of *Coming of Age in Samoa*.

25. F.L.K. Hsu, "Margaret Mead and Psychological Anthropology," *American Anthropologist* 82 (1980), 353; *Time*, March 21, 1969, 60; D. E. Hunter and P. Whitten, *Encyclopedia of Anthropology* (New York, 1976), 5; *Encyclopedia Americana*, 18 (1978), 474.

26. Revelle, "Margaret Mead," 40; Howard, *Margaret Mead*, 390; M. Konner, *The Tangled Wing: Biological Constraints on the Human Spirit* (New York, 1928), 107; W. J. Broad, news report, *New York Times*, September 17, 1993.

27. Plato, *The Republic*, book 3, 414.

# Afterword

1. M. Mead, *From the South Seas* (New York, 1939), x.

2. J. E. Richie, "Ernest Beaglehole, 1906–1965," *Journal of the Polynesian Society* 75 (1966), 110; E. Sapir, *The Psychology of Culture: A Course of Lectures*, ed. J. T. Irvine (New York, 1994), 13; T. Gladwin, "Oceania," in F.L.K. Hsu, ed., *Psychological Anthropology* (Homewood, Ill., 1961), 148; D. Freeman, "Anatomy of Mind," *Salient*, September 6, 1938, 3.

3. E. Beaglehole, "Polynesian Anthropology Today," *American Anthropologist* 39 (1937), 215.

4. R. Firth, letter to M. Mead, May 8, 1950, PMM.

5. D. Freeman, letter to M. Mead, October 21, 1964; for another account of this meeting of November 10, 1964, see P. Grosskurth, *Margaret Mead* (London, 1988), 89.

6. L. Romanucci-Ross, transcript of interview with F. Heimans, La Jolla, Calif., November 5, 1987; D. Freeman, letter to M. Mead, November 11, 1964.

7. M. Mead, letter to D. Freeman, December 2, 1964; D. Freeman, letter to M. Mead, March 20, 1969.

8. In my letter of March 20, 1969, I drew Dr. Mead's attention once again to "instances of obvious internal inconsistencies or errors" in *Coming of Age in Samoa*, about which I had first written to her on May 10, 1968. In a minute to her secretary concerning Derek Freeman and dated April 7, 1969, Dr. Mead wrote: "I am not going to answer this letter at present. At present he seems to be diverting his hostility to Boas and Kroeber, and he may lay off me. I do not intend to correct the statements which he calls errors, but which are by-products of my having to do some tricky double defining of people—like our medical *fitafita*—who was too identifiable if I told all the stories about him in the same way," PMM; M. Mead, preface, June 26, 1972, to *Coming of Age in Samoa* (New York, 1973).

9. D. Freeman, letter to M. Mead, August 23, 1978; compare Jean Houston, who (in *A Mythic Life* [San Francisco, 1996], 247) reported Dr. Mead as having said to her in 1978: "I helped create the current paradigm, and I'm one of the few people who understands how it works. As long as that paradigm is working, I am needed and I cannot die. I will die only when a newer paradigm comes along that I do not understand."

10. M. Mead, conclusion to *Social Organization of Manu'a* (Honolulu, 1969), 227.

11. P. Shankman, *The Colorado Alumnus*, November 1983, 12; D. Freeman, *Margaret Mead and Samoa* (Cambridge, Mass., 1983), xiii.

12. T. Schwartz, "Anthropology: A Quaint Science," *American Anthropologist* 85 (1983), 919; H. Jardine, *Bear Pause* 12 (1983), 19; J. Ziman, *Reliable Knowledge: An Exploration of the Grounds of Belief in Science* (1978; Cambridge, 1991), 8.

13. *Anthropology Newsletter*, American Anthropological Association, January 1984.

14. C. S. Peirce, *Collected Papers*, vol. 1, sec. 55, ed. C. Harteshorn and P. Weiss (Cambridge, Mass., 1960); E. Burke, *A Philosophical Enquiry* (1757; Oxford, 1990), 37; Leo Tolstoy, 1896, cited in Freeman Dyson, *Weapons and Hope* (New York, 1984), 213.

15. G. Hardin, "Is Violence Natural?" *Zygon* 18 (1983), 403.

16. L. Festinger, H. W. Riecken, and S. Schachter, *When Prophecy Fails* (1956; New York, 1964), 4; *The Colorado Alumnus*, November 1983, 12; R. A. Rappaport, "Desecrating the Holy Woman," *American Scholar* 55 (1986), 347; S. Silverman, "Mead's Meaning," *New York Times Book Review*, September 11, 1986, 24; L. Wolpert, *The Unnatural Nature of Science* (London, 1992), 9.

17. L. D. Holmes, *Quest for the Real Samoa: The Mead-Freeman Controversy and Beyond* (South Hadley, Mass., 1987); G. W. Stocking Jr., "The Ethnographic Sensibility of the 1920s and the Dualism of the Anthropological Tradition," in G. W. Stocking Jr., ed., *Romantic Motives: Essays on Anthropological Sensibility* (Madison, Wis., 1989), 208–276; H. Caton, ed., *The Samoan Reader: Anthropologists Take Stock* (Lanham, Md., 1990); E. M. Jones, "Samoa Lost: Margaret Mead, Cultural Relativism, and the Guilty Imagination," in *Degenerate Moderns: Modernity as Rationalized Sexual Misbehavior* (San Francisco, 1993), 19–41; J. E. Côté, *Adolescent Storm and Stress: An Evaluation of the Mead-Freeman Controversy* (Hillsdale, N.J., 1994); A. Kuper, "Male and Female," in *The Chosen Primate: Human Nature and Cultural Diversity* (Cambridge, Mass., 1994), 199–207; L. Hudson and B. Jacot, "Telling the Truth," in *Intimate Relations: The Natural History of Desire* (New Haven, 1995), 30–43; M. Orans, *Not Even Wrong: Margaret Mead, Derek Freeman, and the Samoans* (Navato, Calif., 1996).

18. G. W. Stocking Jr., "The Ethnographic Sensibility of the 1920s and the Dualism of the Anthropological Tradition," in Stocking, *Romantic Motives*, 235–247.

19. Orans, *Not Even Wrong*, 132, 156.

20. Ibid., 143.

21. Stephen Jay Gould, in reference to Samuel George Morton in Lewis Wolpert and Alison Richards, eds., *A Passion for Science* (Oxford, 1988), 148: "If you're fraudulent, you cover up what you're doing."

22. D. Boas, "The Aims of Ethnology," in G. W. Stocking, Jr., ed., *The Shaping of American Anthropology, 1883–1911* (New York, 1974), 71; M. Mead, *So-*

*cial Organization of Manu'a* (Honolulu, 1930), 83; Mead, *From the South Seas*, 212; C. Geertz, "The Impact of the Concept of Culture on the Concept of Man," in J. R. Platt, ed., *New Views of the Nature of Man* (Chicago, 1965), 114.

23. C. Geertz, *After the Fact* (Cambridge, Mass., 1995), 97; Mead, *From the South Seas*, ix.

24. F. Boas, "Race," *Encyclopaedia of the Social Sciences*, 13 (1934), 34; F. Boas, "Genetic and Environmental Factors in Anthropology," *The Teaching Biologist* 9 (1939), 17; in 1935 in the *Proceedings of the National Academy of Sciences* (25, p. 418), Boas gave it as his view that in dealing with the "general organization of the body" a "search for genes would not be advisable," adding: "Is not there some danger anyway, that the number of genes will depend rather upon the number of investigators than upon their actual existence?"; F. Crick, personal communication, 1997; J. M. Smith, *Did Darwin Get It Right?* (1988; London, 1993), 4; E. Mayr, *This Is Biology: The Science of the Living World* (Cambridge, Mass., 1997), ix; F. J. Sulloway, "Darwinian Virtues," *New York Review of Books*, April 9, 1998, 40.

25. J. Tooby and L. Cosmides, "Mapping the Evolved Functional Organization of Mind and Brain," in M. J. Gazzaniga, ed., *The Cognitive Neurosciences* (Cambridge, Mass., 1995), 1185–1192, 1202; W. D. Hamilton, "The Genetical Evolution of Social Behaviour," *Journal of Theoretical Biology* 7 (1964), 1–52; G. C. Williams, *Adaptation and Natural Selection* (New York, 1966); R. Provine, review of *Human Ethology* by I. Eibl-Eibesfeldt, *Contemporary Psychology* 35 (1990), 837.

26. P. MacLean, *The Triune Brain in Evolution* (New York, 1990), 9.

27. J. LeDoux, *The Emotional Brain* (New York, 1996), 21, 174; in LeDoux's view, "The limbic system term, even when used in a shorthand structural sense, is imprecise and has unwarranted functional (emotional) implications"; R. Shephard, "The Genetic Basis of Human Scientific Knowledge," in M. Daly, ed., *Characterizing Human Psychological Adaptations* (London, 1997), 23–31.

28. J. Z. Young, "Choice, Biological," in *The Oxford Companion to the Mind*, ed. R. L. Gregory (Oxford, 1987); J. T. Bonner, *The Evolution of Culture in Animals* (Princeton, 1980); A. R. Damasio, *Descartes' Error: Emotion, Reason, and the Human Brain* (New York, 1994); R. Passingham, *The Frontal Lobes and Voluntary Behaviour* (Oxford, 1993).

29. R. J. Rose, "Genes and Human Behavior," *Annual Review of Psychology*, 46 (1995), 648; M. McGue and T. J. Bouchard Jr., "Genetic and Environmental Influences on Human Behavioral Differences," *Annual Review of Neuroscience* 21 (1998), 17.

30. Geertz, *After the Fact*, 166; D. Dennett, *Darwin's Dangerous Idea: Evolution and the Meanings of Life* (New York, 1995), 20; G. C. Williams, *Plan*

*and Purpose in Nature* (New York, 1996), 170; N. Scheper-Hughes, review of *After the Fact* by C. Geertz, *New York Times Book Review*, May 7, 1995.

31. Compare J. Tooby and L. Cosmides, in L. Betzig, ed., *Human Nature: A Critical Reader* (New York, 1997), 292; W. G. Runciman, J. Maynard Smith, and R.I.M. Dunbar, eds., *Evolution of Social Behaviour Patterns in Primates and Man* (Oxford, 1996).

32. J. H. Barkow, L. Cosmides, and J. Tooby, eds. introduction to *The Adapted Mind* (New York, 1992); Betzig, *Human Nature*; W. C. McGrew, *Chimpanzee Material Culture: Implications for Human Evolution* (Cambridge, 1992); D. Johanson and B. Edgar, *From Lucy to Language* (New York, 1996); L. L. and F. Cavalli-Sforza, *The Great Human Diasporas: The History of Diversity and Evolution* (New York, 1995); A. Lock and C. R. Peters, eds., *Handbook of Human Symbolic Evolution* (Oxford, 1996); S. Mithen, *The Prehistory of the Mind* (London, 1996); Edward O. Wilson, *Consilience: The Unity of Knowledge* (New York, 1998).

33. Geertz, "Concept of Culture," 122.

34. M. C. Bateson, letter, *New York Times*, February 13, 1983.

35. D. E. Koshland Jr., "Nature, Nurture, and Behavior," *Science* 235 (1987), 1445.

# Chronology

| | |
|---|---|
| 1858, July 7 | Franz Boas born in Minden, Germany |
| 1877, April | Boas becomes a student at the University of Heidelberg |
| 1877, October | Boas transfers to the University of Bonn |
| 1879, October | Boas transfers to the University of Kiel |
| 1881, September | Boas completes his examinations in geography, physics, and philosophy at the University of Kiel for a doctorate |
| 1882, April 10 | Boas records in a letter to Abraham Jacobi that he is convinced that his "previous materialistic *Weltanschauung*" is "untenable" |
| 1883 | In Berlin, Adolf Bastian and Rudolf Virchow become Boas's mentors |
| 1884 | Boas arrives in New York after almost a year in Baffin Land |
| 1885 | Boas appointed docent in geography, University of Berlin |
| 1887, March 10 | Boas marries Marie Krackowiser and settles in New York |
| 1889 | Boas takes up appointment as docent in anthropology, Clark University |
| 1899 | Boas is appointed professor of anthropology at Columbia University |
| 1901, December 16 | Margaret Mead is born in Philadelphia, Pennsylvania |
| 1917 | A. L. Kroeber's "The Superorganic" published in the *American Anthropologist*; R. Lowie's *Culture and Ethnology* published in New York |
| 1920, September | Mead enters Barnard College on transfer from De Pauw University |
| 1920 | Herbert E. Gregory becomes director of the Bishop Museum, Honolulu |
| 1921, June | Edward Craighill Handy appointed ethnologist at the Bishop Museum |

| | |
|---|---|
| 1922–1923 | During her senior year at Barnard College, Mead takes a course in anthropology given by Franz Boas, with Ruth Benedict as his assistant |
| 1923, March 20 | Mead talks to Boas about doing a doctoral program in anthropology |
| 1923 | A. L. Kroeber's *Anthropology* published in New York |
| 1923 | Edward Craighill Handy's *The Native Culture in the Marquesas* published by the Bishop Museum |
| 1923, September 3 | Margaret Mead marries Luther Cressman in the Episcopal church at Buckingham, Pennsylvania, where she is a communicant |
| 1924, August 6–13 | Ninety-Second Meeting of British Association for the Advancement of Science, Toronto, Canada; Mead presents her paper titled "Rank in Polynesia" and meets Edward Sapir |
| 1925, April 30 | Margaret Mead is appointed to a National Research Fellowship in the Biological Sciences for 1925–1926 by the National Research Council to undertake "a study in heredity and environment in relation to adolescence" in Samoa |
| 1925, May 8 | Mead passes her doctoral examinations at Columbia University |
| 1925, May 12 | Boas accepts appointment as supervisor of Mead's research in Samoa by the National Research Council |
| 1925, May 21 | Mead is appointed an associate in ethnology of the Bishop Museum |
| 1925, August 1 | Mead's tenure of her National Research Fellowship in the Biological Sciences begins |
| 1925, August 11 | Mead arrives in Honolulu on the S.S. *Matsonia* |
| 1925, August | Edward Craighill Handy, senior ethnologist of the Bishop Museum, gives Mead daily tuition in preparation for her research in Samoa |
| 1925, August 24 | Mead leaves Honolulu for American Samoa in the Oceanic Steamship Company's S. S. *Sonoma* |
| 1925, August 31 | Mead arrives in Pago Pago, American Samoa |
| 1925, October 11 | Mead informs Boas that she has decided to do her fieldwork on the island of Ta'ū |
| 1925,October 19–29 | Mead stays in Vaitogi, a village on the southeast coast of the island of Tutuila |
| 1925, November 9 | Mead travels to the island of Ta'ū with Mrs. Holt, then takes up residence with the Holt family in the U.S. Naval Dispensary |

| | |
|---|---|
| 1925, December 23 | In New York, at a special meeting of its Board of Trustees, Margaret Mead is appointed assistant curator of ethnology at the American Museum of Natural History |
| 1926, January 1 | A devastating hurricane hits Ta'ū |
| 1926, February 18 | An expedition from the Bishop Museum arrives in Ta'ū; Mead accompanies this expedition to Fitiuta, where for some ten days she engages in ethnological research |
| 1926, March 8–18 | Accompanied by Fa'apua'a and Fofoa, two Samoan women from Fitiuta, Mead does ethnological research for the Bishop Museum on the islands of Ofu and Olosega |
| 1926, March 13 | While traveling with them on the island of Ofu, Mead is hoaxed by Fa'apua'a and Fofoa |
| 1926, March 14 | From the island of Ofu, Mead informs Boas about the results of her study of heredity and environment in relation to adolescence |
| 1926, March 19 | In a letter written on her return to the island of Ta'ū, Mead informs Boas that she has decided to terminate her research there about a month earlier than planned |
| 1926, April 16 | Mead leaves Ta'ū to return to Pago Pago on the island of Tutuila, without ever having systematically investigated the sexual behavior of the adolescent girls of Faleasao, Lumā, and Si'ufaga |
| 1926, April 19 | Mead returns to the village of Vaitogi to await the arrival in Pago Pago of the S.S. *Sonoma* |
| 1926, May 10 | Mead sails from Pago Pago for Sydney, Australia, on the S.S. *Sonoma* |
| 1926, May 19 | Mead sails from Sydney for Marseilles on the P. and O. liner S.S. *Chitral* |
| 1926, June 25 | Mead arrives in Marseilles to travel, for some time, in the south of France and to visit Paris and England |
| 1926, September 23–30 | With Ruth Benedict, Mead attends the Twenty-Second Congress of Americanists in Rome |
| 1926, October 11 | Mead and Benedict return to New York City |
| 1926, October | Mead begins work as an assistant curator of ethnology at the American Museum of Natural History in New York |
| 1927, March 4 | In a letter to her mother, Mead reports that Boas is "completely satisfied" with her "The Adolescent Girl in Samoa" |

| | |
|---|---|
| 1927, April 24 | Mead submits "The Adolescent Girl in Samoa" (which is her report on heredity and environment in relation to adolescence in Samoa) to the Board of National Fellowships in the Biological Sciences of the National Research Council |
| 1927, May 10 | The Board of National Research Fellowships in the Biological Sciences approves the publication of Mead's "The Adolescent Girl in Samoa" as a commercial book |
| 1928, March 8 | Mead returns the signed contract for *Coming of Age in Samoa* to William Morrow and Company |
| 1928, July 25 | Margaret Mead's divorce from Luther Cressman signed in Mexico |
| 1928, August | In a revision of her Last Will and Testament, Mead bequeaths her prayer desk to Ruth Benedict |
| 1928, August | *Coming of Age in Samoa* published in New York |
| 1928, October 8 | Margaret Mead joins Reo Fortune in Auckland, New Zealand, where they are married |
| 1929, June–July | After fieldwork in Manus, Mead spends six weeks in Rabaul with Mrs. C. P. Parkinson |
| 1929, August 15 | The manuscript of Mead's "Social Organization of Manu'a" is submitted to the Bishop Museum for publication |
| 1929, September | Mead returns to New York to find herself a celebrity because of *Coming of Age in Samoa* |
| 1930 | Mead's "Social Organization of Manu'a" published as bulletin 76 of the Bishop Museum |
| 1931 | Boas becomes president of the American Association for the Advancement of Science |
| 1942, December 21 | Franz Boas dies in New York |
| 1971, November | Mead returns to American Samoa on a "sentimental five-day visit" |
| 1974 | Mead becomes president of the American Association for the Advancement of Science |
| 1978, November 15 | Margaret Mead dies in New York |

# Note on the Samoan Language

Fourteen letters only are used in the writing of classical Samoan (other than loan words recently introduced into the language): *a, e, f, g, i, l, m, n, o, p, s, t, u, v.* The letters *h, k,* and *r* are used in writing some words of foreign origin. In contemporary Samoa, there are two distinct forms of pronunciation, one formal and the other colloquial. As G. B. Milner notes in his *Samoan Dictionary* (London, 1966), p. xiv, formal pronunciation "is held out to children, students and foreign visitors as a model to follow and is regarded by an overwhelming majority of Samoans as representing an earlier and purer state of the language than that which . . . exists today," whereas the colloquial pronunciation (in which the *t* of the classical language becomes a *k*) is "used by the great majority of Samoans both in their private and public relations." In his dictionary, Milner adopts the formal pronunciation as his standard of description, as did Pratt before him. It is this standard that I have also followed.

The five vowels, *a, e, i, o, u* (each of which is distinctly pronounced), may be phonetically either long or short; long vowels may be marked with a macron. The letter *g* represents a nasal sound, as in the English word *singer*, which in other Polynesian languages is written *ng*. An apostrophe is used to mark the glottal stop that occurs in many Samoan words. This represents a break, or catch in the voice, similar to that found in the Cockney pronunciation of English, in which, for example, the word *letter* is pronounced *le'er*. Further information on the phonology and pronunciation of Samoan may be found in chapter 1 of G. Pratt, *Grammar and Dictionary of the Samoan Language* (Malua, 1960), in the preface to G. B. Milner, *Samoan Dictionary* (London, 1966), and in La'i Ulrike Mosel and Ainslie So'o, *Say It in Samoan* (Canberra, 1997).

# Glossary

*ali'i*   a titular chief

*aualuma*   a group consisting of women (including widows), who are resident members, by birth or adoption, of a *nu'u*, or local polity

*'aumāga*   a group consisting of the untitled men of a *nu'u*, or local polity

*fa'alupega*   a set of honorific phrases that identify in order of rank the principal titles and family connections of a local polity or district

*fa'amāsei'au*   ritual defloration

*fa'aSamoa*   Samoan custom

*faifeau*   a Christian pastor

*fiafia*   an entertainment with singing and dancing

*fitafita*   a soldier

*fono*   an assembly of chiefs

*fono mānu*   a juridical *fono*

*'ie toga*   a fine mat

*lavalava*   a garment consisting of a piece of cloth enveloping the lower part of the body

*malae*   an open space, usually in the center of a *nu'u*, where ceremonies and other activities are held

*malaga*   a ceremonial visit made according to Samoan custom; a traveling party or group

*mānaia*   the son of a titular chief possessing a title with certain ceremonial duties and privileges; when used as an adjective, *mānaia* has the meaning of attractive or beautiful

*masi*   a food made with breadfruit that has been left to ferment in a pit

*moetotolo*   a surreptitious rape or the person who commits it

*nu'u*   a local polity or village

*palusami*   a dish made with taro leaves, coconut cream, and seawater

*papālagi*   a European

*sā*   sacred, set apart

*siva*   a dance

*ta'alolo*   a ceremonial presentation of food and other gifts offered to a distinguished visitor *tafao*  to stroll about

*talofa*  a form of greeting

*talofa e*  an expression of affection and sympathy

*tama'ita'i*  a lady of high rank

*taupou*  a ceremonial female virgin

*tautō*  to swear an oath

*teine muli*  a female virgin

*tuiga*  an ornamented headdress of human hair bleached to a russet hue, the wearing of which is the prerogative of certain titular chiefs and their families

*tulāfale*  a talking chief, or orator

# Index

Culturalism, Boasian, 8, 15, 17, 22, 26, 34, 162, 175, 189, 208, 213, 216, 217
  tabula rasa assumption of, 213
Cultural patterns, 35, 36, 38, 64, 250(n13)

Damasio, Antonio, 215
Darwin, Charles, 19, 20, 22, 23, 214
Darwinism, 19, 216
Defloration, at marriage, 94, 127, 143
Dennett, Daniel, 216
De Pauw University, 29
*Descent of Man, The*, 20
Determinism, cultural, 33, 35, 65, 143, 182
Dewey, John, 36
*Dictionary of Cultural Literacy, The*, 1
Dobu, 185
Dominick, Bayard, 68
Dorsey, George, 179, 182, 185, 198
Dranga, Theodore T., 122
Driberg, J. H., 197
Duelling, 26
*Dunedin*, H.M.S., 84

Edell, Lieutenant Commander William, 84, 115
Eibl-Eibesfeldt, Irenäus, 214
"Eighteen Professions," 25
Eliasara, Tui Manu'a, 95
Eliot, T. S., 197
Elliot, Edith, 98, 107, 175
Ellis, Havelock, 194
Emory, Kenneth, 174
*Encyclopedia Americana*, 201
*Encyclopedia of Anthropology*, 201
*Encyclopedia of Hoaxes*, 141, 169
*Encyclopedia of the Social Sciences*, 25, 195
Engels, Friedrich, 18
England, 169
Environment, 49
Epstein, Jacob, 178
Erdmann, Benno, 21
Ethnology, 44, 56, 119, 125, 242(n13)

*Ethnology of Manu'a*, 230, 231
Evans-Pritchard, E. E., 200

*Fa'alupega*, 109
Fa'amotu, 96, 165
Fa'apua'a Fa'amū, xi, 2, 4, 12, 13, 15, 116, 117, 131, 134, 139, 141, 144, 164, 188, 191, 212
Fagasā, 86
Faleasao, 101, 153
Feuerbach, Ludwig, 19
*Few Figs from Thistles, A*, 52
Fichte, Johann, 19
Firth, Raymond, 200, 204
Fischer, Theobald, 21
Fitiuta, 4, 122, 123
Fitzgerald, F. Scott, 52, 146, 197, 239(n2)
Fleet, U.S. Pacific, 77, 80
Fofoa, 1, 131, 134, 139, 144, 161, 164, 165, 188, 191
Fortune, Reo, 166, 168, 169, 174, 179, 185
  death, 254(n16)
France, the lure of, 106, 146, 151, 158
Frear, May Dillingham, 67
Frear, Walter F., 67
*Freeman*, 29
Freeman, Derek
  "Anatomy of Mind," 203
  *Margaret Mead and Samoa: The Making and Unmaking of an Anthropological Myth*, 207
  meeting with Margaret Mead on November 10, 1964, 205
  meets Douglas Cole at Simon Fraser University, 8
  position at the Australian National University, 9
  research at Library of Congress, 9
  sails for Samoa in April 1940, 204
  talks with Fa'apua'a, 2
  visits Manu'a, 1, 206
Frigidity, 126
Fua i le Lagi, 118, 119, 128